OUT OF PLACE

OUT OF PLACE

Coming of Age in Cold War Germany

Mary E. McKnight

SHE WRITES PRESS

Published 2024
Printed in the United States of America
Print ISBN: 978-1-64742-726-9
E-ISBN: 978-1-64742-727-6
LCCN: 2024917972

For information, address:
She Writes Press
1569 Solano Ave #546
Berkeley, CA 94707

Interior Design by Andrea Reider

She Writes Press is a division of SparkPoint Studio, LLC.

Names and identifying characteristics have been changed to protect the privacy of certain individuals.

To Mom, Dad, April, Laura, and Kitty

To Those I Did Not Know, One Street from Mine,
I Honor You

"Stumbling Stones" project honoring and marking where
Jewish people were ripped from their lives and homes by the
Nazi regime (See the last page of Endnotes/Resources for
their history.)

Ernst, Frieda, und Hermann, Altschüler Hansaalle 12
Elise Hofmann, Hansaallee 146a
Ruth Cohnstaedt, Hansaallee 32
Wilhelm Cohnstaedt, Hansaallee 7

TABLE OF CONTENTS

PROLOGUE

Can and will people ever be able to see Germany as "a good guy"? I can only answer for myself. I do. An important caveat here: I spent *my* years there from the summer of 1974 to the summer of 1977. Thirty years before my arrival, that land, that place, and those people were all part of a horrific past. They were integral to my transformation upon my arrival and three years living there. Memories connected with "place" remind me of who I am, and the reflection, years later, of those memories and that place gave me the space for so many "Ahas!" that inform who I am today.

My story is the love story of a place that brings me back to myself. As life altering as my three years in the mid-1970s in Cold War–era Germany were, upon my recent research for this manuscript, I found myself, my life, and all fifty years of the Americans in Frankfurt, Germany, nowhere. Nowhere but on the side of the former Frankfurt American High School main building. Now it's the Philipp-Holzmann-Schule entrance, way up high.

I had a life, grew, changed, and loved that countryside and the people. The truthful telling of recent times, regarding the horrific actions of the Nazis and the recognition of the Jewish population, was awe-inspiring to me. There was and is a resilience of the German people to regain their culture, heritage, and pride. I think and feel that we, as another culture, helped to heal that land. And in doing so, we encouraged the courageous spirit of so many of the German people to move into a new way of living. Isn't that what transformation is?

The exciting and intriguing thing to me is that both during and after the writing of my memoir of this time, I began to question ideas, motives, events, and history that I did not know while living in Europe and therefore had not asked questions of previously. That's what truth telling does. It does not erase your life; it adds to it. Be brave with me. Come back with me to what I knew then and to what I know now.

No, I don't lose a limb in this manuscript. I am not abused. I do not get hooked on drugs. I do not become an alcoholic. I do not suffer in any accidents. So much modern literature and movies only give the female story credence if some tragedy befalls the girl/young woman. The oddity is that there are many current books and films about boys coming of age where the "normal" is celebrated. Why the difference?

When I read in 2017 of a live World War II–era B bomb discovered in my former Frankfurt, Germany, backyard, I cried. Crying is only done in private—all we 1970s-era Brats know that. This 2017 live bomb unearthed in my former backyard shook me to my core and brought those three years screaming back to me. The shower was my sobbing refuge. I contemplated the possibility of my former home—my former life, the place that sheltered me and expanded me as I grew from child to young woman—being in danger of being destroyed by three thousand pounds of HC 400 live ammunition.

Once I composed myself, dressed, and waited until the proper phone-calling hour of 9:00 a.m., I called my parents. They had not heard of the bomb, so after quickly explaining the details, I uttered the over-the-top emotions I thought I had tamped down.

"Oh, my god! We could have been vaporized!" Apparently, I had not cried out all my emotions, and my father did not appreciate it.

"Well, the German government is well equipped to defuse such munitions," stated Dad. How could he be so calm? How could he not ponder all that could have happened and all that *did not* happen?

Mom's response: "Yes, I guess we were lucky."

Lucky? We were *lucky?* Clearly, those two were not going to share in my desire to mull, contemplate, and dissect this discovery properly! So to contact both of my sisters to share in this drama, I quickly messaged them along with the accompanying BBC News photo.

Oh yes, they would undoubtedly be the two to debrief this event. We would share in the collective worry of it all, peppering it with stories of our time there. Unless you looked way up high on the Holzmann School for the FAHS symbol, the world at large had no idea that Americans built those houses, lived in those houses, and cherished those houses!

"Just think," my older sister, April, began, "if it had exploded, so much of the history each of us has influenced, so many of the people we created would not exist!"

"Sounds kind of sinister to say, 'people we created,'" my younger sister, Laura, weighed in.

"Oh, my god, you two," I said, trying to cut right to the chase. "We could have been playing an innocent game of kick the can, hide-and-seek, or walking to the commissary, and *bam!* Life over!"

I was desperate to find another soul ready and willing to stay hysterical. I was not anywhere near finished emotionally processing this knowledge. Who knows dramatic hysteria better than teenagers? Lucky for me, I had "created" one. When I told her about this bomb two hundred feet from my old house, she grabbed her computer and said, "Do you think the house is still *there?*"

Well, of course, it's still *there.* The bomb was discovered during construction. So what part of this was my daughter not getting? I sought to clarify so we could get back to my train of drama. "Sweets, I told you, the German government is evacuating about 1.8 miles of the city, and then they will try to defuse this massive bomb! But don't you understand? If that bomb had gone off while I lived there, all of history would be different. You wouldn't even exist! If it blows up now, my history is gone!"

She had already pulled up Google Maps while I was dramatically pontificating upon my importance to the thread of history. With her twenty-first-century fingers flying in search of 2360 Wismarer Strasse, I knew I'd have to get my importance in quickly before she was on to something else that caught her eye.

"Sweets! There is a bomb in my backyard!" And then the location popped up. There it was. Oh, sweet, beautiful house. "That's my house, and that's my best friend Jenny's house with the red roof!"

"Mommy, it's not actually *your* house."

But it *was* my house. She couldn't understand because she wasn't an Army Brat. It had been my three-year landing site, where I was on the cusp of turning thirteen when we arrived. And when I left at almost sixteen, I had formed the base and pillars of the truths of feminism and social justice. I had also entered the always colorful world of menstruation and boys while navigating life as an Army Brat in American-occupied Germany. That is a ton of emotional baggage to keep to myself, and that's what I did. There was no "social-emotional learning/sharing" for Brats in the 1970s. "Suck it up and move on"—that was the therapy.

My daughter, sensing my inward historical vision quest, quickly grounded me with, "Mommy, it's been forty-two years. It's not your house."

I had not been back to this street, this curb, this house, and there it was via Google Earth, and there I was, living in my fifty-seven-year-old self and still embodying the depth of feeling and deep cellular meaning that only the innocent age can bring.

We had been an Army family heading for a three-year tour in Frankfurt, Germany. I was to come of age in the birthplace of both Goethe and Anne Frank, just thirty years after the devastation of World War II. I didn't think about all that while I lived there. I was focused on "me" and wanted adventure.

Being an Army family, we traveled as a unit with Dad in the lead and Mom behind him, keeping the proverbial home fires burning. She lived *The Army Wife* (written by Nancy Shea), and as I moved along in my three coming-of-age years, it became harder and harder internally to accept "woman as a second-class citizen." The challenge and journey of my story were separating myself from them and societal norms so that I knew who I was and began learning how to speak *my* truth.

It was June of 1974, and I was a few weeks shy of turning thirteen. I had stopped the games of childhood and was in the fog of the in-between. That's when the five of us went to live in Germany.

TOR NACH EUROPA
(GATEWAY TO EUROPE)

I t had taken Old Blood and Guts George S. Patton's entire Third Army to capture Frankfurt in 1944. I was doing it thirty years later, traveling with my bossy older sister, April, my loving Army-wife mother, my too-smart-for-her-own-good little sister, Laura, and our cantankerous drugged-up-for-the-airplane-ride cat. Dad had relocated there six weeks earlier. The odds seemed stacked against me. Patton had ground troops, military strategy, and tanks. I had anxiety, ignorance, and looming puberty.

When the plane finally landed five thousand hours later, I had only gotten brief periods of dozing off. This length of time in the air left me in a mental fog, with painful neck muscles and zero enthusiasm for anything but a soft bed in someplace familiar. I had neither.

Mom instructed us, "Smooth your hair and clothing with your hands so that you look presentable." I felt sure that even with the gargantuan size of my hands (description compliments of April), no smoothing would alter the effects of the fourteen motionless hours. But, of course, the expectation was that we *must* look presentable.

Mom constantly thought ahead of ways to keep travel peppy and upbeat. She always had new magazines like *Family Circle*, comic books for us, Life Savers, and gum. She just thought of everything and moved through the world with sparkling optimism. She was beautiful, with a ladylike air always about her. Her swanlike neck was always lightly sprinkled with Jean Naté perfume. She was perpetually slim and svelte in the artfully constructed dresses she had sewn. She walked in high heels like they were part of her feet.

With my hands rigid and flat, I started at the top of my head, but when I attempted to fix my hair, my bangs stuck to my now-oily forehead. I was sure this was not a good look, and the derisive cluck from April sealed that thought into truth. Only fifteen months older than me, my sister already had womanly curves. Her sandy blond hair was always straight and cooperative. She had recently traded her ugly-beyond-measure, dark-framed glasses for wire aviators like Gloria Steinem wore. Mom had said that Gloria Steinem was a "feminist." I did not know what that was. Mom's wrinkled brow when she said those words told me that it couldn't be anything good.

The female leisure suit I had donned in my attempt to acquire something resembling denim (as Mom had forbidden our wearing of jeans) effectively contained the BO smell that had stained the white blouse I wore underneath. My training bra had ridden to the mid-chest level, making me acutely aware of the various nerves running through that area. I pulled it down quickly while April looked out the airplane window.

April had blue eyes, and I had brown. Her skin was fair, and mine was olive. April called it "sallow." *My skin is sallow*, echoed in my mind continuously. This was not good. I was not good. I had no beauty. She did. That's what I knew to be valid from her constant verbal analysis of me. Appearance for girls was everything. To be admired by males was everything. That's what society showed us, and I had every reason to believe that even though we were traveling across an ocean, these outward confines would be similar.

These were the constraints I operated under, but inside, oh, inside, I was pleading to get out from under her thumb. I didn't know what that was like—to be free—but I imagined it had to feel better than the crushed spirit I possessed.

Upon our arrival at the Frankfurt Flughafen (airport), it was good to see Dad, as we had not seen him for six weeks. He was posture-perfect, dressed in his usual "off-hours" garb: crisply pressed slacks, collared shirt with a mandatory pocket filled with file cards and a mechanical pencil, leather shoes shined to a glassy sheen, topped off with the once-weekly crew cut.

He and Mom embraced tightly and smooched a loud kiss on the lips. They looked so joyful together. Mom was always quick to laugh, ever the wordsmith, the joy-giver, and the joy-finder to all she encountered. When we left the boundaries of the US, she was thirty-eight. Had she always been as self-confident as she was now?

I adored Mom. It seems she existed only to bring beauty and light to all she met. She had been raised on the South Side of Chicago by her Slovak immigrant parents, flanked by eight older siblings. Mom never complained, cursed, or looked down upon or up at anyone. How could I share with her my fears, my disappointment in myself compared to April, my lack of, well . . . everything?

I didn't. I kept all those revelations to myself. Indeed, since no one else in my family had these deficits, I was the problem. Even my little sister, Laura, seemed to possess the McKnight confidence I lacked.

Laura was two years younger than me, and before our US exit, that age difference didn't matter to us. When she was little, her blond hair fell in little angel ringlets around her sweet face.

Her blue eyes were often rimmed with tears, and her sensitive nature probably refined my empathetic gift/curse.

I think I broke her heart when I no longer found our daily games of Barbies or dollhouse rewarding. I went through the motions of playing but no longer knew what to make my Barbies say: "I feel depressed. My chest is flat. My armpits stink." No, these were not the lines my Talking Barbie used to say, but they swirled in my head on perpetual repeat.

Laura was eleven and still wanted to play. She was lucky. Growing up stunk. Breath, pits, attitude . . . it all stunk.

We had another family member traveling with us on our trans-Atlantic flight, and that was Kitty. We loved Kitty. We had argued among ourselves about her name when we got her in 1967. That verbal family conflict ended, as most did, with Dad announcing loudly and firmly, "Her name will be Miss Kitty. End of discussion."

With my stomach churning and cramping from jet lag, my initial excitement at the landing and seeing Dad was dampened by the extreme pace at which we were required to walk to keep up with the Colonel. This exercise in briskness was punctuated by the carrying of our individual hard-case, wheelless, avocado-green Samsonite suitcases.

Any complaining on our part was met with, "Well, you should have thought of that when you packed your suitcase." Yes, I should have, but I was twelve and packed what I thought were necessities, along with the requisite amount of clothing. The directions given to us from Dad via Mom before the trip were, "Pack what you will need for at least a month while we wait for our household items to travel across the ocean and be delivered by the Army."

With that in mind, my clothing and the necessary items of my youthful self on the cusp of teenagerhood were as follows:

my small Virgin Mary statue in a prayerful pose; a metal bank of the world filled with American coins; Dad's childhood cylindrical, wooden paper-money bank from Shamokin, Pennsylvania; my stuffed bear named Freddy; and my yellow, loved-almost-to-shreds blanket I had snuck along.

Mom had wanted me to pack up my childhood blanket with all the other items to be in "storage" in the States for the three years we were stationed in the Frankfurt, Germany, American Military Installation known as USAREUR (United States Army in Europe). I'm sure Mom meant well in trying to transition me into growing up and growing on, but I knew in my anxiety-ridden heart that I was not *near* ready to do so.

Upon landing, I hoped that we could sit down in some comfortable chairs in the airport and decompress from our trek. "Hoping" always translated into silence. I *wanted* to say, "Hey, Dad, we're exhausted from our trip. How about if we sit here at the airport and discuss what's going to happen next?"

I said nothing, as the scenario above was *not* the established parent–child dynamic laid out within the confines of *The Army Wife*. Dad had gifted Mom with her copy shortly after their engagement. His instructions were for her to read it from cover to cover and to decide if this was a way of life she could and would embrace.

So lucky for us, there was a section in that book with dedicated pages to "The Army Wife in Germany." "As an Army family, you will have tremendous influence overseas, and this influence should at all times be helpful to our national objectives. Courteous, loving, well-mannered children can be a tremendous help in showing foreigners a better picture of American life. Spoiled wives and children, on the other hand, hamper our best efforts at promoting good relations abroad."[1]

Yeah, right . . . that's what I was focused on as we deplaned . . . "promoting good relations abroad." I was only concerned about getting Kitty back, as she had been in the plane's cargo hold.

Upon picking up our furry family member from the Frankfurt suitcase turnstile, we girls took turns carrying the awkward rigid plastic cat carrier in addition to our Samsonites. "Hey, Dad," I cheerfully said with an indoor voice, "they have some carrying carts we could rent. I saw people put coins in a slot and then get the cart." I *know* he heard me and was actively ignoring me. He had glanced at me when I was talking, and then I swear he moved faster to indicate that we would *not* be purchasing any assistance.

I looked at Mom with pleading eyes, but she was in Europe, heart, mind, body, and soul. The smile on her face erased the last fourteen hours aloft, and that was that. April and Laura were walking just a step or two behind Dad. The silent but deafening message was, *See how we don't need help. Mary is such a weakling.* I was sure that by the time we got to our car, my fingers would be rife with gangrene due to lack of circulation induced by inflexible suitcase and cat carrier handles. It would be all Dad's fault. *Welcome to Germany.*

SELTSAM (WEIRD)

The Frankfurt Flughafen was bustling with wide corridors, scads of people, and various shops. The physical airport setup was one we were familiar with, having traveled frequently as a military family. However, I was unfamiliar with the language on all the signs and the people speaking words I did not understand. Dad saying, "Move in the direction of the *Ausfahrt*," reduced us three girls to instant laughter. Why was Dad talking about farting?

A quick stern glance from him and his translation of "That means 'exit,'" was my first German lesson. I have never forgotten it. Then, while heading for the Ausfahrt, my eyes were assaulted with the thoroughly English word "sex."

This shop was something no airport I had *ever* been in had contained. Mr. Somebody's Sex Shop, complete with a display window of nude nipples protruding, pubic hair on proud mannequins, and a variety of tools, the purpose of which I had no idea. A sex shop—just the thing you want to view and experience with your mom and dad. Mom gave her typical "Oh, my gosh!" gasp, elicited by all situations that might scar our virginal brains. The pace picked up to put the sex shop behind us. April and I stifled our laughter, followed by Laura—all of age eleven—bugging us with, "What? What was it? What are you guys laughing at?"

My jet lag liver bile had temporarily settled down upon passing numerous restaurants and carts filled with German culinary delights. I thought about trying the passive approach with Dad, as the direct process clearly was a total failure. "Hey, wouldn't it be cool to try some German food?"

Dad's reply: "We will eat at the local time and not before, so that you all can acclimate to this time zone."

At that point, I did not give a rat's ass about "acclimating." I was starving! I did not, however, protest beyond a slight groan and an internal vow that if I *ever* traveled on my own, I would eat when I damn well wanted to eat! But that scenario would have to wait, as I was currently living under the Colonel Dad Dictatorship.

With the march across the Flughafen completed upon reaching the main Ausfahrt, we arrived at our car. "Everything had better fit," Dad stated. We all stood back as he precision-packed the vehicle. I'm sure I must have been breathing during this spatial-perceptual exercise, but emotionally, I was oxygen-less. I was sure if anyone had packed too much, it was me.

I always carried the weight of fault. It might have been my way of preemptive protection. If I *imagined* things were my fault first, it could lessen the blow of someone blaming me and pointing out my ineptitude.

By the grace of the suitcase gods, our luggage and Kitty in the cat carrier fit in our red VW Squareback—shipped over from the US. "Let's go," was the Dad-directive. With permission granted, I climbed behind the driver's seat and sat on the leather seat I had ridden on since we first bought the car. Laura shoved in front of me. She was forced to the middle straddling her legs over the clutch hump between the driver and the passenger seat. Of course, April rode behind the passenger seat, affording her the most legroom.

The VW packed, we were ready to proceed. When we left the States, it had been a typical hot, humid Maryland June day. Now we were plunged into a cool, sixty-degree gray German day. "Roll your windows down an inch for ventilation," directed Dad, so April and I both manned our window cranks, rolling them down one inch each.

Dad hit the gas, and we soon hurtled down the Autobahn—a series of highways with no speed limits. After sharing his quick Autobahn history lesson, he sternly informed us, "During our three years as guests of the German people, we are not to ever speak of Nazis, Hitler, or World War II."[2]

Why would we? Weren't they going to teach us about it all in school? I kept these questions to myself. No good exchange of ideas could have happened if I had inquired aloud. To have asked would have been interpreted as confrontational.

Mom never said, "Do not provoke your father," but it was just understood. He was not a violent man, certainly no Great Santini.[3] He conducted his life with detail, expectation, and honor. We were to do the same. It was written in *The Army Wife*, so it must be true.

I knew from watching Mom's face what the expectation was in almost all situations. My insides only felt at ease if she was at ease. I never considered what my needs and wants might be over hers. I watched the side of her face as we drove. She had such a glow of excitement.

With no speed limits, our VW reached a pace we had never experienced. The German landscape blurred like the backdrop of a cartoon. Had I not felt my gagging nausea, not heard the deafening yowls of Kitty coming down off her drugs, and Laura wailing, "Are we there yet?" it might have been fun. But instead, all we could do was be thankful that we were packed in so tightly in the back seat that if we *were* to be in a collision, we were certain not to be ejected from the car.

By the time we arrived at the entry gate of the Frankfurt American Military Post, the clothing I had worn for the past twenty-four hours straight had molded to my body. The Ban deodorant I had sprayed stateside had, in fact, worn off, contrary to the claims of the commercial ("Ban won't wear off as the day wears on"), and my hair had taken on the look of an oil spill.

At the gate, Dad had his military ID in his wallet, snapped open and ready to show the MPs (military police) to read and let us enter. A sharp salute ensued, followed by Dad's return salute, and off we drove to our new house.

The 27,000 tons of bombs the Royal British Air Corps dropped had turned most of the medieval city into rubble during World War II. Germany and the Americans had spent the past thirty years rebuilding the city with old-world and modern elements. One of those 27,000 tons of bombs was lying in wait underground, sixty yards from the very place we would soon call home. It would not be discovered until 2017, long after the Americans had decommissioned the Army facilities and grounds back to the Germans in 1995. I would live behind it, play over it, and grow into a young woman, blissfully unaware of its existence.

The time was 1100 hours. All I wanted was a shower and some food. Unfortunately, both would have to wait. Dad's internal itinerary said so.

DU BIST DA
(YOU ARE HERE)

O ut front of each of the big white stucco houses in our new neighborhood was a metal sign with the rank and name of the officer living there. "Col. James R. McKnight" was hung on our new domicile. We were home. *Now* the adventure felt like it was starting. "Place" is a character to me, much more than simply a setting for my life. It lives, breathes, alters, and influences as time does. I carry all these places—the houses, the rooms, the windows, the land—with me in my heart, mind, and in every cell. That's where memory lives for me.

I make mental notes of my new physical surroundings and integrate them with my awareness, taking note of the distinct smells, sights, and sounds. Now that we were on post, all signage was in English, and many people were walking in fatigues and khaki uniforms dotted with US military brass and patches. This looked and felt familiar and comfortable.

Our new living quarters were on Wismarer Strasse, off Miquel Allee. The generals' quarters of 1959 were now housing for colonels (COL), lieutenant colonels (LTC), and their families. Behind our place of residence for the next three years were the BOQs (bachelor officers' quarters), where Dad had spent the past six weeks beginning his duty assignment before our arrival. Little did we know that between our backyard and the BOQ was that live bomb buried by layers of thirty years of undisturbed soil.

I still hadn't peed in twenty-four hours and felt sure that my bladder was beginning to reabsorb the urine. I just assumed we would get out of the car, and I would hit the bathroom upon entering our new home. This was not going to happen. Dad had an internal itinerary that included properly acclimating and keeping a schedule, so it was time to eat lunch. I knew this because after we pulled into the driveway, he said, "We'll go across the street and get some lunch. Leave everything in the car." It didn't matter who was hungry or not. No one was *asked*. No one questioned Dad. This was how it was and how it would be. There was no deviation from Dad's itinerary.

My thoughts at the time: *What an a-hole. Why can't he have already gone food shopping for us and perhaps show us where the peanut butter and jelly are? But no, that "lady task" was to be left to Mom. Because that's what someone feels like doing after traveling way the hell over the ocean!*

Perpendicular to our street was Miquel Allee and the Ambassador Arms Hotel, a 1959 nouveau-ugly, modern, multilevel hotel built to harbor military families while housing was being arranged for new families or families on their way back home to the States. Dad pointed out the details of the facilities as complete with a mess hall (i.e., restaurant), beauty parlor (to attend to the requisite Aqua Net–shellacked bouffants of officers' wives, I mentally filled in), laundromat, and day nursery for little children.

Even though it was well within walking distance, I had hoped we'd drive as the continued tightening of my pubo-genital muscles had almost reached their breaking point. I did *not* want their failure to be my first lasting memory in Germany.

The urgency of bodily functions forced me to utter the rare request, "Dad, I have to go to the bathroom." His response shot me down: "They have a bathroom at the Ambassador Arms. You'll use it there."

Despite my request, we parked on the concrete pad in front of our garage. Dad took Kitty and her carrier into the house. We were told to "Get out and stretch your legs" while he shut Kitty in a bathroom with a litter box, food, and water. With thoughts on mute, off we went across the street.

I found the bathroom, took care of business, and joined my family at their dining table. One hurdle down.

Grilled cheese was on the menu, meaning that was all that was offered. That was it. Well, there was probably soup too, but the grinding in my stomach from lack of food over such a long period of time rendered the odor of all food unbearable. The hunger I had felt at the Flughafen was gone. That always happens to me if I wait too long to eat.

I could barely choke down the toasted Wonder bread/melted American cheese food unit, as it rode up and back in my esophagus. Dad was stern in his command to "Eat now because there will be no food before dinner." I was sure at that moment that he was possibly the cruelest individual on earth!

His responses were nothing new to any of us. It was the dad I had grown up with and the husband that Mom had agreed to in 1959. But nevertheless, the urge to speak up about his curtness, orders, and dominance was rising inside me. Did he think we were stupid women and required these directions to enable our functioning? Would he have treated us differently if we were boys?

The oddity to me in all of this was that he believed to the core that his behavior, word choice, and everything else were for our own good, for the good of the family, and, as a result, good for his career. I looked to Mom for support, but she grimaced and continued picking at her food. I did not know then that, as an officer's wife, Mom had tacitly agreed to Dad being commander in chief of our family. I was beginning to question their power structure and, with it, their relationship.

WIR SIND ZU HAUSE (WE ARE HOME)

Mom was beyond chipper on the traipse back to our new house, post–Ambassador Arms lunch. I swear she labeled everything in sight as though we had never seen anything like it. "Oh! Look at those trees!" "Oh, would you look at that bird!" "Oh, would you look at my three sullen children!" (She did not say that last thing.)

Mom was and still is the most genuinely positive person I have ever known. She finds joy in situations where others see only misery. So how could she be marveling at a sparrow while I felt like nothing but jet-lagged shit on a shingle? The EMO hormones that had begun to take up residence in my soul and corporeal body introduced me to the fine art of sarcasm. Mom's sunny outlook on everything had the effect on me of a sort of Opposite World.

Mom was raised to be a super-Catholic, and the "Wives, be submissive to your husbands" Bible passage fit right into *The Army Wife* way of life. I always wondered what she was think-ing. I would ask but not right now. It could wait.

More awe-inspired gasping ensued as Mom gazed upon the plethora of rosebushes planted en masse in the area next to our garage. We hadn't even walked up to the door yet, and we hadn't gone inside—couldn't we look at flora and fauna later?

No, we could not. April and I shared preteen-invented irritated eye rolls. Surely this moment would never end. But finally it did.

This was not the most prominent house we had ever lived in, but it was close. (Our Victorian folk duplex in Fort Leavenworth took that honor.) This German house was enormous. It was *our* house, and I wanted to get inside, see what everything looked and felt like, and begin making it feel like home.

April ran up the stairs and "called" the most oversized bedroom. I assumed I'd share a room with Laura, as we had always done. Instead, Dad demanded that April "come back down the stairs!" and proceeded to give us the house tour. More oohs and aahs from Mom.

The Army had furnished the house from top to bottom. These furnishings included crystal goblets for wine in the dining room. Mom had tears in her eyes as she cradled one in her hands. *That's lovely, Mom, but can we keep going? Boring!* Ah, the internal selfishness of one with two weeks to go before turning thirteen. I was filled with the requisite preteen urgency of "What's next?"

Mom labeled *everything* contained in each room as we walked. April and I couldn't understand what the "big whoop" was. We had seen furniture before. We did not know that Mom's "orders" via *The Army Wife* were to make our living quarters into a showpiece. We just thought she was overreacting to the heavy, olive-green, thick fabric-upholstered couch. *It's a couch, people. Now, where's the bedroom I'll share with Laura?* My comments, of course, were strictly internal.

Couch, two chairs, coffee table, floor lamp, table lamp—check. We could function. Chandelier and large, heavy mahogany buffet piece for the crystal and china—check. Small kitchen ...with no dishwasher! Dad supplied the answer: "You girls will be the dishwashers." *Thank you, Dad. Way to solidify our gender roles.*

When we got to the bedroom off the kitchen, Dad proudly stated that this was the "maid's" room from the days of yore. It would become Mom's sewing room. We would have no maid. Oh, no, wait a minute—we three *girls* would be the maids!

When we were finally at the upstairs portion of the tour, Dad pointed to the various bedrooms and gave us our assignments. Laura had a small room with a window facing the front yard. April had the small room at the other end of the hallway with a window facing the front yard, and I, I was gifted with the large (as in two-closets large with a double bed) bedroom with a window facing the side yard *and* a window to the backyard.

I will never know why I was given this advance in space, but suddenly, Dad went up in my mental book of points and demerits. That room would become a retreat, a daydreaming space to process the next three years. I took a moment to revel and pass April a quick, "Ha! I got the biggest room!" glance. She must have known it was coming because she averted her eyes from mine.

She *always* had the upper hand. So why did I even try? For many years, I fought this inner conflict of sticking up for myself versus giving in for the greater good (as I perceived it). It took a toll on my spirit and my body.

Whether Mom and Dad had discussed the room assignments ahead of time, I don't know. I didn't ask, and they didn't tell. I suppose this is how leadership keeps the troops in line and the unit functioning smoothly.

It's not like Dad *never* showed a pleasant, engaging side, as he did to Mom and all others. On the contrary, Dad treated everyone with the utmost respect and kindness, and we were to do the same. I did like that about him. I just couldn't understand why he did not openly extend this to April, Laura, and me.

When Mom opened the refrigerator later that day, there was food in it. Dad had grocery shopped. I had called him an a-hole in my head, and he had gone food shopping. *Now* who was the a-hole?

Later that first evening, we met our "sponsors," a family who had been in Germany for two-thirds of their three-year tour and were responsible for helping us get settled in this new culture.

Off we went to meet their young daughter, Laura's age, and their son, my age. The expectation was that the children would show us around the local town (walking, of course) and the parents would enjoy sipping fine German beer and talking about whatever officers and their wives verbalized in 1974. Before leaving, the boy donned a beret, cleverly tipped to one side. April and I shared an annoyed "What a dufus" glance, and off we went. We were *not* in France. What was with the beret?

We McKnight girls had no idea where we were going but followed Beret Boy down the streets of Frankfurt to a *Schnel-limbiss*. This establishment was akin to a newsstand, with sex magazines front and center, candy and other food, cigarettes, and beer.

He bought us some gummy bears, something we had never heard of before, and some gummy cokes (my new favorite). His generosity was most likely the result of directions from *his* Colonel Dad. I imagine it sounded something like this: "You will be an accommodating host. You are to provide your guests with a positive, pleasant experience of the local culture. Understood?"

He was clearly trying to impress us with his "worldliness." On our first day of school a few weeks later, he pretended not to know who April and I were. *Idiot.* Apparently, his father had yet to give him a direct order to acknowledge our existence beyond our initial meeting.

Upon our return from this "off-post" German jaunt, Mom and Dad were all smiles, I'm sure helped by the hoppy goodness of the Bitburger beer. Mom had her German phrasebook and felt compelled to utter her first phrases on our way home from the sponsors' house. Her effort was not helped by us, her snickering daughters. It's not like we knew any more German than she did. We just knew that she was doing it all wrong. This hyper-analysis of others is a highly annoying trait of adolescence. The secret Mom held was that she had the freedom to try new things, unfettered by the opinion of others, and we were in the adolescent mindset of self-imposed limitation.

DAS IST MEIN SISYPHUS
(THIS IS MY SISYPHUS)

I assumed that on day two on foreign soil, still jet-lagged but wanting to get the lay of the land, we would head out on some recon around town. But nope, first we needed to get our living quarters up to snuff.

We were all on "maid status." Even though the Army had spic-and-spanned our house before our move-in day, Mom insisted that we clean it Slovak style. Mom's mother and father were immigrants from Slovakia, and apparently in that culture, cleanliness was indeed next to (or right behind, so as not to be blasphemous) godliness.

This Cleaning Revolution began with the prep work, which included the individual removal of the living and dining room thermal-lined, thousand-pound, harvest-gold filigree-designed curtains provided by the military. Each hideous panel was attached to the curtain rod by "rollers." To take down and clean the drapes lined with crisp white canvas as per Mom's orders, you had to disengage each roller from its metal apparatus. My shoulders screamed with a burning buildup of lactic acid as I struggled to pop the five million rollers from each weighted curtain panel.

When a family on post was a month away from going back to the States, the children wore a set of those rollers on their collars. I am still determining how this tradition got started, but I learned about it from our next-door neighbors at the time, the Balls. They had their rollers on and were headed back to the States toward the end of summer.

After the curtains were down, Mom mixed her toxic brew, ripe with ammonia, to wash the windows. We females were on the inside, and Dad was on the outside with a ladder. Dad had proper ventilation to dispel the toxic fumes. Unhappily ensconced inside, we took turns balancing either up on a stepladder or on the marble mantel over the bay window, always on the verge of an ammonia gas faint-fest. There's a reason Windex was developed and used by the modern world. Why Mom decided that we needed to clean old-school is beyond me. Due to the massive inhalation of ammonia, I have no recollection of cleaning the rest of the house, but I am sure we did.

The mental exhaustion and brewing agitation created by this tedium of cleaning tasks were only escapable in my room. It was the first time in my life that I had ever been alone! Well, save for bathroom visits. I wasn't sure what to do with this newfound freedom. My double bed provided a landing area for me and any of my writing and reading.

The solid wooden desk in the corner by the side window was to be more of a storage area. This was the first time I had my own desk, and I took time to arrange the few items I had brought overseas. What to put on my walls? I had no idea. I had never considered what I liked, what I found inspiring, what I loved. Anything and everything in the past had to be cleared with Laura as my roommate.

How could I be almost thirteen years old and have no defined likes? I felt lost as to how one cultivates this. I turned to my Archie Comics Spectacular to look at Veronica's bedroom versus Betty's bedroom. I was more of a "Betty," but even Betty was beyond me. She was beautiful, even though she thought she wasn't. There was no character like me in the Archie comics. As far as I could tell, I was one of a kind, and not in a good way. My walls stayed bare for months.

I knew some of the things I did *not* like! I did not like cleaning. As far as I could tell, any "pride in task completion" would only last for a maximum of one week. The dust, grime, and clutter built up, and the tasks were repeated. It was my Sisyphus—rock up the hill, clean, crash down on me, repeat. *How did women get stuck with this? This is hell!* I hated being told what to do, but honestly, I did not know how to motivate myself. I wanted to change the world but wasn't sure how or why. Changing the world seemed far easier than changing myself.

The Army-issued, olive-green wool blanket covering my bed was not exactly inspiring. It looked like something borrowed from the set of *Hogan's Heroes.* No curtains, just metal off-white venetian blinds on my windows. Mom instructed me that at twilight, I was to twist the apparatus on the side of the blinds so that the individual slats faced down. This was so that no one could see in. Who was going to be looking? I didn't ask, and Mom did not volunteer any information.

The haze of jet lag, along with the inhalation of cleaning chemicals, leaves the timetable of the following events a little sketchy, but suffice it to say that in the coming weeks, we began to venture out some on post and on "the Economy," the land not part of the Army post.

UNSERE WELTERWEITERT SICH (OUR WORLD EXPANDS)

Culture Shock. Yes, it was a significant culture shock, and I had skipped right to Stage Two, labeled "Hostility and Irritability." Mom was in Stage One, "Honeymoon Stage," and Laura was just going with the flow at age eleven. April was always hostile and irritable, so did that mean she was in constant culture shock? No, I think she was just a developing dictator. Dad was in his own stage of "maintaining." It was still the summer of 1974.

Our home goods shipment had finally made it across the ocean, and because of this, our house felt more like home. However, it was most important to Mom that we experience life beyond the confines of the Little America of the Frankfurt American community and the neighboring military installations of Rhein-Main and Wiesbaden Air Base.

How did she become so adept at fearlessness? Was she a natural explorer? I liked spending time with Mom because she always made me feel grounded and solid. Her eyes looked at me with such love and kindness that I couldn't get enough of it. The pull of confusion came from my desire to escape her rules and constant insistence on "ladylike behavior and appearance."

I did not know the terms for personality preference at the time, but I was a grade-A introvert. Mom and Laura were previously my havens wherever we traveled; it was no different the first German summer. April tagged along on our jaunts off-post, because she had "nothing better to do."

Life off-post was just a street away on Hansa Allee. We walked with a giant paper map, Mom turning it to face what-ever direction we were walking, and April chastising her for not being able to orient herself without that maneuver. Why Mom didn't tell her to shut the hell up, I do not know. I guess Mom was so used to Dad bossing her around that she had tuned April out and did what she needed to do to see the world at large.

As we traversed these ancient ways, only recently rebuilt after the devastation of World War II, Mom looked about in wonder.[4] April countered Mom's cheery narrative by quickly noting the apparent "oddities." The dialogue went something like this:

Mom: "Oh! Isn't this such a quaint street?"

April: "Geez, MaCrow, Mom, it's an alley. Hope we don't get mugged!"

That "country bumpkin" exaltation of April's was developed in lieu of "Oh, my god!" Mom informed us it was taking the Lord's name in vain. Why April decided to mimic how a south-ern scarecrow might talk, I do not know.

I didn't usually chide Mom aloud. I was the good daughter. Surely Mom could see that. Ah, but inside, when Mom praised the virtues of cobblestone, my inner critic cringed and said, *It's a rock, Mom. Get over it.* The difference was that I only *thought* these things. April said them.

Shortly after we arrived in Frankfurt, it was my thirteenth birthday, and Dad introduced us to Bologna's, a restaurant at Eschersheimer Landstraße 273. None of us other than Dad knew what to expect from the place we were walking to, and despite our thousand questions, Dad kept replying, "You'll see when we get there." He must have talked it over with Mom because she looked very pleased, and I trusted her taste in food and her ability to know what I liked.

I was not a picky eater, as Laura and April were. On the contrary, I prided myself on liking everything I had tried thus far. However, April did strike a chord of fear in me, suggesting that the restaurant served "haggis."

"Oh," I said with wide eyes, "what's that?"

April, with a shit-eating grin, replied, "Sheep guts stuffed into stomachs."

As there were no smartphones in 1974, I had to take her word for it and began to worry that I would be forced into trying this vomit-inducing dish. Dad defended me (or perhaps he was just defending the truth) with, "There will be no haggis!" He was not smiling. Conversation-thread over.

Upon entering the small restaurant, we were all pleased to see and smell the all-familiar Americanized version of pizza and other Italian food. The decor was café simple/sparse, with square tables covered in white tablecloths, accompanied by metal chairs with attached plastic-like cushions. I certainly hoped the food would indicate "celebration" because the decor did not.

The menu was in German. *Great. Way to go, Dad.* How were we supposed to know what was what? Mom had her handy-dandy "Welcome to Germany/Willkommen in Deutschland" phrasebook. This was going to take *hours*; I was sure of it. For once, Dad's impatient attitude was going to pay off in his efficient ordering of "*Zwei große Pizzen mit Peperoni, drei Cola, und ein Krug Bier*" when our waiter came to the table.

I heard what I was pretty sure was "pizza and Coke." The waiter quickly served us our beverages. I was sure some mistake had been made as the three dark-colored drinks for us kids had no ice, and there were obvious lemon slices rimming each glass. I guess our collective confused looks caused Dad to quickly announce, "In Germany, the beverages are served at room temperature. Better for digestion."

Thank you, Mr. World Traveler, but if it tasted horrible, who cared about digestion? This was *not* how we drank it in America! Finally, April piped up, "Well, can we at least request ice?"

Dad shut her down quietly with, "No! We are guests in Germany and will do as they do. Acclimate!"

Message received. I was still in the "whatever is American is better" mindset, as were my sisters. I did not know that the first day of turning thirteen was when I received a gift that only time and retrospect would make clear. It was the gift of an expanded lens through which to view the world.

But on my thirteenth birthday in 1974, my narrow lens had me stuck with warm Coke and a lemon slice. Weird. Mom, ever the cheer-filled conversationalist, asked, "So, Mare, what are your dreams for yourself now that you are a year older?"

What? Dreams for *myself*? I hadn't considered that. I thought I was just supposed to "acclimate." But I could not leave Mom hanging, so I answered, "Well . . . I have always loved writing. I think I'd like to do more of that."

In one of his rare tender moments, Dad spoke up with a huge smile, "Yes, I remember the story you wrote and sent to me when I was in Vietnam—about Mr. Cookie. It was excellent with the accompanying illustrations."

Mom concurred with, "Oh yes, and you were only eight years old!"

April could not let me have the spotlight and quickly chimed in, "Yes, and I edited it for her!"

She did. It's true. But did she have to say that, *then*? I could not spell or get the gist of grammar. It seemed tedious, and I was only interested in the creative output.

The pizzas came, and it only took one bite of the warm, salty heaven that was this German/Italian wonder to begin to alter my view of this restaurant. It was the best pizza I have ever eaten. And yes, I have eaten pizza in New York City, and that German pizza wins!

I imagine that Dad had this restaurant picked out to ease us into the heavier German cuisine I grew to love and cherish—especially in its absence—once back in the States, where my sisters and I became Euro-snobs. Good job, Dad. I hope I told him, but I don't think I did.

I was thirteen. Thirteen is selfish. Thirteen views the world through the lens of "What about me?" With this lens, I looked at myself in the various store-window reflections on the walk back to our house and saw my still-childlike stick figure with enlarged hands and feet. When would I be transforming? April seemed to ease into herself. One day she did not have breasts, and the next, she had cleavage. I swear it happened that fast. She was all, "Wait, I have to get my purse . . ." while I just shoved my required military ID card into my front pocket. She carried a brush and lip gloss.

Should I be doing the same thing? Did she ask Mom to get her those supplies, or would I need to request them? All my disappointment, my questions kept to myself, my missing the familiar, and my anger at myself for not being more adventurous erupted in an epic silent sob into my pillow once I was back in my room that evening. I did not want these changes. My body felt foreign—like I knew it, but it did not know me. I never used to think about it, and now I couldn't stop. Why didn't Mom swoop in to help me? In the past, she always seemed to anticipate what I needed, or at least some of it. I was going to be on my own in this.

Nothing like feeling the double whammy of foreigner-in-a-foreign-country coupled with foreigner-in-a-now-foreign-body. Mom's answer to just about everything now was to keep busy, which meant sojourns "on the Economy."

DER TREK (THE TREK)

Our first big jaunt on the Economy (which meant going off the US Army post) forced an expansion of my understanding of "place." The previous stateside locations we had lived in did not look, smell, or sound anything like this. As a family, we had never lived in a big city before. The closest I had ever been to this atmosphere was my childhood immersion in the book *The Little House* by Virginia Lee Burton. It was where I first saw streetcars.

I was witnessing these streetcars (called *Strassenbahnen*) moving effortlessly on wires held above the street. The "Strasse" ran up and down Hansa Allee, the street parallel to ours. This was exciting: leaving the Army post so quickly and being in this foreign atmosphere. However, I wasn't sure what to focus on to orient myself.

There was a human bustle to the main streets, even though Germans walked steadily, accentuated by their hands clasped behind their backs. How odd. It looked to me like they were holding themselves hostage. Knowing the history now, I suppose they were. I knew a thing or two about self-suppression, but I was not trying to stifle a Nazi salute. I was required to sublimate any notions unbecoming of a young lady. Who was this mythical, perfect "young lady"?

The dress of the city locals depended on age. The young children dressed in short shorts, brightly colored knit tops, and white bobby socks with sandals. I had never seen *anyone* wear socks with sandals. It seemed counterintuitive to me. Wasn't the point of sandals to *cool* your feet from the heat of being previously enclosed? In addition, the children wore leather bags reminiscent of briefcases on their backs. What was that all about? Were all German kids carrying classified documents?

The young people and teens wore well-tailored, denim bell-bottoms and primarily white or brightly colored tight-fitting knit T-shirts, again with the sock/sandal combo. There was not a lot of facial hair on the teen boys. The adult males wore what looked like khaki or olive-green wool trousers, coupled with long-sleeved dark-colored dress shirts and socks with sandals! The women wore cotton dresses over the knee with the black schoolmarm-style closed leather shoes. I guess women in Germany were no further along in fashion liberation than American women in 1974.

Everyone besides us spoke what I assumed was German and was fair-skinned like my sisters, except for the dark-skinned, dark-haired men who dotted the streets behind portable tables selling trinkets. They were "Turks," as told to us by our American neighbors. Officially, they were *Gastarbeiter*, or guest workers, of the German people.[5] No socks with their sandals for these people. I never saw any women or children with them, just men. I was highly uncomfortable with the way their eyes undressed me and lingered on me, followed by a smile that reminded me of an evil character in a Disney movie. Was I supposed to smile back? If I didn't, was I being rude? They didn't follow the "nod rule"—they spoke to us in English. Were we supposed to answer back? Mom usually did. I noticed that our pace quickened to bypass their tables with a fly-by "hello" from Mom and Dad, ever the good American ambassadors.

At what point, as a female, was I allowed to shout, "You are gross! You have no right to look at me that way. Shut the hell up!" It seemed, never. I felt scared to the bone in a way I had not felt before. Fear was no stranger, but this was a new *type* of fear. I'd had sex ed in sixth grade. I knew about getting a period but had no knowledge beyond that. Mom had never sat me down for the "birds and the bees" talk. That's what April called it. I think she must have read a book. I did not have this book. But I had a deep feeling in my gut that those men were not supposed to be looking at me that way, and I hated how they leered at me.

This was confusing. I wanted to be "noticed," but not like that. But like what? The looks the Turks were giving me were not the stuff of romance. I did not know what it was, and I wanted no part of it. I should have asked Mom about this confusing, scary feeling, but I did not. I did not think we were supposed to discuss "such things." I should have asked April, but I was sure she would laugh disparagingly at me, pointing out yet again how inept I was.

The scenery and Mom's cheer-filled commentary temporarily shaded the deep gouge inside me created by the visual undressing. I was thankful for the diversion. Off the main drag, the narrow Frankfurt city streets, initially forged by horse and pedestrian traffic, were filled with small cars parked halfway onto the sidewalks. There were no behemoth Cadillacs or Buicks. Apparently, the German people were cool with cramming their bodies into tight spaces to commute, unlike Americans. I guess we should have known this, as the Volkswagen brand offered no luxury sedan in the US. But like so much of life before our German stay, I had not drawn any conclusions or observations. Now I was incapable of shutting them out.

During this first Saturday morning on-the-Economy trek, I noted rows and rows of German apartment windows filled with pillows and down comforters. Dad filled in as junior tour guide and announced, "This is how the Germans air out and whiten their bedding in the sun."

Didn't they have dryers or at least a clothesline? If we commented aloud like this, Mom quickly came to their optimistic defense with something like, "Isn't that an ingenious idea?" *Oh, my god, Mom! Can't you be slightly grossed out like I was at the open viewing of other people's drool-stained pillows?* No, she could not. Note to self: Always have enough money and space to afford a dryer.

As we continued our walk, I took copious visual notes. I had done this all my life, and that propensity always made it easy and fantastic to picture scenes from books in my mind. However, the women actively scrubbing the front steps of buildings with metal washbasins and scrub brushes seemed odd to me; that was something I had never seen. What—was there going to be an inspection? They wore floral housedresses and full aprons, just like both of my grandmothers wore.

When we walked by these industrious souls, they met our eyes and nodded. We had been instructed before our walk by Mom to do the same. Apparently, the German people didn't appreciate the vivacious "Good morning" greeting we were accustomed to, or in our family's case, *required* to do as Americans. I was good with the nod, but how stupid did we look if we passed a large group of people and were just all nodding and nodding like an army of bobbleheads?

Sweet *Konditorei* (confectionary) scents were aggressively smudged out by the odor of putrid urine, compliments of men openly peeing in the alleys. Perhaps they had indulged in beer all day and night. We were informed by Army families familiar with local customs that this was acceptable behavior. I guess if beer is served at the *Trinkhalle* during the wee hours of morning and night, one *must* pee frequently.[6] Still, it was super gross, and when I caught a glimpse of some guy with a stream of yellow piddling at his feet, it evoked raucous laughter from my sisters and me and a pinched face on Mom. Sorry, Mom. Dad just smiled. It was nice to see him smile.

He had a good smile. He liked it when we were well-behaved. Really, who doesn't like it when children are well-behaved? No one likes a *brat*. Still, it's hard always to be well-behaved. It was *so* hard when I was hungry. My blood sugar drop meant a total rise in my cranky factor.

The street-side food offerings, perhaps precursors of the American food trucks of today, laced the Frankfurt streets. This was "fast food," but not what we Americans defined as McDonald's-era fast foods: bratwurst on *brochen* (a hard roll), *pommes frites* (french fries), warm Coke with a lemon slice, warm beer, and many other German specialties graced the daily menu.

I knew not to ask Dad if we could stop and get something. The McKnights didn't do that. It wasn't lunchtime, so there was no eating. Even though we were walking at a fast clip, we were not on a "hike," so there was no GORP (good ole raisins and peanuts). I would just have to allow my body to go into ketosis and begin eating itself.

Dad had some destination in mind or some allotted number of blocks we were to walk that morning, but none of us accompanying him were privy to that information. I think Laura was the one who finally whined, "Dad, when can we go home?" She was still little at age eleven and seemed to be able to get away with the cute cheeks, slightly turned head, and eyes glistening with possible tears. Dad responded, "We still have a bit more to see, and then we'll take a different route home."

"Oh, Jim. This is all *so* lovely!" Mom probably could have walked forever on the cloud of happiness. When we finally turned onto another street, I guess Dad thought it was essential to show the multitude of neatly arranged items like chairs, small tables, and metal trash cans sitting near the curb down a side street. Our Army-family neighbors back on post had previously described this scenario, informing us that anything left on a curb on the Economy was meant to be taken for the use of others. Mom informed us that "that was for poor people to begin to improve their surroundings, not for greedy teenagers wanting freebies for their rooms." I was sure she was wrong, but it didn't matter what I thought. It never mattered what I thought. We were *instructed* on what to think.

But inside, oh inside, I had much to say. Why the hell did we always have to live with this honor code that the rest of the world did not seem to follow? What was the point of living with such high standards? Who made up these standards? Who would it hurt if I took this free, super-cool, folding wooden chair that would be perfect in my new room? The family that put it out on the street wouldn't have done so if they hadn't *wanted s*omeone to have it. *Were* there poor people in Germany? So far, if there were, they did not look any different than anyone else. What did poor people in Germany look like anyway?

There was no time to ponder those questions because we reached a stopping point at Eschenheimer Turm, a crazy castle-like edifice that looked entirely out of place with the modern buildings surrounding it.[7] Dad quickly filled in with a short history lesson, "This tower was part of a much larger fortification complex built in the early fourteen hundreds."

More important to me at that moment was the fact that this was also a stop for the U-Bahn, the underground transportation system. We boarded there at Eschenheimer Turm. Excellent tour, Dad! He had planned this outing to the last detail for the maximum on-the-Economy experience. So down the U-Bahn steps we went, holding the railing, moving at the brisk pace we permanently adopted when out with Dad, and descended deeper under the city. I had never been on any underground transportation and was not at all sure what to expect. I was just glad to be going back home where I could get something to eat!

We purchased tickets at an automated booth. If Dad explained the procedure that day, I don't remember it. He gave each of us our ticket, and when we got to the turnstile, he showed us how to insert it to enable the bar blocking our entrance to move forward.

I was glad he knew what he was doing because I had no idea where we were going, despite the bright overhead lights and copious signage. He instructed us, "Keep back from the edge of the platform. When our train gets here, you are to wait until the passengers on the train exit, and then we will proceed in a line to board. So stay together and keep your purse in front of your body."

What? Purse in front of our body? What was going to happen? Was this going to be dangerous? It was all so clean and orderly. I didn't have a purse, so no worry there. Still, his warning left my Spidey-senses tingling.

The train pulled up, and an automated lady's voice announced something in German. Dad said, "This is us. Move with a purpose." So we boarded efficiently with the others, sat in the seats Dad pointed out, and moved toward what I hoped was (and ended up being) home. I fell asleep and was awakened by April's elbow in my ribs.

After reaching our stop and exiting with purpose and order, April suggested, "Let's race up the stairs," but Dad put that idea to a quick rest with, "There will be no racing." *Okay, let's plod up step-by-step with the little blood sugar we have left in our systems. Great.*

A short walk from the Miquel-Adickesallee stop, then across Hansa Allee, and we were home. Mom put together a quick spread of lunch meat, cheese, bread, butter, and lettuce, and we each made our own sandwiches at the dining room table. After I'd consumed enough calories to enable me to speak again, I asked Dad if he knew more about the Eschenheimer Tower.

April rolled her eyes at me. Why did she have to roll her eyes? I was genuinely interested! It looked like part of a fairy-tale castle. Dad said, "We can look in your mother's guidebook later." He always referred to Mom as "your mother" when he talked about her to us.

I did not know the history of Frankfurt, either before World War II or after. I had only my experiences and a few stories from Mom and Dad about their childhoods. I wanted something exciting to happen to me. But I didn't want it. I wanted to experience something I never had before. And yet I didn't want to. I did not have words for that suffocating duality, but I learned some years later that it was called generalized anxiety disorder. I don't think there is anything in the *Diagnostic and Statistical Manual of Mental Disorders* for the opposite drive to "see stuff." That was all Army Brat.

SOUNDTRACK MEINES LEBENS (SOUNDTRACK OF MY LIFE)

After returning home, the newness of the long trek on the Economy necessitated a period of retreat. I went up to my room and recalibrated with music. My nervous system required an activity that allowed a return to homeostasis.

USAREUR had one English-speaking radio station: AFN, the American Forces Network. It consisted of various blocks of modern music alongside the music of yesteryear and, late into the night, old radio serial shows from the World War II era. AFN was one of the ways the US military kept the US forces and their families entertained, while boosting morale with the connection to "home."[8]

I listened on the only portable music device available in the mid-twentieth century. It was my prized Sharp transistor radio Dad had brought back for me when he returned from his tour of duty in Vietnam in 1970. It had a single ear-speaker plugged into the side and was fueled with a 9-volt battery.

With no ability to choose when a favored song came on, I spent hours listening to musical groups and singers I had never heard before. All I could do was hope that "my song" would come on; sometimes it did, and sometimes it didn't. Moreover, my favorite song changed as I heard more music.

I am beyond thankful to AFN for those years, because it forced me to experience various musical genres. All that self-imposed waiting and listening defined and expanded my musical tastes. (My playlist is provided for your listening pleasure at the back of this book.)

The disco era was in full play, and Donna Summer was front and center. I can assure you that her extended version of "Love to Love You Baby" with the moans and groans simulating sex is not a song you want to hear over breakfast with your dad. The one time that happened, he glared at me over the *Stars and Stripes* newspaper like I had chosen the song!

Oh, my god! I didn't write the song, and I didn't sing the song. I didn't even turn on the goddamned radio that morning! How was it then that I felt so responsible for Dad's discomfort and anger at that moment? Why couldn't I turn off the Mary-as-Martyr behavior loop in my mind? That song could not end soon enough for either of us.

Dad carefully screened any albums we purchased from the PX, the Army post exchange, by listening to and evaluating all the lyrics. Anything that he deemed inappropriate was banned from airing over the stereo speakers. We had one stereo system purchased at the Frankfurt PX. Unfortunately, it was in the living room, and we were only allowed to play our records aloud when Dad was at work.

The stereo also had a cassette player and an 8-track player. The 8-track was Dad's favorite listening device. His "Ray Conniff Orchestra" library was on full blast on weekends. This was one musical genre I never gravitated toward, ever! I swear the man listened to that music to get on our nerves. Even Mom hated it. It didn't matter.

Mom's musical tastes were formed in her Chicago family home in the wee hours of the night in the early 1950s on her little radio. As she described it to me, "I had to listen to my music in secret. I loved the blues with Muddy Waters, B. B. King, John Lee Hooker, and Little Richard."

I did not understand what had to be so secret about it and asked her. "Secret? You mean like your dad listened to the lyrics like Dad does and censored your choices?"

"My father didn't speak English. It was society doing the censoring. It was scandalous for white people to listen to Black people's music in Chicago."

More questions from me: "What was scandalous about it? Music is music."

Mom's response through a pinched face: "Well, things were different back then, and white and Black people did not associate with one another."

Me, with wide-eyed fascination and wonder: "Why? People are people."

Mom, still visually taut but trying to open: "Yes, but not everyone sees it that way. We do, but some don't, and you don't want to mess with those people."

Me, with indignation: "Well, I do not even want to know 'those people.' How stupid can you get?"

Mom, with the sword of truth by her side: "Mare, hate makes for hate. We can't change some people and their ill-informed attitudes, but what we can change is ourselves. That's work enough."

I'd like to say that the conversation continued in a give-and-take of in-depth information, but I was thirteen and did not want to feel any more uncomfortable than I already did. I just loved music and didn't care what the artist looked like; they just looked how they looked. If I didn't like a genre of music or a song, it was because it did not speak to me emotionally. If I liked it, it either woke something inside me or enhanced the way I already felt.

Because of the eclectic AFN playlist, which included soul, classic rock, classical, jazz, and country, my musical taste and appreciation encompass a variety of genres.

The soundtrack of my life from ages thirteen to sixteen still elicits the emotions celebrated, sorrows cried over, and memories forever sealed in my head and heart during that time. As I listened, I saw movies of my own making in my mind. It was such a lovely escape from the teen angst loop of my thoughts.

My first musical loves were heavily influenced by my second-grade teacher at Occoquan Elementary in Virginia, Mrs. Hoxie. She had played "Hey Jude" for us, and, at age eight, I knew that something had awakened inside me. Music created pictures, scenes, and ideas in my mind. There, I belonged and felt no fear, anxiety, or panic. This retreat, with volume and bass on high, is still the one thing that gives me deliverance from the crushing weight of anxiety.

We had no TV for the first two years in Frankfurt. Our only connection to the States (other than AFN radio) was via written paper correspondence sent and received by airmail. No long-distance phone calls were allowed on our Bakelite black rotary phone, as the price was cost prohibitive, according to Dad. The mail was delivered to Dad at his place of work—the IG Farben Building. That meant to get the mail, we had to wait for Dad to come home.

There was a day shortly after we arrived in Frankfurt when, meeting Dad at the door as we always did with the greeting of, "Hi! Any mail for me?" he expressed an approximation of previously unknown (to us) feelings.

"It would be nice," he spoke calmly, "if you girls were happier to see me than to see if you had mail."

Ugh—this was an emotional hit to the solar plexus for me. I had hurt Dad, and I had not meant to. He made me crazy, and sometimes I really did not like him, but I had not set out to hurt him. April just looked annoyed at his comment. Laura's eyes welled with tears, and Mom quickly countered with, "Oh, Jim, they're just young, and I'm sure they are glad to see you. They will alter their greeting, and all will be well." Mom was like a UN ambassador/mediator extraordinaire with her de-escalation skills. I do not know where she learned or honed this ability.

It annoyed me at the time because it never seemed like she won. Didn't she want to win? Didn't it bother her that she was always compromising? Now I am genuinely in awe of her knowledge of power play and her ability to quickly assess a "hot" situation and calm it down.

I learned this skill from her and have used it numerous times in professional situations. However, the part she never learned (and I did not learn until late in my teaching career) was that a person eventually needs to vent the anger they had kept at bay until a later time—not keep it forever stuffed inside.

Calm on the outside, boiling on the inside is a perfect storm for the body learning to see itself as the enemy. Autoimmune issues, addiction—hmmm . . . suppressed emotions, anyone?

ALLES DREHT SICH UM DIE SCHUHE (IT'S ALL ABOUT THE SHOES)

B eing a "happy subordinate" was easier as a child when I was not questioning everything internally. I do so appreciate Mom's playing mediator between us sisters and Dad all those years. Dad was used to the chain-of-command mentality, which came with the expectation that those with lower "rank" should not be insubordinate.

I understand now why he was the way he was because of the nature of his work during my growing-up years. But in 1974, I thought he yanked my chain and that of Mom and my sisters for some other power-hungry reason.

Dad's work at the IG Farben/Abrams Building was within walking distance of our house. Until recently, I only thought of the IG Farben Building as Dad's place of work—nothing else—though the halls I strolled had been where Zyklon B (the gas used by the Nazis in the concentration camps) was developed. The only history in the mid-seventies I was interested in was my own.

There was a mini PX in the IG Farben where I bought Toblerone candy bars, and where I also acquired my first pair of Adidas. White leather with three red stripes on each side of the shoe, the brand was made extremely popular in Deutschland by the West German athletes during the '72 Olympic Games in Munich.[9] I came to Germany with deck shoes and soon realized that to have a hope of looking cool, those Adidas were a necessity.

Mom was very hard to convince. She was not at all sure that Adidas conformed to and conveyed a genteel, proper look. Her staid attitude may have been fabulous in the 1950s, but in the mid-seventies, I was going to be a social outcast if I did not dress in some approximation of the style of my peers. I was sure of that.

My Barbies were far better dressed than I was. They were back in storage in the States, but I knew each of their outfits by heart. Every ensemble had a name, like "Lemon Kick." If they had names, my own outfits were "Boring and Banal" or "Chic for a Nun."

April was the driving force behind our clothing transformation, beginning with the acquisition of the coveted Adidas. She appealed to Mom with health reasons to purchase the shoes. "Mom, they are made of leather, and leather breathes better than the cotton that our deck shoes are made from." *Very smart, Ape. Know your audience and appeal to their beliefs—let me file that tactic away for future use.*

With Mom giving us permission to buy the Adidas, April and I were off to IG Farben.

DIE SUCHE (THE QUEST)

To acquire my cool shoes, I needed to overcome my fear of the paternoster, a constantly moving series of elevators where you must step off when it comes to your floor. There were no doors, and it never stopped! It's really a wonder I weighed anything during the Frankfurt years because I was constantly sweating in the face of all these new experiences, the paternoster being one of them.

Dad thought it was an efficient method of intra-building transport, and he easily rode it to his office day after day. We didn't know what Dad did at work. We never knew. We still don't know! When he returned from the Vietnam War in 1969, and I asked him what he had done there, he said, "Soil erosion control." Asked and answered. Any follow-up questions would not have been gladly entertained or elaborated. Dad was in the Army. That's all we ever knew. Mom said that when he returned from Vietnam, he never said a word about it, and she did not ask.

Now, on reading that, many people will probably say, "Your mom is such a saint!" I believe the by-product of so many unanswered questions and unsaid truths is why women contract addictions and autoimmune disorders at such an alarming rate.

When I have not spoken my truth but instead suffered in silence, I have developed an array of autoimmune diseases. For example, vitiligo, a condition where one loses the color in their skin, began to show up on my exterior when my interior knew that I had given up my own "color," my own voice, my own demands and requirements, and knew I should be with some-one who wanted me to express—not suppress—myself.

Mom attributes the longevity of her marriage to my dad to this self-imposed editing. Well, I tried, and I tried, and I tried in my adult relationships, but after contracting Graves' disease from one relationship debacle, vitiligo from another relation-ship gaffe, and finally two frozen shoulders from the last tango with self-imposed suppression, I stopped doing it. But in 1974, I was pretty adept at suppressing my emotions. My stomach, oh, my stomach, knotted and shook so violently that my shirt moved.

With my shirt moving compliments of adrenaline-fueled anxiety, pits wet with sweat, and the chide of April—"Come on! I'm going up and getting those shoes, and if you don't, you will be forced to continue wearing those rinky-dink deck shoes!"—I picked up my pace. My desire for fashion was more potent than my fear that day, and I leaped onto the paternoster, almost plowing into an officer already standing in the moving compartment.

"Oh! I'm so sorry, sir," I quickly said while looking him in the eye and absorbing the mortified look on April's face—made just for me and at me.

"That's all right, young lady. It takes some getting used to." Even though it was so kind of him to say what he did, it still bugged me that he called me "young lady." Yuck. What a stupid, stifling term.

After purchasing our glorious all-leather, three-stripe "Vienna" Adidas, April and I sat by the reflecting pool and changed into them for the walk home. This was the begin-ning of my fashion transformation and my love of most things European.

JUNGE VERRÜCKT
(BOY CRAZY)

I n our 1974 overseas neighborhood, living by the stifling *Army Wife* handbook, I sought opportunities for freedom. The only answer for self-preservation was to engage in an activity that already had prescribed rules and fun. We were quickly brought into the fold by two of the families on our street. Wherever we lived, neighbors were a large part of our daily lives.

We were no strangers to the freedom of unstructured time and place that the outdoors provided. The lack of air-conditioning in our German living quarters invited many an evening of kick the can. The boundaries were set anywhere among our three houses, thus providing a triangle of possibilities to run and hide.

I was never a fast runner or a good climber, so I spent many an evening as "It." Unfortunately, I'm probably still "It." I could only escape that moniker when the younger kids played with us. The game was fabulously exhausting, and the filthy ring around the post-game bathtub proved my commitment to the whole experience.

The value of this activity for me was the instant friendship it provided. No intimate conversation was necessary, no revealing of anything—just establishing the game's rules. The social construct of military Brat inclusion was a real boon for an introvert like me. I didn't have to extend myself to anyone in any way beyond "Where all have you lived?" Our youthful interactions easily crossed lines of ethnicity, race, class, height, weight, and age.

Dad had established his own set of compadres during the six weeks he was without us, and we soon met a family that had a lasting impact on me. Enter Colonel Motsko, his wife, Liz, and their three gorgeous sons, who were a few years older than us.

Young Mike was on summer break from college, Greg had just graduated from high school, and Nick was going into eleventh grade. I was smitten with each of them from the get-go, and thus began my entry into boy craziness. It was an absolute, instantaneous intoxication for me at the cellular level.

The Brut cologne, dark, longish hair, tender eyes . . . What was a girl supposed to do? Sweat. My initiation at the Motskos' into the Boy Crazy Club was the pit-to-waist sweat stains on the dark cotton blouse I had chosen to wear to their house. The Ban roll-on deodorant was no match for my overactive sweat glands. Ugh, those huge, dark sweat stains. What an impression I must have made. I was not used to this lack of control over my bodily functions; the nervousness that precipitated it was an old frenemy.

I kept my growing interest in the opposite sex to myself. April and I did not have a conversational relationship. She was only fifteen months older than me, but we were vastly different temperamentally. This dynamic can be traced back to the moment in Altus, Oklahoma, when Mom brought me home from the hospital as a newborn. At fifteen months old, April had not walked a step yet, but she began walking the day I came home. There are numerous slides of this event, but none of me coming home until a few weeks later. She seemed comfortable with her Queen Bee status and never missed an opportunity to let me know this. I imagine there is a reason why so many firstborns and only children become presidents or dictators.

At the Motskos', the adults were served hot buttered rum, and we kids were given hot buttered water. Having never had this beverage, I slurped down the semi-melted butter pat in the first silent "Oh, my god, this water is burning the roof of my mouth" sip. I said nothing so as not to call attention to myself, but I could feel the skin peeling from the roof of my mouth.

I can't recall a time when I have not felt the heavy responsibility of protecting people from myself. My life was rife with shape-shifting, activity acquiescing, and staying quiet on the outside to please others. Inside I felt loud and opinion-filled but continued to internalize what should have been externalized, so as not to disappoint anyone. I have spent a lifetime absorbing wincing looks and pursed lips and wearing them on my skin, losing my color and giving up my color, unable to answer the questions of expansion and fearful of any and all responses answered with a loud chorus of "What will I do if . . . ?"

I always kept my frailties to myself. And yet there was this drive inside me to be free. And with boy craziness coursing through my veins, I was given a gift and a challenge.

The age difference between us, along with the staggering good looks of the Motsko boys, rendered me mute. April managed to talk with them, and Laura just hung by Mom. I . . . I just produced sweat. On the walk back across Hansa Allee to our house, April felt it was important to describe my sweat stains to me. "Uhh! Did you forget to use deodorant? You have huge stains from your pits to your waist!" *Thank you so much, April!*

She was right. My dark cotton blouse was marred with such dark stains that, forty-five years later, I don't ever wear blouses. At the time, I didn't come back with some verbal cut to her esteem. My peace-loving heart absorbed the verbal analysis. I never questioned her opinions of me and carried my anger and views of myself via her with me through the writing of most of this book.

Mom always wanted us to bond as siblings, and to assist this process, she sent us off on short sojourns together around the post, aka Little America.

IN DIE TIEFE
(INTO THE DEEP)

The post had built-in activities to keep the troops happy and discourage them from engaging in tawdry off-hours pursuits. Many an afternoon was spent at the bowling alley, close to the BOQ (bachelor officers' quarters) from our house on Hansa Allee. Laura and I went there together to bowl, with our neighbor Jenny often joining us, but April only sometimes accompanied us. She did grace us one day with her presence, which provided a most memorable afternoon, still told in story and song. I'm sure she thought she was doing us a favor, and truth be told, we were always glad when she joined us for activities.

She brought a new level of competition wherever she went. I volunteered to show her how to throw the ball, as she had never bowled before. I was getting pretty good and scoring well, but she rebuffed my offer with, "I already know how."

Fine! Throw the damn ball. I was expecting her to make a strike on the first try because that's how it always worked for April, no matter what she tried. Instead, what transpired next was an epic failure. She chose her ball off the rack, put her three fingers in, and threw it *overhand* like a baseball down the lane. Laura and I erupted in laughter that filled the alley. I can still see the ball flying and landing with a bomb-like thud about mid-lane. The rest of the outing is lost to the ages, except for the fact that I beat her that day. She never bowled with us again.

It resulted in a permanent hollow in our lane. It was probably still there when the Frankfurt post was decommissioned and dismantled in 1995.

Our forays off-post were frequent, as Mom was ever determined for us to experience the German culture. However, we were not interested in doing this because it meant that Mom would speak her fractured German, and we (as young teens) looked stupid by association. It was far better if we went off on our own.

That first summer, Mom allowed us to walk to the PX/ commissary complex if we went together. With my military ID shoved in my pocket and a little American money for spending, off we three went.

"We stay together. I know the way." April sounded confident, so there was no need for me to be anything but a willing participant. We crossed Hansa Allee, mindful of the two-way automobile traffic, plus the Strasse. This was not my favorite part of the walk, as I don't think the drivers remembered that this was not the Autobahn!

Once across Hansa, we passed a Trinkhalle. Men, garbed in their wool pants and long-sleeved shirts, were already drinking beer. It was ten in the morning. Weird. Shortly after the Trinkhalle, we descended the steps of the U-Bahn station.

"Now, we will walk quickly past the Turks. Do not speak, do not make eye contact, just keep walking," were the firm directives from April.

"I thought Mom told us to nod," I responded.

"Look, they are creepy, and if you know what's good for you, you'll follow my lead."

This was not good—creepy men in an underground station. I was not going to like this. As we continued through the station headed for the exit near the PX, little tables filled with trinkets appeared. There were the men.

"Hey, pretty girls. Where are you going? Stop to look. We have some lovely things."

There was no way in hell we were slowing down! April maintained a steady pace, and we three whisked by the Turks.

Shortly afterward, we slowed down, and April said precisely what I was thinking, "They are so gross." Then we came upon a person, the likes of whom we had never seen before. This person was super tall, very broad shouldered, wearing a dress, and sporting a full beard. This individual wore makeup. This human was smiling and singing to themselves. We three said nothing as we passed.

We said nothing as we ran up the stairs into daylight and walked into the PX/commissary complex. Laura, the youngest of us, was the only one who dared to speak about what all three of us were wondering.

"Was that a man or a woman?"

Then we all burst out laughing. That was the early teen years in 1974. When faced with someone dressing and acting in a way we had not seen or heard about before on the three TV channels back in the States or in any type of reading material, we laughed.

April summed it up: "It was an It."

I am embarrassed to say that the entire three years we lived in Frankfurt, we referred to that individual as "It." At the time, I felt frightened, just not knowing their motivation or how to respond to them.

None of us ever mentioned "It" to Mom or Dad. My goodness. What must it have been like for that transgender individual in 1974? I am not an overly remorseful person, but I am genuinely and deeply remorseful for referring to another human being as "It." We never spoke to him/her. We only ever walked quickly by, just as we did past the guest workers.

Due to the teachings of my parents (to whom I am so very, very thankful), I knew even then that the behavior of one person does not generalize to all the other people of their race, religion, or lifestyle choices.

I did talk about the Turks with Mom and asked where their wives and children were. She did not know, but in researching this era recently, I read that the men generally left their country of origin to obtain a visa and go to work in Germany. In the 1960s, Germany needed cheap labor and so established a two-year visa system with Turkey. The men were originally to be unmarried, but by the 1970s, the visas were extended, and families began joining or coming with their husbands.

Mom was very firm and clear when she told us, "You are not to adversely judge the Turkish people based on the inappropriate behavior of a few Turkish men." I am truly grateful to her for always being a vocal and behavioral advocate of making judgments of people based on their individual character and actions.

TAGESAUSFLÜGE
(DAY TRIPS)

Life on post became quite familiar that first summer, but there was a whole big Europe out there, and Mom was determined for us to experience it. That meant going counter to Dad's wishes. My parents *never* argued in front of us growing up. I truly had no idea that they were ever mad at each other!

That probably seems like an amazing way to grow up, but the downside was that I grew up with absolutely no idea how to argue with a loved one and come out okay on the other side. I thought I just had to absorb whatever bad feelings I felt via sublimation and move on. That is a hard way to live life!

Mom shared many years later that, after the first European June of going nowhere, she had sternly said to Dad, "Now, Jim, I did not fly all the way across the Atlantic Ocean with three girls, many suitcases, and a cat to be in Europe and go nowhere! Now, either you take us places, or I will start going with the girls myself!"

An officer's wife back then was the glue of the family, but she took a back seat to the officer's career. His word was law. He made all the final decisions, so this was quite bold of Mom to speak up, and I am forever grateful to her for her stance on that subject. What must it have taken for her to rise up and speak her truth? I asked her once recently, but she does not remember ever saying that. I mentioned it to my two sisters, but Mom had never told them about that solitary Mom–Dad confrontational incident.

As a boy-crazy teen, I was more interested in the comings and goings of Nick Motsko than visiting places of antiquity, but off we went. One early trip was to the Palmengarten in Frankfurt with the whole family. *Great, a flower garden.* We knew how this would play out. Mom, oohing and aahing over all the flora, greeting every human she met along the way with a cheery, "*Guten Tag,*" despite the nod rule. She couldn't contain her enthusiasm. Oh no! A breakdown in Rule Land! Did that mean we, too, were supposed to speak now rather than nod? I thought the modus operandi was "When in Rome, do as the Romans do."

Did this mean that we could also bend the rules? This was a question I asked only internally, as I was pretty sure I knew the answer. There was no rule bending.

Dad seemed to take joy in Mom's verbal expressions of happiness while wandering the floral paths. As rigid as he was with us kids, Dad adored Mom. It showed in his eyes. The way they looked at each other said they were in it together. How was this possible? She was like a servant. Was that how men and women got along? And when the woman stopped agreeing, was that when divorce happened? Did I have to keep men happy to get and keep one? What about me? When did my needs get met? There was no time to stand and ponder, as my loitering held up the ability of others to view the floral displays. We couldn't have that.

We were forced to endure this trip with Dad taking five thousand color slides, all of which we were required to view once they were developed. Dad's cameras weighed a ton, and he felt compelled to carry *every* lens imaginable. This consumed an inordinate amount of time, with us all waiting for him to get the perfect shot, as we were not allowed to walk ahead. It was the day and age of "film," so there were no wasted shots.

For this required floral fest, we three sisters had decided to wear shorts, football jerseys with our first names printed on the front (why the names were not on the back, I do not remember), tube socks, and those dreaded deck shoes. Why not the stylish Adidas? Mom thought the deck shoes were more ladylike.

The Germans stared at us the whole time; I think it was because we were woefully underdressed in their estimation and according to their tradition. Or perhaps our disastrous matching outfits led them to believe that we were going to break out into a three-part Osmond Brothers harmony. What were we supposed to come in, lederhosen? At our age, we didn't consider (or really know, for that matter) how one was supposed to dress to walk around and look at flowers. *Get over it, people—it's summer.* Mom noticed the stares, and we weren't allowed to ever go beyond the confines of the military post dressed "like that" again. McKnight girls for the epic fashion fail.

Being good American ambassadors in Deutschland, to enhance and grow our cultural boundaries required us to dress in long pants, not jeans. Mom was concerned that if we went out in jeans, we would be perceived as "hoodlums." I can guarantee that even if we *had* worn jeans, no one was going to perceive us as anything but awkward kids.

I had begun to question aloud, while one-on-one with Mom, the rules on appropriate dress. "Mom, I don't see everyone else following these rules!"

Mom's response was, "Well, people judge others. They just do. And they make these judgments based on appearances at first. It's a fact. You want to make a good first impression so that others will want to get to know you."

This made no sense to me and I countered with, "If they don't like the way I dress and judge me adversely because of it, why would I want to know them?"

Her answer: "It's just the way it is."

"What? Who made that rule?"

Mom's final response to this moral volley-and-return was, "Men did. Men . . . are a disappointment."

Whoa . . . a disappointment? This was not good. What the hell? She had to be wrong. Maybe she had just met the wrong *kind* of man. That had to be it. Otherwise, what was the use for women? Well, I was not going to be held down. *I* was not going to be defined by a man. But I was to not honor my promise to myself time and time again. In 1974 moving toward 1975, I was still heavy in "Man Land."

DER DIALOG
(THE DIALOGUE)

When I did have the opportunity to pick out my own style, I did so. With my maroon bell-bottom corduroy Levi's, short-sleeved T-shirt with a faded blue VW logo, and Adidas on, I was ready to accompany Mom on a walk to the PX that fall of 1974.

On that walk, Mom met one of her Officers' Wives' Club friends. The friend looked at me and said, "Oh, is this your son?" Your *son*? Great.

After this graceless encounter ended, Mom quickly responded to me with, "I think she might be going blind."

"Mom, she was not going blind! She saw my flat chest and stupid face, and she just assumed I was a boy!"

"Oh, now don't be so hard on yourself. You are a beautiful young woman, and you will grow into yourself."

What did *that* mean? "Grow into myself?" Who had I grown into so far? Apparently, according to this Wives' Club friend, a boy. I had grown into a boy.

Awkwardness was not only played out in my style of dress but in required interactions with the locals. A trip to Mespel-brunn Castle, a medieval moated castle between Frankfurt and Wurzburg, is most memorable to our family in retrospect for the "Violin Incident." They remember it for the "humor," but I recall it for the outright humiliation. I only tell it to my family as a funny incident. That is the way I have forged my memories to get past the abject pain and humiliation—with comedy. Isn't that how all comedy is created?

Out front of this schloss we visited was an elderly man playing a violin. I had been studying a bit of German and had memorized a dialogue that Dad thought rendered itself useful at Mespelbrunn.

The dialogue went like this: "*Was machst du? Ich übe Geige. Bist du müde? Ja.*" This loosely translates to, "What are you doing? I'm playing the violin. Are you tired? Yes."

Dad said to me, "Mare, go up to him and use your German dialogue."

At first it was a request, but I rebutted with, "Dad, this is going to be *totally* embarrassing. I think I'll pass."

One did not "pass," and Dad then ordered me, "Go up and use your dialogue!" Oh, my god! This was going to be mortifying! I was so angry inside, but what was I going to do? The overwhelming powerlessness gave me a brief thought of drowning myself in the moat just to escape this Dad demand.

But off I went in my required pants—not jeans—to the native German man to speak in the worst possible German accent—as I had no formal training—with a dialogue asking a question to which I already knew the answer.

The man looked up at me after I asked him, "*Was machst du?*" like I was possibly the stupidest person on the planet. I have no idea what he said in retort because it was vastly different than the German text dialogue. I think he was saying, "You dumb American. This is a violin; now take your elitist occupier status and get the hell out of here."

When I returned to my family after this memorable exchange, Dad eagerly asked, "How did it go?"

"He said he was playing the violin and looked at me like I was an idiot."

Mom helped me try to save face and filled in the long silence with, "Oh, I'm sure he was pleased you took an interest in him!" Mom always thought the best of people. I wish she had said in private, "Mare, your dad is who he is. I'm so sorry that you had to go through that. It must've been so hard. It will not always be like this. You will go to college and make your own way in the world with no one telling you what to do but yourself." She didn't, and I did not know enough to think those thoughts at the time.

April was beyond amused at my being forced into that clumsy exchange with Herr Violin. She didn't even know German! She knew French. How was that going to help us in Germany? It didn't matter what I said or what I thought. I was always going to be fumbling and bumbling. The only thing that April and I had as a common denominator was teen hunger and the quest for food.

IN DER ÜBERSETZUNG VERLOREN (LOST IN TRANSLATION)

If Dad was with us, there was no *Schnellimbiss* food, but if he wasn't, Mom was fine with us filling up German style. It meant less work for her at home, and it also meant contented teens as traveling companions.

If we were out at lunchtime, I opted for a bratwurst on *brochen* (a hard roll) slathered with spicy mustard and *pommes frites* (french fries). I was getting used to warm Coke with a lemon slice. We didn't drink soda at home, so even lukewarm Coke was a treat.

If we were out in the late afternoon, it meant a pit stop at a *Konditorei*. Monday through Friday at midafternoon, business locals closed their shops, and people flocked to these bakeries for coffee and dessert.

My first bite into a plum kuchen made my face squish up with sourness. This was not the sweet dessert of Hostess Twinkies and Ding Dongs I was used to from the United States. Mom marveled at the lightness of the crust, so I decided to be the one sister who liked it. Mom had this childlike innocence about her, and I felt it needed protecting and validating. This "coming to the rescue of the underdog" was something I had always felt.

It confused me, as the drive to do so ran counter to my dad's "pull yourself up by your bootstraps" mentality. I could not control the truth, though, that if others were bullied, neglected, or forgotten, then it was up to me to show them their self-worth.

When I was four and April was five, a girl named Diana used to make fun of April. I thought I could help this situation by being Diana's friend, so I set about including her in our Nebraska games. The bullying stopped. People need kindness. Hurt people need a lot of kindness. That lesson in being kind to others defines the one part of me that has never altered. It is perhaps my core truth.

To be more of Mom's friend meant that I had to step up in the chores department. As young teens, we were forever hungry, which meant frequent food shopping—and that was a chore. To continue with Mom's desire to appreciate the great big Europe at our doorstep, we periodically went to German stores.

It was just one Strasse ride to the Kaufhof, a multilevel Frankfurt shopping experience. Upon our entry, a pungent odor smacked me in the face. This full-stop shopping experience, with clothing and home goods on one level and food on the other, was complete with hanging sausages everywhere. I assumed the fetid odor lacing the air on every floor was due to these tubes stuffed with meat parts.

I never wanted Mom to buy me any clothing from there because I was sure the essence of wurst would linger. You don't want to smell like dead meat products when you are thirteen.

The first time we went, we all loaded up our cart with various fresh fruits, vegetables, and bread unavailable at the American commissary.

The cashier must have taken one look at us and known we were American. I think it was Mom's super bouffant hairdo that gave us away. The cashier asked with a sweet smile, "Your bags?"

Mom answered with a full-on smile of kindness right back, "Oh, yes, thank you."

The cashier then had a quizzical look on her face and said in broken English, "You have them?"

None of us had any idea what she was talking about, but then she pointed at the people in the line behind us and said something in German. The customer held up a small string fishing net stuffed with other string fishing nets. What was with the fishing nets?

Mom understood that they were bags—shopping bags, reusable shopping bags. They were a staple of the German shopping experience. Mom's face was crestfallen. We did not have these bags. We had no bags. We just assumed everything would be bagged up in requisite brown Kraft paper bags.

"Oh, my goodness. We did not know. I am so . . . *Entschuldigen.*" (When Mom said it, it sounded like, "IIIIn shulding.")

Our phrasebook had supplied, "*Entschuldigen Sie bitte,*" but none of us knew that was only one of many "Oops, sorry, we are stupid Americans who need to apologize" phrases used. There was *Entschuldigen Sie bitte meine Fehler.* > Excuse my mistakes.

Entschuldigen Sie . . . / Entschuldige dass . . . > Excuse me that . . . / Sorry that . . .

Entschuldigen Sie bitte, dass ich Sie störe. > Excuse me for disturbing you.

Entschuldige bitte, dass ich es vergessen habe. > Sorry for forgetting.

And if that weren't enough, *Entschuldigung / dich um Entschuldigung* > Sorry / Please excuse me.

I felt so helpless and desperate to assist Mom with her heartfelt apology. I thought she was going to cry, and I quickly said, "Mom, it's okay. We'll know next time." Then I turned to April and Laura. "Come on, guys, let's put this stuff back." *Must alleviate the suffering of others! Must protect those who need protec-tion!* I could have slapped the irritated look off of April's face. Who the hell kicks people when they are down?

What the hell was wrong with April? Mom had only ever exuded the kindness attributed to a saint to every goddamned person she had ever met and to us! It oozed out of Mom, and April was some stupid anomaly I was embarrassed to know and, worse yet, have as an immediate family member!

We returned to the cashier with the few items we could carry in our hands and then boarded the Strasse to head back home from "the sausage emporium." There were no seats left, so we stood, awkwardly, each with one hand holding onto the poles in the middle of the aisle. Laura was plastered under the arm of a burly German gent in a sleeveless shirt. The dank odor wafting from his hairy pits quickly spread across the tight area we all shared.

The German standard of personal cleanliness was a mite bit different than the American standard. This smell-a-thon ride on the Strasse was a quick lesson in German "no deodorant" hygiene. Mom tossed us looks meant to quell our snickering. I hope that we did, but I think we did not. Ahh . . . the Ugly American.

DER EINGESCHLAGENE WEG (THE PATH TAKEN)

Mom and Dad were determined that we regularly engage not only with the local population and with the city proper but also with the German landscape. Dad was quite enamored of the backpacking craze of the seventies, and hiking in the local Taunus Mountains provided the breadth of experience that Mom wanted and the physical challenge Dad needed. We kids were forced to go along.

Dad was in his early forties, and I was a spry thirteen, ready to experience our Family von Trapp "Climb Every Mountain" experience. To gear up for the trek, we had made a trip to the Rhein-Main PX, which had a dedicated outdoor department. Dad said we needed "proper hiking boots." That meant classic leather, metal eyelet, and brown-laced ankle-high boots. Cool.

My feet were already up to their total growth at size eight and a half. The boots were German, so that meant European sizing. Prior to our Taunus Mountain hike, Dad instructed us to manually bend our boots over and over to break them in.

Oh, my god, this was so much work! Why couldn't we just go on the damn walk? I was sorry later that I had not put the proper amount of time and work into the "breaking-in process."

Dad had also purchased a daypack into which Mom had contributed individual bags of GORP. Dad added the trail map, and we each carried our own old Girl Scout metal canteens of water. Dad did not give us any details of the trail. He did say that we were going to be stopping somewhere to eat while hiking.

How was that going to be possible? What, was he going to shoot a squirrel, skin it, and cook it over an open fire? I did not ask.

As we passed other hikers on the trail, I noted that the men all had on long leather shorts and wore wool-rag knee socks with their leather hiking boots. I wore a stiff pair of Levi's and white cotton bobby socks with my leather boots. I paid for this error in sock wear, along with my shoddy "boot break-in" efforts, in the form of massive and copious blisters.

Luckily Dad had also packed a first-aid kit complete with moleskin. Was it really made from the skin of little moles? I didn't know and didn't care at that point, as I was so glad for the relief it provided me.

"Well, I guess next time I give you directions, you'll follow them," Dad said with a smile.

"I don't know what happened," I said defensively. "I did what you told me!" (No, I hadn't.)

With my blisters covered, we were back on the trail. Dad walked like we were in some type of competition. I kept trying to walk beside him, but whenever I got close, he went into some walking warp speed.

That man *never let me catch up to him* on any part of the hike. How was this possible? Why couldn't we walk side by side, chatting away? There was no talking, as far as Dad was concerned. He always marched along like we were on some mission.

If it had been me, and I were leading the trek, I would have turned to the others and said, "How's the pace?" Or if I noticed that others were falling behind, I would have slowed down. It was not a race!

I hate competition. I did then, and I do now. It seemed to me that when you were competing with someone else, the goal was to dominate and destroy. This was not good. This was, I was pretty sure, the reason that we had wars. This greedy mindset of "beating others" seemed like the reason for the world's woes.

I did share this thought with April while on the trail, and she countered with, "What are you, some kind of communist?"

I, of course, had heard of communism because of President Nixon's trips to China and Russia but wasn't sure how that related to me and my belief that we as humanity should share, rather than compete, with one another. It wasn't like I could go to the post library and check out a book on communism, because then it would have looked like I was conspiring with the enemy.

I simply thought there was no good reason to pit oneself against another. Someone always ended up feeling bad. And if that person was me, my loss did not inspire greatness—it inspired defeat and the abandonment of whatever activity in which I was the loser.

I eventually gave up trying to catch up to Dad and strolled back a ways with Mom. The day was gray, and a perpetual mist surrounded us. Every breath I took was happy with the conifer aroma. Well, happy until I was starving.

"Dad, when are we going to eat?"

"When we get there," said Dad, answering the question and yet not really.

"Jim, could you give us some indicator of time until we eat? Even I'm getting hungry!" said Mom with unusual urgency. Mom was never hungry.

After we had walked for what felt like an eternity, we rounded a corner, and there ... there in the middle of the forest was a restaurant. It was either that or someone's private home, but with Dad leading us up to the door, I was sure it was our lunch destination.

We looked around, and I know I was confused at the lack of individual tables. There were just long tables, so we sat at the end of one by ourselves. A group of people already at one of the other long tables motioned for us to come over and sit next to them. Oh no! Mom was sure to try out her German, and she did. They must have appreciated her effort because they answered in very fractured but confident English. Mom, the world's best person. She would have made an excellent United Nations diplomat.

On this first post-hike meal, none of us had thought to bring a German–English phrasebook, so any chance of our translating the menu was nonexistent. Dad took it upon himself to order for all of us. We all had what our German tablemates were having. I can eat just about anything and enjoy it, but Laura was a super-picky eater. When she tried a new food and did not like it, she gagged very loudly, and Mom would usually end up sweeping it out of her mouth with an index finger.

We were used to this, but I think our German tablemates were rather confused. After her first gag and mouth sweep, our seatmate locals ordered a soup for Laura, seeing that the dish (what turned out to be Wiener schnitzel) was not to her liking. Goulash soup ... a dark brew guaranteed to please the most discriminating palate, coupled with a deep dark bread and unsalted butter. Success. The clink of crystal Roemer glasses, green-stemmed goblets filled endlessly with wine, sealed the afternoon, adding to my growing love of Germany.

The intoxicating scent of evergreens will forever bring me back to that day. Standing in the California Redwoods on my forty-ninth birthday some years later, wearing those very same Taunus Mountain boots, I gulped a melancholy I can only imagine was the remembered promises of financial independence and being my authentic self that I had made to myself, forged during those German years and broken over the years since. That, and knowing that Dad had begun to slow his pace, and my wishing I could get back the days when I could never catch him.

DIESER MANTEL IST HÄSSLICH / CE MANTEAU EST LAID (THIS COAT IS UGLY)

Memories of Laura's food-gagging will stand out for all three sisters in Strasbourg, France, a city on the western edge of Germany (hence the dual language translation). This area was returned to the French people after World War II. Public service announcement: Hey, people worldwide, stop conquering and forcing your ways on other countries. It should never have happened in the first place. Mom told me that wars are started by men who still think life is a "Who Can Pee the Farthest" contest. And now, back to our story.

We three had on these stupid matching London Fog brand trench coats that Mom assured us was "a wonderful brand and necessary for the weather in Europe." No one else was wearing them, so I began to think Mom had no idea what she was talking about when suddenly a fellow trench coat wearer came walking down our side of the sidewalk.

He passed by Mom and Dad, and when he came up to the three of us, he opened his matching overcoat and flashed us! It was the first time I had ever seen the male anatomy, and if his was representative of the average "junk," I didn't care if I ever saw it again! Shriveled and sad . . . just shriveled and sad. It was awful, and all we did was burst out laughing! We did not tell Mom or Dad what we had just witnessed. Mom kept saying, "What, what, what is it?" We did not tell her until many, many years later.

Mom was right. Men were a disappointment. So why weren't women running the world? My only thought as an answer to this was the physical strength of men over women, and they are using that as their power play time and time again. That, and that they, as a gender, had brainwashed my gender into believing that we had to spend all our time and resources looking "pretty" for them. Apparently, men felt no pressure and had no beauty standards to maintain, because I can assure you that The Strasbourg Flasher was hideous and yet felt comfortable enough in his manliness to "share" it.

After the horrid flasher display, I couldn't say I was hungry, but Dad announced that it was lunchtime, so we ate. Laura scanned the menu and determined that the only food she could possibly eat was the Black Forest ham. When our food arrived, hers was in log-shaped rolls, kind of like the Flasher's pathetic penis. She took one bite and began audibly choking and gagging. Hardly the "Rick Steves' adventure through Europe" experience. She never ate Black Forest ham again. And me? I hear the word "Strasbourg" and can only picture the flaccid Flasher.

ZEIT FÜR DIE SCHULE
(TIME FOR SCHOOL)

I had tried to eat, but every little grain of Rice Krispies that early September morning made me retch with the oh-so-familiar fear of the unknown. It was time for the new school year to begin. Waiting at the bus stop steps away from our house to be transported to a building we had only been to once (to register) was an exercise in vomit control. Even though April and I were going to the same place, I knew I would not see her again until it was time to go home.

We would know two people: Beret Boy and John from across the street. We had all hung out with John and his two younger sisters throughout the summer, but I didn't know that he would pretend not to know us. I was so hurt, so very hurt, when we met him at the bus stop and he just muttered, "Hi." *What the hell? That's it? That is all you're going to say to us?* I should have said this out loud, but that would not have been ladylike. That would not have been appropriate. Why did girls and women always have to be the "keepers of the appropriate"? At what point did males become responsible for their own f-ing behavior? We had played together *all summer*, and now he was acting as if we barely knew one another?

I looked at April for some sort of . . . well, I don't know what the hell I was looking for from her. She barely talked to me either. It was possible that she was just as stressed as I was at that point, but I was sure they were actively ignoring me because I was not worth talking to and that to associate with me would incur some unspoken social minus.

I balanced my new plastic binder filled with blank, wide-ruled notebook paper, two number two pencils, and one Bic pen against my growing hip bones, along with the lunch Mom had lovingly made and housed in a brown paper bag.

With darkness parting and daylight beginning to shine through, the olive-green Army school bus ride at O-dark-hundred rolled up, ready to head for Frankfurt Junior High School. As soon as the bus door opened, I was hit with cigarette smoke. Because it was still semi-dark outside, the interior lights came on, and there, in the back of the bus, sat the smokers.

Boys and girls alike slowly dragged on cigarettes, attempting to make smoke rings by popping their jaws and, unbeknownst to them, creating skin damage that might result in premature aging from vertical lines around their mouths. Before this, I had never seen kids my age smoke.

My first impression was that they looked like pretenders. *Oooh, look at me smoke, aren't I so grown up?* Then I wondered if their parents knew. They were military Brats like me, and smoking seemed like a break in proper protocol—but there was no time to ponder more, as I needed to find a seat.

April and I sat together, with me looking out the window. I was sure my shaking stomach from nerves of worry about getting lost in the FAJHS building would cause me to vomit, but I didn't. In fact, I have never actually vomited from the intense whole-body anxiety I experience, but that fact has never stopped me from swirling the possibility of hurling.

The driver had on AFN radio, broadcasting some weird serial program called *Chicken Man*. "Chicken Man, he's everywhere, he's everywhere!" I tried to listen to take my mind off my concerns, coupled with attempts to generate saliva to wash away the taste of the chalky Gelusil chewable antacid tablets Mom had given me. But unfortunately, *Chicken Man* and Gelusil were not settling my nerves.

I was not a smoker, but my porous dark hair smelled of it by the end of the ride. I hated riding the bus and had a stomachache the whole first week. Perhaps it wasn't the bus I hated but going to school.

I had never felt like I belonged in school in any meaningful way since entering kindergarten in 1965. Being at home with Mom provided an environment of safety and, for the most part, a place where I could be the best version of myself. Perhaps at home I did not have to pretend to be enjoying what I did not enjoy. School was an extroverted dynamic, and I was an introvert, drained by the energies of others. It was years before I learned how to use boundaries with people and situations to preserve myself. As a result, I got labeled as "antisocial." No, I was just selectively social.

Other students reported that Frankfurt American Junior High School had been a German jail during World War II. However, in researching it, I can find little or nothing about this facility. It was a no-frills place—asbestos-tile floor and painted with "Army light-green" walls—filled with the most dynamic group of teachers I had ever encountered.

AUSSERHALB DER LINIEN
(OUTSIDE THE LINES)

"*Verstehen und Sprechen*," or "Listen and Speak," read the cover of my German textbook, which I thought sounded like a dog command. My German teacher was Mr. Siemaszko—a long-haired, long-mustached forty-something who was determined to teach us about modern German culture along with the language. Since I had little or no prior information about Germany, I was initially open to his ideas and methods.

Shortly after the school year had begun, my openness quickly began to shut down as Mr. S. instructed us to "Break the confines of the straight lines" by forming our previously arranged rows of metal-framed, wooden-topped desks into a circle. We screeched across the floor, with all the extroverts wondering aloud what we were doing and why. I said nothing and wished I had chosen another language that would not require me to interact with others. Was there such a class?

Shortly before the end of class that day, Mr. S. walked silently to the middle of the circle, forcefully threw our class textbook down on the floor, and yelled, "Freedom!" (long before Mel Gibson in *Braveheart*). He announced, "We will be freeing ourselves from the limitations that the German text requires."

Hmmm . . . what did this mean? How would I know what was coming up next if we had no textbook? How would I know on any given day what was going to be discussed? Were we just going to make this up as we went along? Where was the structure? What was the expectation? Oh, my god, this must be what anarchy is like! At that moment, I realized that the same rule structure I had been internally hating was the very thing I craved.

The next day after our classroom makeover, he had students from a local German school come in and have a class with us in our circle. As the fair-skinned teens entered the room, my heart rate accelerated, my underarm deodorant was put to the test (and failed), and the next sixty minutes felt never-ending. I was unsure of my German skills (not that I ever studied hard at home) and just as unsure of myself. Who would want to talk with me?

Talking to people who spoke English as a first language was daunting enough. The angst of believing that whatever I had to say might be boring and inconsequential usually reduced me to agreeing with whatever someone else uttered and producing the requisite sounds of active listening. This translated for me into a lot of "Ja, ja," accompanied by affirmative head-nodding with my German compatriots.

The upside to my frequent self-imposed observation-status behavior was my cultivated ability to read people. If I listened long enough to what was said and not said, I could quickly gain insight into the motives behind a person. Or at least, that's how I saw it. But unfortunately, since I never spoke aloud about my analysis, I had yet to learn if I was right or wrong.

Now, if I had gone into a crime-fighting career, I guess that would be a highly valued skill. I did not. I became a teacher of young children. But at FAJHS in the autumn of 1974, I was tasked with communicating with this ragtag group of German youth.

They each spoke way better English than I did German. I wish I had viewed that experience as an opportunity, but like so much of life, I experienced it as a sweat fest with liquid released and freely flowing from every bodily pore.

I made the mistake of telling April about the unconventional way that Mr. Siemaszko was conducting this class, and April, of course, took it upon herself to report this deviation to Mom and Dad. Oh, my god! My sister was a morality narc. Why did she have to tell Mom and Dad? The better question was, why did I keep thinking she was going to change and keep putting myself out there to her in the hopes that she would talk with me rather than rat me out? And at what point should I stop hoping that April would change and start believing she was the person she was showing me to be?

I had not yet learned that I could be hopeful and yet still protect myself. So, because of my unprotected hopefulness, I just kept sharing Mr. Siemaszko's methods of transformation and my excitement about the events, and April kept reporting to Mom and Dad. As far as I know, they did nothing about it but listen.

KEINE RICHTIGE ANTWORT
(NO RIGHT ANSWER)

To ponder and then question, or to regurgitate and say what others want you to say—that is the question. FAJHS was the first place where I became aware of the distinction between the two teaching methods. Something stirred inside of me with this possibility of a flexible truth. Many years later, this type of learning was called "intuitive inquiry," but in the mid-seventies, it was called "radical" by so many, including my big sister and her "color within the lines" mentality.

The day that Mr. S. played "The Pachelbel Canon in D" demonstrated the painful pull between my innate ability to imagine and my heartbreaking reaction to strangle myself silent simultaneously.

"Johann Pachelbel was a German composer. I'm going to play you a piece of his music known as 'The Pachelbel Canon.' Clear your desks and then just listen," were the directions from Mr. S. He carefully placed the needle on the vinyl album and out poured a song filled with such a joyful melancholy that I thought I would shed tears in front of others.

I managed to fight my salty emotions back by using Mom's method of driving my fingernails into my palms. Mom had told me that public tears were inappropriate because they put the attention on me and not on whomever or whatever the experience was that I was attending.

Our post-song instruction was to "Simply talk about what you felt and what you pictured while listening. What did that song mean to you? How did it reach you? What did it make you wonder?"

I had so much to say, so many images to free, but I remained an observer during the pontifications of others. I could not risk making myself vulnerable to criticism. April's systematic analysis of my every action, inaction, and innate introversion rendered me a functional mute.

My classmates kept using words like "sad," "alone," and "down," referencing the song, whereas I had had just the opposite reaction. The visions in my head had elicited a joyousness, a lightness as the music rose in dramatic melody. Not being a student of music, I lacked the proper terms to describe this, but I was struck by my reaction versus that of my classmates. Was this a competition? Was I losing? It certainly felt like losing. What would happen if I gathered my courage and spoke my truth? Unfortunately, I did not gather my courage and did not speak my truth aloud then.

Perhaps Mr. S. was making up the curriculum as he felt would best benefit us: by purely absorbing what Germany had to offer us in the mid-twentieth century, reflecting on times before the Nazi fascism that modern movies portrayed with frequency. Or maybe he just felt like doing whatever the hell he wanted. Regardless of the reason, his free curriculum opened me to places and experiences that had been previously unknown to me. But because I remained silent, neither he nor my classmates knew that—or much else—about me.

INNERE GEDANKEN
(INNER THOUGHTS)

The bittersweet ache induced by Pachelbel was so intoxicating! I wished to feel this joyous angst as often as I could. Or perhaps I was already feeling the "bitter" part by virtue of rising puberty, and the "sweet" part was compliments of the simple melody Pachelbel had put forth while strolling through a German mountain range. I had to write . . . I had to attempt to put down in words this feeling, these feelings, but not in rhyme. The rhyme was too restrictive and lacked the flow that my emotions required for a written rendering.

I knew that April kept a diary because she had received one before we left Rockville as a going-away gift from one of her friends. It came with a little lock and key, and April wrote in it at her desk. As per Mom's instructions, we were not allowed to close our doors all the way. So I guess she wanted to keep an eye on our "private" goings-on to keep us on a virtuous track that a closed door would not allow.

I needed a diary. The PX did not have any, so I was forced to use loose-leaf paper in a notebook that I hid in my underwear drawer. Underwear was "eww," so I figured it was the safest place for it to be.

In this diary, I would carve out a place for myself to record my inner thoughts. If I had kept these diaries, I would have such a treasure trove of my hero's path. But I threw them away prior to leaving Germany to meet my part of the back-to-the-States-moving-weight restriction, as per Dad's orders.

The experiences—even without my diaries—have stayed with me. Mr. Siemaszko added some more to my awakening with a class trip to the Romerplatz in downtown Frankfurt to watch the movie *Fahrenheit 451*, based on the book by Ray Bradbury. The Allies had heavily bombed the Romerplatz during World War II, but the Germans reconstructed it afterward to look very much like it had before the devastation.

Before entering the movie theater, Mr. S. spoke of some of the history of Frankfurt and the sidewalks on which we were standing so casually with our deck shoes and three-stripe Adidas.

"Goethe was born in this great city. Johann Wolfgang von Goethe. 'Knowing is not enough; we must apply. Willing is not enough; we must do.' His words, his city. This city also held a book burning during the Nazi rule. Censorship is the downfall of any society. When we begin to tell others how to think and restrict their access to reading material, we have committed moral treason. The movie we are about to see deals with this very travesty."

At age thirteen, having watched only G-rated movies by Disney, I was so uncomfortable with this movie. What the hell was "moral treason" anyway? After viewing it, I experienced such a confused disconcertion to thinking of the government as controlling its people. As a military family, the government controlled so much of our lives, and we considered ourselves lucky to live the life we did. Well, that's what Mom told us, and since she was happy, we figured she was right.

We debriefed the movie in our eighth-grade classroom the next day. Mr. S. warned us that the movie portrayed how our US government was moving. The class scuttlebutt was that Mr.

S. was a "radical" and that our government was only looking out for our best interests despite his take on the movie.

Questioning the motives of those in power was something I had not done as part of any study. But the door was open now, and my internal and private written inquiry began. What were people's motives? You mean not everyone had my best interests in mind? People in power wished to control me? Was *I* a lemming? How did one become "not a lemming"? These were not the sorts of ponderings I shared with Dad, or even Mom, for that matter. She would have felt compelled to tell Dad, and I would probably get in trouble for "conduct unbecoming." The "trouble" would be the outward disappointment on Dad's face, a stern lecture, and all the negative vibes I felt coming off him.

I did not understand it at the time, but I was a highly empathetic person, and because of that, other people's "stuff" became my "stuff." I just thought—well, believed—that I was weird, too sensitive, and to avoid feeling worse than I already did about myself, I needed to keep people's moods either neutral or pleasant. It was exhausting.

It wasn't just the emotions of people in front of me that I absorbed. It transferred itself to movies as well. Mr. S. showed *Future Shock* in class—a film based on the book by futurist Alvin Toffler. The author maintained that the way society was going in the seventies was leading us all to a complete psychologically overwhelmed status, i.e., massive stress.[10] I think I had always felt overwhelmed when in the company of others beyond my own family, and lately, I could not find a peaceful refuge there either.

As a young teen in the seventies, I found Toffler's view of the future bleak at best. Why would anyone with independent thought, and therefore independent action, choose to run their society, and consequently themselves, into ruin? Mr. Siemaszko explained that *Future Shock* echoed the fate of the Roman Empire. To elucidate this point, off we went on a field trip to Saalburg, Germany.

It was winter when we toured the Roman ruins and accompanying museum. That meant raw chill, fog, and a general "Why the hell are we here?" feeling among us, the Siemaszko tribe. Basically, the lesson for the trip was, "Before the fall comes the pride." The museum's focus in 1974–75 was all on the ingenuity and architectural wonders of the Romans.

I was more interested in the forest and wondered about the people who had walked that way for many years before the marauding Italians. I kept my opinions to myself. My mind was being formally expanded and was anything but silent. I was receiving an education about the world beyond what I had known thus far, and this "question everything" curriculum caught me and sent me into a tailspin. It upended the message of "Do as you are told," which I had swallowed and followed for the first thirteen years of my life. My fellow students did not seem to be engaged in serious thought like I was.

My classmates seemed as alien to me as I sometimes felt about myself. They were "cool," and I couldn't figure out how they could be from military families as I was and yet be allowed to wear hip-hugger jeans and tight T-shirts, revealing their growing figures. They were already spending time brushing their hair, applying lip gloss, and flirting with the boys. And they were engaging in all these shallow, vapid behaviors while we were walking the very land that the Romans and the Germanic tribes had walked! Why was I the only student concerned about the way these people had lived? I felt like the ancient ghosts were rustling the branches for only me to see and feel. Yes, I was weird. That was the only answer.

KERNWUNDE
(CORE WOUNDING)

My belief in my oddity among my peers did not end in German class, where I came out with an expanded mind but little or no German-speaking ability. It was blatant in my assigned business math class that year.

I believe the academic translation for the class level was "Math for Dummies." I'm sure my big sister provided this translation for me. I was the only one from my social group in that class. Math had always been a struggle for me. Whatever the core reason, I could see the numbers, follow the process, and then not remember. It just didn't "stick." Because every other school subject came relatively easily to me, it was a mystery and an embarrassment that I could not grasp the math curriculum.

It did not help that April and even Laura found math such a breeze. April had tried to help me understand concepts but inevitably dissolved into an exasperated, "Oh, my gosh! How can you not understand this? It's so easy! You need to try harder!" I just saw a blankness in my mind and no amount of trying harder broke through to any "Aha!" moment for me.

I have had this mathematical inability forever. I could not see mathematical patterns or logic. As early as the first grade, word problems rendered me paralyzed. I could read them easily but could not assign numerical values or formulas to derive answers. I blamed this inability on low oxygen during an operation when I was four. That slice-and-dice provided the terror-stricken personality I live with daily and, worse, nightly. This was my core wounding.

Apparently, the reason for the operation had been my many infections with high seizure-inducing fevers. The tangy orange Johnson's baby aspirin was a much-too-familiar taste for me.

As preparation in 1965 for the impending operation, I had a pre-op visit where I was given a book explaining in very happy terms and pictures what would be happening to me. I was so very proud of my little book, and April was bilious green with envy.

The envy was short-lived, as was the pride when I entered the hospital and Nurse Ratched explained to Mom that she would not be allowed to stay in the hospital and would need to come back in the morning. I overheard the conversation and saw Mom put her hand up to her mouth.

There are no pictures at all about an *operation* where the nurse has to pry the four-year-old's stubby little fingers off the sobbing mother as she walks out the door, leaving her with strangers. How confident the little girl in the booklet looks in her hospital gown.

Fear gripped my every muscle and breath during the entire ordeal. I had been falsely led to believe by the *OPERATION* book that having an operation was going to be a wonderful experience. But unfortunately, they forgot to include the page that states, "Your mother will not be allowed to stay with you overnight. You will be alone with strangers and in horrid pain for the first time in your life." Maybe the writer thought since she capitalized the word *OPERATION*, that it was code for, "This is going to scar your child for life," and it did. As a result, I still have periodic nightmares of waking up alone.

The hospital staff must have had someone skilled in tran-
quilizer guns shoot me quickly, as the next thing I recall is
waking up in a shared room with a girl who was under a big
plastic tent. I could hear her labored breathing and could see
the plastic move up and down as she did so.

I spent many days and nights all alone, clutching my yellow
blankie. I would ask the nurse to tie it around my neck so that
I could try to be brave like Batman's trusty sidekick, Robin.
I cried a lot, covering my face so no one saw. I did not want
to disgrace our family with my overt weakness. My teddy bear
named Freddie accompanied me on this trip of torture. The
nurses made me keep him in the little brown hard suitcase with
the mirror on the inside during the day and only allowed him
out at night. I was sure he could not breathe, and when they
weren't looking, I snapped the latch quietly so that he had air. It
seemed more important to break that rule than let Freddie die
from lack of air.

Freddie and my blankie were the only two things that kept
me safe during my hospital stay. I knew the phony smiles and
lifeless eyes of all the hospital staff were there to stab me with
anxiety, the effect of which has lasted my whole life. When
Mom came through the door to visit, I thought my heart would
shatter.

She looked so beautiful in her short, frosted coif (complete
with additional hair called a "fall"), the brown-and-white dress
she had tailored, shiny spectator pumps, and her Grace Kelly–
style black wool coat. I begged her to take me home, and she
bit her lip, telling me that it would not be long and that I could
have all the ice cream I wanted upon my return home. I did
not want ice cream. I wanted my mommy. The two of us went
down to the hospital playroom, but I just wanted to sit in her
lap, feeling that if I could bury myself deep enough, she could

take me out the door with her. The nurse on duty kept encouraging me to play, but I knew I was in no mood to play with kids scarred with various skin diseases, attached to large oxygen tanks, and talking way too loudly in public. Clearly, they were not representing their families well. I thought if I held on tight enough, Mom would not leave, but the nurse led us back to my room and escorted Mom out the door. There was little or no healing for me during that hospital stay, although all my vitals said otherwise.

Low oxygen damage or not, I was faced with many a math challenge during my school career. My FAJHS business math teacher was such a patient soul. Ms. Bobbye Geary was the first female African American teacher I had ever had. I didn't think anything of that fact back then. She was just another math teacher bound to be internally frustrated at my lack of math skills—I was sure of it.

She never showed if she was ready to explode out of disappointment in me. Instead, she always had a smile, a kind word, or an additional explanation to encourage me. She was the kind of teacher I wanted to be—and I hope that I was to all my students once I had my own teaching career.

Leaving her class, I could calculate simple operations more efficiently. Still, I had no better understanding of the art of math, the science of math, the . . . probably something else, but since I don't "get it," I-have-no-other-words-for-it type of math.

HÄSSLICHE JEANS
(UGLY JEANS)

Thank the education gods of the mid-seventies for their belief in student choice. Sorry, millennials, that you are saddled with the government-knows-best-common-core-no-student-choice curriculum. At FAJHS, we tested into our math class and English levels. We created the rest of our schedule based on interest.

The break built into the morning allowed time to go to the cafeteria to buy a snack. The twenty-five-cent Long John was my favored treat, akin to a chocolate éclair. The break gave me a chance to calorie-load, switch my books for the afternoon classes, use the bathroom, and of course, brush my hair.

The break also gave me a respite from having to be with others. I finally purchased a purse from the PX and loaded it with a brush and some rolled-up dollars for snacks. No amount of brushing ever rendered my hair silky, shiny, and controlled like all the pretty girls at school. They went to the bathroom first before going to the cafeteria to hang out with the popular boys.

I went into the bathroom and up to the mirror after them to try and de-static my hair. The pretty girls must've had some magic elixir that I didn't know about because the more I brushed, the more flyaway it became.

I still had the long hair and bangs that I had arrived with in Germany, but halfway through the year, I decided to grow out my bangs. I became the typical 1970s girl with long hair parted down the middle. I was getting closer to "cool," but Mom still forbade us from wearing jeans to school, as only "hoodlums" wore jeans. Somehow, every other student wore jeans, and there were never any of the fights or gangs about which Mom had cautioned us. Maybe the strong commonality of us all being military Brats overrode any divisive influence.

April finally wore Mom down to allow us to dress in denim once a week. I don't know when or how she did it, but she did. "Thanks, Ape!" I offered cheerfully.

April countered with, "We could have worn them sooner if you had contributed anything meaningful to the argument for jeans. But you're too busy trying to be Mom's friend. No one is friends with their parents. You are so weird."

Now, if she had just said, "You're welcome," with a kind smile instead of her Grinchy smirk and vocal slam, the door might have opened for us to create a sisterly bond. She was not the least bit interested in that. April was in Aprilville, where only her interests and opinions were deemed important. She knew how to cut me even with a compliment.

Despite Mom's continued efforts to keep us locked in a bygone decade, the once-weekly wearing of jeans did not give way to a lifetime of gang activity. I was still Weirdo Mary with ideas and thoughts that I did not hear from others anywhere— even way the hell across the ocean.

I had decided on Friday for my freedom-from-dresses-and-slacks day. This was because of the flexibility that Fridays offered at our junior high. The FAJHS Friday mini-course days were where each student chose an area of interest from among the vast offerings of the classroom teachers and enjoyed learning something new every eight weeks.

FAJHS gave me so many opportunities to make decisions on my own. The responsibility of our Friday mini-courses was ours and was not directly influenced by anyone else. Despite this opportunity for free thought put into action, I did not base my choices on my actual interests. So as not to be alone, I went with whatever course my friends wanted. I never spoke of my decision-making process, and no one ever asked me. There were no questions from elders or contemporaries and, therefore, no growth in my decision-making process. I pursued this often ill-fated whatever-you-want-to-do method well into my thirties.

The non-decision decision-making required no bravery or risk-taking. What it did involve was the self-destruction and sublimation of my own unique characteristics. I justified this to myself with the carefully crafted construct of being a "relationship person." The relationship I had woefully negated was the one I had with myself. And I knew that. I knew it not overtly but in the discomfort that I lived with each time I said, "Whatever you want is fine with me."

MIT DER MENGE GEHEN
(GOING WITH THE CROWD)

The decoupage mini-course that my friends wanted to take seemed benign enough, so I signed up for it. This popular seventies craft experience involved cutting and gluing pictures from magazines onto a painted slab of shaped wood. Then we spent many weeks adding layer upon layer of Mod Podge (a wonder-shellac that was a glue, sealant, and finisher, all in one), with time spent sanding between layers of finish to remove the air bubbles. I made a hideous Holly Hobbie plaque. Holly Hobbie was a Kewpie doll–looking set of illustrations with icky sweet sentimentality that was somewhat appealing to my naive eighth-grade self.

It wasn't like I saw enduring beauty in Holly Hobbie. I didn't know to ask myself the all-important question, "Why?" Why do you like that? What do you like about that? Somewhere in a German landfill lies my decoupaged plaque, preserved in all its Mod Podge greatness.

I was very busy trying to survive in the extroverted dynamic of school. I had really wanted to take the guitar-playing mini-course, but no girls were signed up for it. I had checked the roster on Mr. Noon's door . . . all boys. Clearly, guitar playing was for boys. What would have happened if I had signed up for his course? Would it have changed the direction of my life in some cosmically transformative manner? If it would have, I never gave it the opportunity to do so. What I failed to understand at that time was that I was transforming by my very questioning and pondering of possibilities. I just didn't "see" it.

To be "seen" by others, I was determined to improve my wardrobe. *Seventeen* magazine assured me that this was the way to popularity. Did I want to be popular? It seemed like I should. Unfortunately, the opposite was what I was, which was not so great, so I signed up for a home economics sewing class as one of my yearlong electives. That class was only for girls, so it eliminated the need to jockey for a chance to speak without being interrupted by a male with the inherent desire to dominate.

Boys took shop class, where I guess they learned how to make birdhouses. Perhaps the thinking was that if there was going to be a Cold War–induced apocalypse, the males would be experienced in building back the cities, and the women would keep us clothed. I was just glad that with the home ec curriculum requirement, I was in a scenario where there would be no whole-group class discussions.

Ms. Janice Fowler was my teacher. Was it a requirement for a female DOD teacher to be the nicest human on the planet? It must have been, because Ms. Fowler maintained her saintly demeanor among all those loudly whirring Singer sewing machines.

She gladly circulated around the room checking on progress, helping wind bobbins, clearing out jammed needles when we stepped on the sewing pedal too hard, and answering my eternal question of "How do you make a buttonhole?" once again. So many directions were involved, and trying to orient my buttonhole to the right and left of the machine presser foot was constantly confusing. Each time I had to make a buttonhole, I struggled with the same damn problem. Repetition of this spatial perceptual task did not solidify the method.

It was beyond frustrating when my machine stopped working and a project due date was coming up. I guess the DOD budget did not allow for frequent maintenance, so I did a lot of sewing at home, and much to Mom's delight, I began to love it. It was the common factor that gave my mom and me a language and activity to navigate my teenage years.

I was a grade-A procrastinator where so much was concerned, which did not exclude sewing-project completion. I read a quote once that too much patience, i.e., procrastination, is fear. Yep. My final project for home ec sewing class and the essence of my grade was a project I had put off until the weekend before it was due.

I had purchased a rayon/polyester red fabric with elephants that I artfully crafted into a two-piece wonder that April coveted and begged to wear once it was complete. Sewing was the one thing I could do better than her. She was not naturally good at the fabric arts and therefore decided they were not worth pursuing.

Mom stayed awake late into the night with me that sewing-project weekend in case I needed her artful assistance. I felt such guilt at her commitment when I had previously shown so little. When sometime at O-dark-hundred I sewed the back to the front of the bodice, I could have ripped the whole thing to shreds. Mom sat there with a seam ripper, muttering, "I hope you are learning your lesson from all this."

It was perfect when I finally finished this grade-making-or-breaking project. It was perfect with the eight buttonholes up the front (there was no buttonhole maker on the sewing machines back then) to the crisp pointed collar so expertly attached to the unseen hand-stitched hem. I had reached perfection status and hadn't learned a damn thing about life, except that I could wait till the last minute and pull a stellar project out of my ass if I needed to.

I wore this outfit with dark blue platform shoes, previously ordered from the Sears catalog. Unfortunately, when they—my first attempt at stylish dress shoes—arrived, they were nearly a size too big. To exchange them for another size would have required sending them back to the States on a boat, and the return shoes would not have reached me for months. However, I was so close to being fashionable that I was willing to modify them by stuffing the toes of the shoes with layer upon layer of Kleenex to bridge the size difference.

April informed me, "Your feet look like pontoons in those shoes." That's all I could think of as I looked down at what was supposed to be a happy, fulfilled fashion triumph. I should have said, "You're just jealous. Shut the hell up. No one cares what you think, least of all me!" But I didn't. I just accepted her verbal barb as the truth, and I wore them anyway, as I had begged Mom for them.

Mom was so outwardly happy at being able to help me reach my fashion dreams. She understood shoes and had often regaled me with the story of her working at a carnival after graduating from high school to buy a pair of spectator pumps.

I'll bet Mom looked stunning in her black-and-white pumps while all I could visualize were my enormous feet swimming in the navy-blue platforms. How would I ever drive out April's critical voice? I would only be able to do this by developing my own. It had not yet happened, but my internal barrage of questioning was driving it closer.

The periodic audible ankle *snap-crunch* when walking fast or going over uneven sidewalks in the four-inch-high, one-size-too-big platforms was inevitable. The key was to keep moving and walk it off.

This "crunch and go" scenario was made more prevalent by trying to avoid every FAJHS boy imitating the then-popular Bruce Lee. Boys with nunchucks, untrained air kicks, and punches coupled with the classic Bruce Lee high-pitched scream made for an interesting dodge-and-duck walk down the school halls and stairwells. It was a good thing I had excellent connective ankle tissue because I frequently twisted my ankles in those concrete humanity-packed stairwells.

I was willing to put my own health at risk for the attention and acceptance of peers to try to "fit in" instead of joining the path of truth. Ahh . . . my path of truth. I knew more about myself than I was willing to admit, even in the private writings of my journal. I wanted to bust out, not fit in. I wanted to do, say, dress, sing, dance, and live without all the rules—but with kindness and justice for all.

Or did I want to return to the days of childhood? Those weren't perfect either. If I could just return to a moment when life was sweet, simple, and accepting, I would be all right. But, no, that wasn't right either. I tried on people's opinions like other people tried on clothes.

DIE VERGANGENHEIT IST VORBEI (THE PAST IS GONE)

There is a desire inside me for roots, to know where I come from, and to have a place to return to that never changes. That place for me for the first twelve-plus years of my life was Dad's childhood home in Freemansburg, Pennsylvania, where my grandparents had lived since 1925. But unfortunately, this place would change forever for me in the fall of 1974 with the death of my cherished Grandma McKnight.

It was three thirty on a typical gray Frankfurt afternoon and Dad was already home, so I knew something was wrong. Mom had been crying. I could tell because her nose was red and her eyes were bloodshot. Dad had us all sit down at the dining room table.

His face was in its usual emotionless expression, but his eyes had a sad tenseness. Then, finally, he announced, "Your grandmother has died." That was all he said. It was probably all he could say without crying himself. But when he told us, I felt like he had dropped an anvil on me and left me to bleed out. He was bleeding too; I am sure of it now. But at the time, all I had room for was the stark reality that I would never see her again.

I sat there in that hard, solid wood chair, leaning forward physically but emotionally blown backward. Grandma McKnight was my favorite person in the world next to Mom. We'd had our last visit with her and my grandfather just under four months before while still living in the States. I am named after my grandma, and this is our story:

My paternal grandparents lived in Freemansburg, Pennsylvania, on Green Street. I loved that house—it never changed. No matter where we moved, that house stayed the same. I depended on that sameness for a sentimental longing, for a happiness I would only feel again with my daughter, while trying to recreate that life for her so many years later.

It was the horrible-tasting horehound drops in the Depression glass candy dish, the plethora of house plants in the dining room windows, the metal tray installed outside the kitchen window filled with sunflower seeds for the cardinals, the metal tin of crayons in the bedroom where we three girls slept, doilies on the backs of each living room chair and on the back of the couch—all items in their forever places and all contributing to a bittersweet portion of my heart.

I loved my paternal grandmother, with her soft olive skin, silver wavy hair, and copper hoop earrings. I knew I was her favorite grandchild. She never said that; I just knew. When we visited, she got up at O-dark-hundred, turned the light on in the bathroom, and waved to me as I sat up in bed. We kids were in the room that had been my dad's when he was growing up. My two sisters were late sleepers, and when Grandma came out of the bathroom, we descended those creaky stairs together to the kitchen. My footy pajamas covered on the bottom with rubber grabbed and peeled up on those thick wooden stairs with a most satisfying sound.

Once in the kitchen, Grandma pulled out an enamel washbowl from beneath the sink, placed it in the huge cast-iron kitchen sink, and washed her face with Dove soap. Then she closed the door partway from the porch and combed her hair in the mirror behind it. Finally, she opened the medicine cabinet hung there, swiped her face with powder from a compact, had a teaspoon of cod-liver oil, and put on her copper hoop earrings.

Breakfast was a bowl of Cheerios, and afterward, she opened the basement door to get the tin of Windmill almond cookies. Then she drank her black coffee made from a percolator on the stove and had two of the cookies. Her beautiful, olive-skinned hands wrapped around the cream-colored mug and my little-kid hands tight around my cookies are forever a memory so sweet that it seems I must have made it up. Once everyone else woke up and came downstairs, the aura of the two of us in our ritual vanished. It was a ritual I will never forget, and it chokes me up and makes me ache each time I recall this.

On that beautiful, emotionally devastating fall day in September 1974, I walked with my memories up the stairs to my room and closed the door. I had written her a letter just a week before she died, and I never knew if she had received it. The only memory of that last visit—the one that seared into my soul with a deep and confusing sadness—was when we were leaving. Grandma had cried and said, as she hugged me so tightly and sobbed, "I'll never see you again." My heart imploded. I needed to protect her. I quickly countered, "Oh, no, you'll come and visit." But she never did, and when we did go back three years later, she was gone.

MAMAS BÜCHER
(MOM'S BOOKS)

"This is not a discussion. You will stay in school, and I will go back for the funeral," Dad had said. He was the law of our land. Mom kept life normal for us in his absence for the funeral. She had done this just a few years earlier when Dad was stationed in Vietnam. That was Mom's superpower. Did she sacrifice herself for our comfort? Did she love this "single parent" role with no one to provide guidance or unsolicited input with her decisions? I don't know. When I dared to ask her recently, she replied only, "I don't remember."

How could she not remember how delight-filled she made life? "There is nothing like a good book to take one's mind off of their sorrows," she often said with chipper intent.

We were off to the post library for literary mind-numbing. I struggled with what to read, as I was no longer in the children's section stage. There was a small teen section that April frequented. I stood beside her one day while Dad was still in the States attending the funeral, perusing the titles. I was blank. The teen section was devoid of anything resembling my cherished *My Side of the Mountain* or *Island of the Blue Dolphins*.

"Here," April said, quickly pulling out *Run Baby Run* by Nicky Cruz and shoving it into my arms.

"What's it about?" I asked, as it seemed like a reasonable question.

"You'll find out once you read it. So here . . ." she said, plopping S. E. Hinton's *The Outsiders* and *That Was Then, This Is Now* on top of my growing pile.

Reading those books certainly expanded my understanding of gang culture, but I was sure that the lifestyle depicted was one I would not encounter in my lifetime. They also did not give me any window into the female experience and left me with the undeniable realization that women just did not count.

Ironic that S. E. Hinton is a woman and was only sixteen when she wrote *The Outsiders*. It was a man's world. If I wanted "the female experience," it was only available through crafts and cookbooks. So I added a few of those books to my pile.

Standing at the checkout line, Mom commented on my choices. "Oh, *The Vegetarian Epicure*! That sounds enchanting. You'll have to try some of the recipes out on us while Dad is gone. Your father would never consider a meal without meat."

It made my insides happy that I had pleased Mom. Mom's preferred genre during our teen years was nonfiction. The subject matter usually concerned social issues and/or self-improvement. So I was sure that anything that exposed her to thinking beyond *The Army Wife*'s advice was progress for her.

I soon regretted my delight in her mind-expanding genre. *Games People Play* by Eric Berne became her companion, and that stupid book made my life even more irritating than it already was! Mom took it upon herself to analyze our every sibling conversation with a book in hand.

"Mary! Did you use my bathroom? Your gross hair is all over the bathtub," yelled April later that afternoon from the top of the stairs.

"Yes, but—" I did not get to finish my rebuttal as Mom jumped in.

"The game you're playing is 'Yes But'—as in, 'Yes, I did do that, but I did it because I had to.' If you did something, you must own up to it. April, the bigger issue is your assumption that the first-floor bathroom is yours. If you are not using it, any family member may use it. Now, Mary, you do need to clean up your hair, no matter whose bathroom you use."

April was not about to lose an argument to pop psychology and finished the conversation with, "Oh, does that mean I can use your bathroom, Mom, without asking?" But of course, she knew damn well that was not what was meant.

Mom should have said, "April, the game you're playing is 'I've Got You, You Son of a Bitch,'" but she didn't. Instead, she just gave April a smile that said, "Don't even try it," and walked away.

I thought Mom showed weakness by not verbally standing up to April that day. But in fact, Mom had dropped the mic long before it was a twenty-first-century thing, leaving April to twist in the wind.

DAS SPIEL, DAS DU SPIELST (THE GAME YOU'RE PLAYING)

With Mom's new stack of self-help books from the library, I was sure that *The Army Wife* cleaning schedule was not keeping her satisfied.

Ha! I'm sure it did not. How could it? A woman finishes whatever menial task, like scrubbing the kitchen cabinetry with Fels-Naptha soap, but cannot put her feet up like her husband and children. She then whips up some homemade fried chicken for her husband and family for dinner and then is forced to clean the post-cooking grease splatter, and there she is—rolling that familiar Sisyphean boulder back up the same damn mountain.

Mom's next epistle was *I'm OK—You're OK* by California psychiatrist Dr. Thomas Harris. Really, I think as a woman in the 1970s, the internal battle cry of the military wife was probably, "You're all okay because I am definitely not okay, working my ass off while you all relax!"

I remember thinking that I should really help Mom but did not want to because Dad would not help, and by helping, I would just be continuing the oppression-of-women cycle. Flawed as that logic was, I was formulating my stance on women's liberation. I was not ever going to be "liberated." No woman would ever be liberated until freed from the confines of constantly taking care of the other household members. When was the time for a woman to pursue her own interests?

I was not going to spend my entire life trying to figure out what everybody else wanted and needed and pretending that it fulfilled me. Mom's books may have been her attempt at letting us know that her maid-status-for-life was not all it was cracked up to be. Perhaps by leaving her books out where we girls could view them, she was subversively helping expand our minds and, hopefully, our life choices.

Was that possible? Could Mom be breaking ranks with the legions of Army wives? Maybe these books were what they discussed at their Officers' Wives' Club meetings. Perhaps they all sat around in their well-fitted shift dresses, pantyhose, and high heels and conversed on how to break away from this shitty life.

I just knew that I was never going to get married. Being married seemed like a death sentence to a woman's freedom. This thought was one I kept to myself. It would have been like slapping Mom in the face if I had announced it aloud.

It hurt me that Mom let Dad have the last word on everything. How would she ever fulfill herself if his voice always overshadowed hers? If a dinner conversation was getting too heated in Dad's estimation or getting too something else he didn't like, he would raise his voice and say, "This conversation is finished." The room would fall silent, but the internal tempers still flared. I vowed I would never let a man tell me when a conversation was finished.

Mom was closest to me temperamentally, at least when I was in "Can't we all just get along?" mode. It had always been hard for me to physically leave her, but the tug I felt toward growing up was straining that relationship. How could I be close to Mom but still flex my growing independent thoughts and desires?

VERBOTEN (FORBIDDEN)

This inner dialogue tore at my already-shredded stomach. I needed someone else to share my daydreams and my thoughts (edited, of course, so as not to become vulnerable), and Jenny H. became one of those people. Jenny's family had moved in next door to us after the Ball family left. The H's were from the South: heavy smokers, sociable, kind, and welcoming.

I had never met anyone from the Deep South before. The closest I had previously gotten to any understanding of the culture was from singing folk songs in music class. The lyrics were all, "Frogs, fishin', and fun." Of course, no frogs and no fishin', but the fun factor was always present at the H's.

Jenny was about four feet tall with a six-foot personality. She was Laura's age but shared my boy-crazy tendencies. Jenny vacillated between spending time with Laura, playing board games and badminton, and then with me, talking about our boy crushes and hanging out together at the PX.

She was a smoker, and I was not. However, during one of their vacations, when I was taking care of their Siamese cats, I wandered down into their basement. Jenny's older sister had turned it into a self-described hippie haven. I had no idea what transpired down there when Kathy was with her high school compadres.

I just knew there was a steady stream of burnouts coming in their back door, smoke billowing out the basement windows, teens leaving with red eyes, smiles, and a fixed look of self-satisfaction.

The ashtray down there was filled with cigarette butts, and I had decided to see what all the commotion was about. So I turned on the Led Zeppelin album I was not allowed to own because the band took drugs. How my mom knew of this band's drug use was unknown to me. "Black Dog" blaring, the cats already fed, the plants watered . . . me, a match, and an unfiltered Marlboro.

The long and short of it was I loved it. I knew I had to stop. I enjoyed it right away—the taste, the motion of my fingers to my lips, flicking the ashes, seeing the smoke leave my lips . . . There would be no way the Colonel would allow this activity. I knew this was to be a one-time-only event. It's a good thing, really, that I had his strong influence, or I probably would have joined the mindless ranks of Kathy's "friends."

Jenny and I spent hours in their basement, listening to records. Before Jenny, I hadn't heard of Southern rock before. Now it was a steady diet of Lynyrd Skynyrd, the Charlie Daniels Band, and anything else where the singers were slinging back Southern Comfort while riding in an old pickup truck on a warm summer night.

Jenny brewed gallons of sweet tea from Lipton tea bags to accompany our frequent music fests. I was acquainted with iced tea, but only as a lightly sweetened beverage to be consumed in the summer at a restaurant. Her caffeinated sweet tea was the perfect accompaniment to our vinyl fests.

When I was at Jenny's, we sang all the lyrics to Elton John's "The Bitch Is Back." That song would never be allowed in the hallowed halls of the McKnights. Jim Stafford's "I Got Stoned and I Missed It" was sung at the top of our lungs. I had never been stoned, but singing these lyrics made me feel free.

We each introduced the other to various musical artists. My contribution was Bob Dylan. I had become acquainted with Bob's poetic, nasal ramblings while over at the Motskos' with Mom. I don't know which Motsko honey was playing the records, but the lyrics from Bob Dylan's *Greatest Hits Volume II* spoke in a literary language that rattled my heart.

Jenny and I read all the liner notes on each of our albums, poring over lyrics, analyzing, comparing them to our lives, wishing, dreaming, and planning. All the records we listened to, with the exception of Kathy's Janis Joplin album *Pearl*, were by male artists. We did not plan it that way and did not even think about this. I wasn't really aware of the gender inequity in our listening habits.

I was internally railing against the oppressive male, yet I was blindly supporting this dynamic in my musical purchases. We can only know what we know, and life in the military community supported women as adjuncts—not the main event. But to Jenny and me, we were listening to music, not making any overt or covert political or societal statement.

Our conversations usually revolved around boys and inevitably followed this structure:

"Bob Dylan is hot," Jenny contributed.

"Oh, yeah. What do you think Nick is doing right now?" I asked her.

"You have got to let him go, Mary. Kathy said he was bad news, and for my sister to say that it must be true. Her standards are not that high."

The conversations rambled on about various boys and how "cute" or "gorgeous" they were. Personal transformation is almost impossible while spending one's time extolling the attributes of others rather than experimenting and refining the strengths and gifts of one's self.

While Jenny and I drank sweet tea and sang loudly in the basement, her mom was upstairs chain-smoking, doing what all moms did—cooking from scratch and cleaning. Again, total status quo lifestyle, and Jenny and I were well on our way down the same route.

SCHWESTER BOND
(SISTER BOND)

The air at the H's was punctuated by Jenny's parents' persistent deep, liquid, gravel coughing, kept constant by the perpetual cigarette lit in an ashtray. This auditory phlegm only bothered me when I went to their house for dinner. It was tough to eat the novel-to-me fried okra and black-eyed peas when I was sure a piece of one or both of their lungs was being expelled into the common air we were breathing.

On the rare occasions when Mom agreed to let me sleep over at Jenny's, she and I tuned into the single AFN-TV channel to watch old, scary black-and-white movies. Sweet tea and Jiffy Pop popcorn punctuated our late-night viewing. One evening, we were in her living room with the lights out, eating the Jiffy Pop extra buttered and highly salted.

We sat in the avocado-green Quartermaster-issued side chairs, leaning forward, each hanging on every word of *Cry of the Banshee* when we heard a knock on the front window, accompanied by a shadowy figure pressed against it.

We were first scared into silence and then screaming, ending in a sound that only dogs could hear, until Jenny recognized the figure as Kathy's latest boyfriend. He was looking for her, but she was with another guy. With no cell phones invented yet and it being much too late to call the house phone, he had just been wandering around the streets of Frankfurt searching for her.

After Jenny said that she didn't know where Kathy was and the boyfriend left, Jenny informed me that Kathy was with some local German guy who went by the name of "Rom-bee." The guys Kathy hung out with did not look like the sort that a father hopes and dreams will end up with his daughter. The movie ended during this "Where is Kathy?" escapade, and there was nothing left to do but talk about boys. The conversation continued into the night, with us each describing our ideal guy and the ideal date.

I was sure my guy would be tall, dark, and handsome. This was a description I had read in an Archie comic. He would be impulsively romantic and yet would do all the cooking and cleaning so I could write. Wow, this setup still sounds ideal now. But it turns out that guy does not exist.

Jenny informed me, "That kind of guy is gay. You want a gay guy as your ideal man?" We fell back, laughing to tears at her instant analysis. Once we had composed ourselves, we defined the parameters of the ideal first date.

"Oh, that's easy," I started. "A picnic on a perfect summer day. He packs it, plans it, and I just show up. We talk, laugh, and share our dreams."

"Yep," Jenny confirmed with a nod of her head, "your ideal guy is gay. My first date would be at a concert. We would make out during our favorite song and end the night under the moon, planning the next time we could be together."

I thought it improper to kiss on the first date (not that I had any experience at all), and Jenny was emphatic that any date that didn't involve making out was not worth it. Of course, she had no actual experience either, but it was clear we were moving in two different directions.

Jenny was most anxious to grow up, and I was scared to. But scared or not, it was happening. So now the question was, what was I going to do with it?

WACHSEN UND SICH VERÄNDERN (GROWING AND CHANGING)

I was gaining weight but still had no discernable curves. This weight first became apparent in my thighs. I noticed the horrible dark red jagged streaks on the back of my legs one day in the bath. They were hideous and had a slight indent when I finally mustered the courage to investigate them physically. What were these wounds that were not open but were not closed? They did not sting as a scratch did.

I said nothing and hoped no one would notice. They were probably some sort of silent killer anyway, and I would be dead soon. I was sure of it.

April to the rescue: "Oh, my gosh! You have stretch marks! You must watch your weight! Gross!"

Stretch marks? What was that? Oh, Mom had those on her abdomen, only they hadn't been red, just slightly wrinkly, skin-colored indents. Yuck! Were my legs going to look like her belly? I risked humiliation by asking April what to do, and she recommended leg exercises. How did she know this? I started in on the leg lifts right away, but no matter how many reps or how many weeks of side lifts, front lifts, and back lifts I did, the stretch marks remained.

Mom noticed them one day when she came barging into my room while I was dressing.

"Oh! Stretch marks!"

Thank you, Mom. I already knew that.

"They will fade. Not to worry."

Not to worry? Yeah, when you're forty, and no one cares what you look like, that would be easy to say! Now I felt fat! Our family was never overweight. Not because Mom dieted; she never did. She was just naturally thin, as was April. In looking back at photos of myself at that time, I realize I was thin too. But those damned stretch marks and April's stinging observation made me feel flabby. She took it upon herself to guide me in additional specialized exercises to draw attention away from my matronly legs.

This tutelage consisted of "bust exercises" to increase my April-labeled "egg yolk–sized" breasts. "We must, we must, we must increase our bust," I chanted countless times as I pressed my palms together and my elbows out in the assuredness that this would move me into the "attractive" echelon. It did not. I would continue to be an embarrassment to her.

Unfortunately, styling compliments of the PX stymied all of my efforts to echo looks seen in *Seventeen*. Mom forbade me from buying that magazine as she felt it "did not encourage ladylike behavior." I read it at the PX in the book area as if I were reading contraband, always looking over my shoulder to be sure Mom or April was not around.

I had thought that sisters were supposed to "cover" for one another as Jenny did for Kathy, but apparently, April never got that memo. Instead, she was ever-vigilant in her quest to keep me contained in a life reminiscent of Rebecca of Sunnybrook Farm. Part of me was comforted by the safety that her over-watch provided, but another part of me wondered what was on the other side. I wanted to be noticed, and *Seventeen* was ever helpful with their "Ten Ways to Dress to Impress" articles.

The clothing represented on those pages was not what Mom had in mind for us. The bell-bottoms split up the side to the knee, with fabric insert and frayed ends, were not allowed in our house. I loved that look. What was a girl to do? Why, add "extenders" to my pants, of course!

Mom had a box of "trim" gathered over the years, each with such exquisite color and design. I talked her into letting me embellish my maroon corduroy bell-bottoms with some of the trim added to the flared bottoms. I finished my look with a black turtleneck channeling a fifties-beat vibe and a large medallion on a leather cord. (Think of Peggy Lipton as the Julie character on *The Mod Squad* as my style icon.) The light pink corduroy shirt I wore as a jacket was the pièce de résistance.

April failed to see the impending style trend I was about to set, as did the rest of the world. No one said anything about my outfit at school, and by day's end, I had removed the medallion and pink jacket by unceremoniously stuffing them into my locker. So now I was just a girl whose high-water pants, unsuccessfully disguised by old-lady trim and topped off with a Barry Manilow turtleneck, screamed, "Fashion Emergency!"

SCHÖNHEITSROUTINE
(BEAUTY ROUTINE)

Despite this devastating setback in my quest to become noticed, I sought my individuality by acquiring all the popular skin and hair products of the day available at the PX. How could I resist the Max Factor Fancy Fruit Mask scented with synthetic green apple, a product promising to remove my growing population of nasal blackheads? I was sure that the alcohol sting of the chartreuse-green, translucent face mask would cleanse my pores. I had done the requisite pre-scrubbing with Noxzema and a washcloth, stiff from being dried out on the clothesline.

No matter how hard I scrubbed or how often I used the mask, I was just left with a red, dried-out epidermis and black, pinprick-sized nose pores. Jenny had said that Kathy got her blackheads out with a needle and alcohol. I tried this. Kathy's skin was beautiful, with not a blemish in sight, so this should work for me, right? It didn't. It just left me with small red scabs all over my nose.

Okay, if I couldn't get my skin to cooperate, there was work to be done on my hair. Herbal Essences shampoo, in all its forest-green glory, promised luxuriant locks. So how did all the pretty girls at school get their waist-length hair to move as one unit when they turned? How did they escape the ever-present static cling that caused my hair to cloak my face like a beard? I have yet to find out.

All my beauty efforts were complicated because I had no shower in the bathroom I shared with Laura, so hair washing was in the tub. I could never completely rinse my hair that way, and I spent three years with hair that stuck to my scalp like a skullcap. I'm sure Mom thought I had developed some tic, as I spent the better part of each day flipping my hair over my head to add "body."

When my hair and skin failed me, I was led to believe by advertisements in my bible—*Seventeen*—that Wind Song perfume would render the opposite gender helpless and cause them to fall hopelessly, romantically in love with whoever dabbed its heady floral scent on their wrists and ankles. ("Her Wind Song stays on my mind . . .") It came in an enormous glass spray container shaped like a crown. April informed me that it smelled like cat food on my skin. This was not the scent experience I was going for in life.

It was on to Sweet Honesty via Avon, a very icky-sweet concoction I felt compelled to douse myself with each school morning. "Can sweetness and honesty find happiness together?" asked the print advertisement. If I were to embody these two qualities, this concoction would help. Or maybe it would distract others from my abject gawkiness. What a disquieting desire to be noticed and to be left alone at the same time.

DAS IST SO PEINLICH (THIS IS SO EMBARRASSING)

My quest for beauty and acceptance required many a trip to the PX/commissary complex, which was a hub of activity for the entire post. When we wanted to shop American style, off we'd go to the commissary (grocery store) with two shopping carts. Now, it didn't hurt that Greg Motsko was a cashier there. I always volunteered to help Mom with the food shopping because of him. It was just wonderful to be in his presence, although I don't think I ever said anything beyond "Hi."

I regretted my insistence on accompanying Mom on one occasion when the mega-box of Kotex sanitary napkins we had on the conveyor belt did not have a price tag. This was well before the days of computer-coded labeling for prices. Greg had to go to the shelves to get another box for the price. I suspect incidents like this spurred the creation of online shopping so teenagers could save face.

As Greg was off down the aisles searching for Kotex, Mom attempted to counter my mortification with, "Not to worry, this too shall pass."

Thank you, oh wise one. Now I feel relieved that Greg Motsko is associating me with stinky period blood! Just the magic moment I was searching for—not.

I was a sanitary napkin gal. This was the day and age before self-stick pads. Mom gifted us each with a "sanitary belt" upon the onset of our first period. This elastic apparatus still maintained its original design from the 1880s! The user would have to carefully thread a ginormous cotton pad with tails at both ends (another design from the 1880s) through each plastic holder (at least an upgrade from the 1880s metal holders).

What a horrible labor-intensive process! The multitude of steps necessary to attach the cotton tails securely at both ends, and the bulky product itself, prevented me from wearing "anticipatory pads" during the initial years of menstruation when I never quite knew when I would get my period.

I got my first period on a school day, wearing my one-day-a-week, light-colored bell-bottom jeans. I headed to the bathroom when I felt a trickle of liquid and noticed a rust-colored stain on my white undies. Panic ensued as I was sure gushes of crimson blood were about to pour down my legs. I took the Army-issue toilet paper, created as thick a pseudo pad as possible, and spent the second half of the school day praying that I could get home with no one finding out I was bleeding.

I felt shame and relief at the beginning of my trip into womanhood. Ditching my stained-with-shame underpants in the trash and creating another mock pad from toilet paper delayed the inevitable cringe-inducing admission to Mom. The following day, my cleanliness-driven mother entered my bedroom with the most awkward expression I had ever witnessed. Oh shit . . . my secret was out.

She uttered, "Welcome to womanhood," and passed me an industrial-sized box of Kotex pads along with my sanitary belt. Then she told me to ask April if I had any questions. Yeah, that was never going to happen. Forty more years of cramps, bleeding, a bloated abdomen, and referring to it as "the curse" would never leave me feeling comfortable with "that time of the month."

DER SCHMERZ VON WENN ALLEN (THE PAIN OF IT ALL)

The sting and embarrassment of bleeding was never discussed in complete sentences at home or with friends. The single word "cramps" embodied the humiliation of a bodily function taking over our lives for one or possibly two weeks a month.

Was it any wonder that I felt such a grounding relief when my ovaries made their last stand at age fifty-five? With menstrual cessation, I would never be caught off guard again by the dribble of blood or be rendered bedbound by nausea-inducing uterine contractions.

All my Catholic training was supposed to make me believe in some benevolent male God figure, but would a Supreme Being really design women with such faulty parts? Now, who the hell was I going to ask this question? A celibate priest? A celibate nun? April? I chose to keep my question to myself.

You know, I wonder if the reason why our periods hurt is that we try to hold them back to make men comfortable. What if we talked about them openly, passing pads and tampons as effortlessly as we pass Kleenex to someone with a stuffy nose? What if we celebrated our uniqueness in the ability to shed the lining of our life-giving parts and lorded it over men? But, no . . . life is about making men comfortable. Until we disrupt that, it's just 1975 all over again.

And in 1975, we had to anticipate that not only would Mom be heavily involved in her champion-of-the-domicile day-to-day but also that there would be the ramp-up week-before-a-party duties too.

This required the active participation of all four females, scrubbing walls, ceilings, and grout with a toothbrush! How the hell was I going to write the great American novel, learn to play the guitar and write music, or do anything meaningful if I was brain impaired from Clorox and ammonia? Oh yeah, it was "the man" at work again, thwarting any efforts by females to liberate. But I couldn't leave Mom alone to endure this fate.

I told myself that my participation would only be for as long as I lived at home. Then I would pay others well to do this once I was rich (from some undefined career). I did not antici-pate that almost fifty years later, it would still be women doing this drudgery.

FALSCHER STOPP
(WRONG STOP)

Walking was a way of life for me on post, but there were times when public transportation was necessary for distances longer than a stroll back before dark allowed. The German mass transit system and its rigid punctuality were nothing foreign to our Army-run family. But the freedom that mass transit gave me and my sisters was.

Before Germany, I walked to local stores in Rockville, Maryland, but anything beyond a mile meant that we depended on Mom. I hadn't wanted to go anywhere without her, so it wasn't like I was missing out on anything, but April assured me we were.

She was like a mini grown-up from the time she was little. She operated with such confidence and desire to experience life. Her exasperated sighs and pseudo whispers of "This is so boring!" accompanied each family activity. Her discontent with family outings increased in Germany. I couldn't imagine that the fifteen-month age difference between us was the defining factor in her maturity versus my immaturity. I just assumed I was a genetic anomaly. Well, I assumed this after April surmised this aloud to me.

I felt that I needed to "grow up," and I guess Mom did too because she dropped me off at my on-the-Economy friend

Laura's family apartment and informed me that I needed to take the Strasse home. Mom made sure I had the required money and knew the specific place where I would later board the streetcar for home after my time with my friend.

I was mentally obsessively going over my trip home the entire visit. This ability to simultaneously operate in two conscious states had been honed by my years of anxiety. The internal state of consciousness elicits the visceral vagal response, and it's never pleasant.

When the time came for me to leave, my friend Laura walked me to the street to board the correct Strasse. As a native of Germany, she was so adept at traveling the mass transit system alone, as were the gaggle of young German children accompanying me on my Maiden Maturity Voyage. I watched eagle-eyed out the window for familiar places but soon realized that I had no idea where I was.

I had not paid any attention previously when traveling with Mom, as she was always the one in charge. I had been a passive passenger, and now I was ill-prepared. This was not going to end well if I didn't take hold of the situation.

I had failed to write down the name of my stop, and all the stops sounded the same. Not speaking enough German to understand someone after I asked for help, I just got off at the next stop and walked . . . and walked and walked and walked. There were no cell phones then—just a fourteen-year-old walking very quickly, sweating, and hoping to get home.

I tried to look like I knew where I was going and that I liked doing it for fear of being mugged or worse. I had learned about mugging in the Nicky Cruz books. I think that walk induced my first full-on panic attack, but I never told anyone. With stomach acids riding up into my throat and my heart rate increasing to a level where I could see my shirt moving in and out, I had to attempt to look confident so as not to invite unwelcome advances from leering men.

Coursing through every pore, every vein, every available sensory cell was the belief that death would have been preferable to this experience. I had little-to-no spatial perception as it relates to directionality and depended on landmarks to guide my navigation. The streets looked unfamiliar, as I had only ever viewed them via car travel as a passenger.

I kept glancing up at street signs, hoping for a familiar name, and at buildings, praying for that I-know-where-I-am recognition that would guide me home. But unfortunately, fear leads to doubt, doubt leads to panic, and panic leads to . . . Nope, I had to stay focused because the only way I was ever going to get home was by staying on that street, Reuterweg.

My whole body toggled back and forth between "I am going to die" and "I know I can do this." The "dying" was my heart palpitating rapidly and then skipping beats, a gripping pain in all my joints, a noose-like tightening around my neck that made breathing shallow and difficult, muscles trembling throughout my body expending more energy than a walk ever should—all capped off by an internal terror that I could not control.

Only the stalwart McKnight upbringing allowed me to override my well-developed anxiety. I kept repeating in my mind, *Just keep walking. You can do this. Just keep walking. You can do this*, all while continuing to endure the physical manifestations of the prolonged panic.

When I looked up and saw the street sign reading "Gruneburgweg," I knew I was saved. It sounded like Gruneburg Park, which I knew was near-ish to our house. So it would not be that much farther to Hansa Allee, Miquel Allee, and then to our home, to my bedroom, where I could hope to release the pent-up trauma from this experience.

I made it home, but I said nothing other than that I'd had a good time at Laura's house. If I had only explained to Mom what had happened, I feel sure now (but did not then) that she would have gone over the route on a map with me. Or maybe she would have figured that I was incapable of the same freedom privileges as April, who traveled by innate echolocation.

That walk has stayed with me and serves a dual purpose. It has been the scene of many a nightmare but also a beacon of strength for me. I know I can find my way home, and I can endure even while in the grip of panic. Years later, when my then-husband had spent every penny I had in our "joint" bank account, I would repeat that mantra, *I can do this. I can do this. I can figure this out.* I did. There were many other complicating factors. It was awful, and I'm sure I disappointed my family with my divorce.

HABEN WIR SCHON SPASS?
(ARE WE HAVING FUN YET?)

The Ambassador Arms Hotel was right across the street from our house; somehow, our maid's quarters became the holding ground for various officers. One of our guests was the new pastor for the Catholics on post.

Chaplain (COL) Corbin W. Ketchersid was a robust man with an enormous laugh and a biting sense of humor, the only priest ever who made church worth going to for me. He stayed in our maid's quarters for a week while his quarters were being readied.

Mom had been taking French cooking lessons, and Father Ketchersid's visit was the perfect opportunity for her to try out myriad recipes. At age fourteen, I was always hungry, so I was ready and willing to eat whatever she put in front of me. The breakfast of marinated French toast was a velvety concoction of eggs, sugar, cream, and a hint of nutmeg poured over slices of thick French bread, then left to soak overnight in the refrigerator and finally fried up in the morning. The result was sublime, really—the crater in the middle was a perfect holding place for the butter to melt.

Father Ketchersid was the first priest I had ever personally had dealings with beyond the pulpit railing. He laughed easily and deeply and seemed more like a Special Forces officer than a man of the cloth.

He was to be the new head Catholic priest at the post chapel. When I went to a Mass that he led, he always made his way back to me while singing the last hymn. He strolled down the aisle, holding his hymnal, and purposely sang at the top of his lungs. He was a jokester, but I did not appreciate the extra attention.

The Adjunct General was also a visitor at Chez McKnight, and he, too, was treated to Mom's excellent food and hospitality. It made me feel so good to hear him gush over her cooking. So finally, Mom was being verbally rewarded beyond our family members for one of her talents.

The preparations in our household pre-visitor were epic. The top-to-bottom cleaning of our quarters was a real irritant as far as I was concerned. It's not like "Colonel or General Whoever-The-Hell" was ever going to come into my room. So why did I have to clean it up to specs?

The Adjunct General returned Mom's kindness by arranging a Christmas trip for us all that year to Garmisch, a picturesque town in the German Alps of Bavaria. We owe that trip to Mom. However, I know I did not see it that way at the time. It might have been so meaningful to have heard from Dad that the Garmisch trip directly resulted from her hospitality. Perhaps it also could have gone a long way toward my early understanding of the importance of her contributions as an Army wife. It is only now that I have come to the realization that the lasting Garmisch memories are due to Mom.

We celebrated Christmas-present-opening the night before we left for our trip. We three girls had all left the magic of Santa behind a few years before, so there was no need for that ruse. April had spoiled it for me anyway when I was eight years old. She had unceremoniously announced that Santa was made-up. That news had rocked my world and sent me into a deep existential crisis. The 1975 Christmas trip to Garmisch brought back the magic that April had robbed me of so many years earlier.

My matching hat and scarf à la Ali MacGraw in *Love Story* were from Mom and Dad. April informed me that the hat "elongated [my] already oblong face," and the wool it was made from made my forehead itch, along with flattening my hair. The Alps were going to be cold, so I had no choice but to wear them—that, and Mom was so pleased with the purchase. I just couldn't hurt Mom's feelings. She always tried so hard for our family. I was willing to risk April's derision in support of Mom. April was a mean person. I was not.

The four-and-a-half-hour ride seemed endless, crammed into the back of our new Peugeot, but it was sweetened by a classic Sylvia McKnight lunch. It was the bottomless brown shopping bag of tasty delights: sandwiches, pickles, candy, nuts, cookies, gum—she'd thought of everything! Now of course, Dad being Dad, we had to wait a certain amount of time before consuming anything. If we were hungry, Dad claimed it was our fault for not eating enough at breakfast.

Who could eat a 4:00 a.m. pre-trip breakfast? Dad . . . Dad could eat at 4:00. I tried to choke down a few Cheerios but felt they would come right back up if one more soggy loop met the back of my throat.

Throughout our Auto Alpine Adventure trek, we sang songs April had learned as a member of the FAJHS choir, many of which were popular songs at the time. There is nothing like three girls singing, "Ain't No Woman Like the One I've Got," at the top of their lungs in an enclosed space to point out the fact that we were Americans.

The singing abruptly stopped when the first view of the jagged, snow-covered Bavarian Alps came into sight. They were natural monuments, and the sky was crisp, blue, and cloudless as I first gazed upon them. This alpine range was oh-so-different from the rounded, hilly Appalachian Mountains we had hiked back in Maryland and Virginia. It may have been at my internal point of visual comparison that all things American suddenly paled to all things European.

The mistake I made was then verbalizing this comparison, which precipitated a lecture by Dad on the geological history differences between the two chains. *Ugh . . . lesson learned, now can we just drop it?* This last thought was, of course, not one I articulated aloud.

After Dad's diatribe on the value of "appreciating where you are, rather than comparing and ranking one experience above the other," we returned to singing. I guess the sparkling snowcaps inspired the start-up of Christmas songs, as the whole family joined in the revelry.

Our quarters for the week were the General Patton Hotel. Was it Mom, Dad, or the Army concierge who decided our daily itinerary? Whoever it was, the day after we arrived, we traveled to the Zugspitze. The only "Spitz" I knew of was Mark Spitz, the über-gorgeous, thick dark-mustachioed American swimming ace of the '72 Munich Olympics. I was quickly instructed that we would be spending our day traveling to the Zugspitze and then sightseeing atop this pinnacle of the Wetterstein Mountains—the highest peak in Germany.

This jagged point was only accessible to us tourists by cable car. For me, being trapped in a metal "car"—pulled by what I hoped was the strongest steel imaginable and no way out but a death plunge—was an exercise in breathing while breathless. *What will we do if the car stops in midair? Who will rescue us? Will we have to grab hold of the cable and climb hand-over-hand? What if I must pee? What if I vomit? Why couldn't we just have viewed this from the bottom of the mountain?*

I tried to distract myself with the utter beauty—glistening snow, piercing sunlight, and Mom narrating the *entire time*, "Oh, look at that. Aren't we lucky to be here?" If you call being held at 9,708 feet in the air with no MacGyver skills "lucky," I guess that was us.

Once at the top, we were ushered to the observation deck. Enter Dad with his industrial-sized camera case artfully filled with every lens and filter ever created by mankind. Unfortunately, at a certain point, even a goose-down coat loses its ability to insulate against gale-force winds and below-freezing air temperatures, allowing no detectable living things beyond the stupid people snapping photos of snowcapped mountains. My coat was long past that, and my wool mittens could not shelter my hands and long fingers from starting their descent into frostbite.

Mom finally gently suggested to Dad that we "proceed down the mountain to eat lunch." So why is it now that I would give anything to view those slides of the summit of the Zugspitze? Is everything for me truly better in retrospect? Perhaps it's easier to look fondly on an experience when all danger of losing a limb or digit due to frostbite has passed.

MALERISCH
(PICTURESQUE)

Our Tyrolean vacation continued on Christmas Eve. Mom decided we would all go to Midnight Mass. Dad, the Protestant, accompanied us, which was a real rarity. We walked from the hotel to the chapel. The snow-covered town lined with classic wooden chalets and Christmas greenery was enchanting. While we meandered our way to the chapel, it was snowing—dry, heavy flakes that glistened and iced the already stunning alpine scenery.

I am sure that is where the current Hallmark Channel standard for romantic winter sets originated. We girls sang all the way, with Mom reminding us that "not everyone is awake at midnight, and not everyone will appreciate your rendition of 'Santa Baby.'"

Prior to entering the church, April snickered and said to me, "Don't get your foot caught under the kneeler." She was referring to my gaffe a year earlier during my Catholic confirmation when I got my little toe broken by my classmate's quick descent onto the kneeler, post-Communion. Not one of my finer moments. I was careful in Garmisch not to catch any appendage under the kneeler.

The Alpine chapel was candlelit and very full. I had on six hundred layers of winter clothing. Coupled with potent incense, German body odor, and being dead tired, it was the perfect storm to induce fainting . . . and faint I did, at least for a moment.

I ended up sitting for the rest of the Mass, feeling green and wishing I were in bed, sleeping. Mom remembers that Mass as one of her favorite Christmas experiences ever. I was puce green, and she was overcome by the Holy Spirit.

The day after Christmas, we traveled to the nearby town of Oberammergau. This ancient city is known for its wood carvings and passion plays to ward off the plague. I wonder, in this age of COVID, if that would help? But I am being irreverent.

Now, I like good craftsmanship as much as the next person, but the entire city was woodshop after woodshop. It was Geppetto's dream. We each got to buy something, and I settled on a "tree face" (a face carved into a tree branch). My sisters got religious items, olive-wood crosses if memory serves. I was the sole Druid in the bunch. Mom had her heart set on a dirndl, a classic Bavarian folk dress, and Dad purchased a woolen loden coat worn by Bavarian hunters.

Unless Mom was planning on part-time waitressing for Oktoberfest and Dad a mid-career change from Army officer to medieval hunter, I couldn't understand the purpose of their purchases. What were they going to do with those things? Wear them about town? Ward off the plague? Dad switched into his loden coat for the duration of the trip, and Mom hung her alpine treasure in our hotel room and only again brought it out at Halloween.

Garmisch–Partenkirchen had been the site of the 1936 Winter Olympics. April mentioned this during some part of the week and was quickly silenced by my parents. "That period of history was a complete embarrassment to the German people," Mom and Dad explained back at the General Patton, and we were not to speak of it. We didn't. I did not think of it again until writing this book.

I found this utterly confusing. Why the hell couldn't we talk about this time within the confines of the General Patton Hotel? What was going to happen? Was the ghost of Hitler going to be summoned? Were some of the former Nazis working at the hotel?

These were all questions I had but dared not ask. Besides, where was I going to get the answers? I doubted the Frankfurt post library had a section on Nazis. It truly felt to me that by not talking about something, it was like it never existed.

With our 1936 Olympic questions quashed, we were free to enjoy our blissful ignorance. We did not go skiing while in this playground for snow sports. We did not do any sports while there. I'm not sure why that was so. I know Dad had enjoyed many a winter escapade while growing up in Freemansburg, Pennsylvania. He had spoken of sledding down the super-steep Green Street and of ice-skating on frozen ponds growing up in the 1930s and 1940s, so why weren't we pursuing those adventures in the Snow Capital of Germany? I'm sure he had his reasons, but we never asked what he was thinking. If he wanted us to know something, he would tell us.

MEINE GRENZEN TESTEN
(TESTING MY LIMITS)

The trip home was quiet. Christmas was over, and we would return to school in a few days. FAJHS was arranging an Outward Bound trip sponsored by Mr. Siemaszko. As Mr. S. described it, Outward Bound was going to be "a wilderness program designed to challenge your notions about yourself while confronting tasks requiring problem-solving and physical endurance previously unknown and/or unattempted." It sounded great to me, as it would be a week away from school. It's not that school was awful; I just wanted something "different."

I entered the lottery for the twenty or so spaces available and earned a slot. In theory, the lottery was random, but I have a feeling I was chosen to help me overcome my self-imposed limitations.

As soon as I was chosen, I realized I wanted to get out of it. The idea of a novel experience thrilled me more than the execution of such. This was one experience I would not be able to dodge. I had told Mom about being chosen and she told Dad, and they both decided it would be a wonderful "character-building exercise" for me.

The drive to the camp was the longest bus trip known to mankind. Being on that tour bus for hours on end, sitting alone, as no one sat near me, was like being in class feeling like the weirdo I always was. Only this was now that experience on wheels.

We arrived in the dark at the facility, and each of us was assigned a bunk and a job. I was on KP, or kitchen patrol, the first night and felt so homesick I thought I would surely hurl. There were no cell phones or computers in this mid-century experience. I missed the familiarity of my room, my bed, my mom, my irritating sisters, my stern dad, and our cantankerous cat.

Why? I had this internal desire to leave what I knew but a stronger pull to return to it. After being awakened in what still felt like the middle of the night, we were all instructed to dress and to meet outside. I was anticipating a hot breakfast to keep me from passing out from low blood sugar, but that was not to be.

The first "challenge" was a two-mile run through the snow-covered forest trails to an icy stream. Upon reaching this stream—which was a raging arctic river—we were to *lie down in it* and then run back to the camp soaking wet in below-zero air.

What the hell? How was this going to build character? I was sure this was how the author of *Lord of the Flies* had found inspiration. Perhaps today's performance fabric would have assisted in this forced march-and-dunk, but I can assure you that wet goose down soaked with icy water is not a recipe for anything but terror and whole-body shivering. I believe the medical community calls it hypothermia.

After lying back on the rocky stream bottom, gasping for air, being pulled up by the instructors and told to run, I was sure that the last activity of the week was going to be digging our own graves.

That same afternoon, we were paired with German kids, also on their Outward Bound experience, for a "Find your way through the forest with a foreigner" challenge. We were each given a German partner, a compass, and some written instructions. Cue the *MacGyver* theme song. Oh no, wait, this was 1975: no MacGyver and no skill set for me beyond expert blackhead popping and professional procrastination. I was in trouble.

I was so angry at myself for not having practiced to perfection my past German dialogue homework, failing to seriously commit to my studies. Because I was now stuck with Johann, who spoke broken English at best, in a desolate forest with nothing but a compass I could not read, impaired spatial perceptual ability, and the task to find our way back to camp before darkness arrived. I have no idea how we made it back, but I was convinced that this trip would kill me. So I played sick. I felt sick but knew it was nerves, not some weeklong flu. I would have to severely cut down my food intake while I was there to keep up this anxiety-induced charade.

I did go back and forth internally about how long to maintain my ailing status, but I got my period there and knew that river-soaked sanitary napkins were not going to change my experience for the better. So I spent each of the remaining five days in my bunk, alone with nothing to do but worry obsessively.

Different classmates brought food up to me when they returned from various activities, which must have been fun, proven by all the laughing and comradery. Each afternoon, I made the decision about whether to remain "sick" or to have a miraculous recovery and join in on the team-building/push-yourself-to-the-limits experiences. I always opted for my sick-out.

The last morning, the counselors decided I was well enough to do the dreaded two-mile, run-plunge-get-back-before-frost-bite challenge. Unfortunately, due to spending the week in bed,

I was in worse aerobic shape than I had previously been and was the last one down the path of Frozen Hades. The group clapped for me upon my completion, but I knew I was a fraud. What had seemed like a good self-preservation plan had only solidified my self-loathing. I wasn't any better or any more independent than I had been before this week.

What if I had pushed myself to override my familiar panic and participated in all the Outward Bound activities? Could that have been a defining moment of change for me? Was it possible that if I had done that, it would have allowed me to control my anxiety—possibly gotten rid of it? These will always be questions left unanswered.

The shame I felt—the disappointment in myself—sat on me so heavily that I thought I would break in two. I could not let my family see this. I needed to quickly invent a narrative palatable to me that was equally so for them.

I have never been so glad to see my family as when we pulled up to FAJHS in the dark of night and I was able to go home. I never told my family that it was homesickness that had plagued me during that week. But I guess if they are reading this, they know now.

Mom enveloped me tightly and I her. I think it didn't matter to her how the week had been, just that I had survived it. She did not ask me too many questions, and I had just enough stories about the polar plunges to keep them all entertained. *Keep them laughing . . . then they'll think I'm all right.*

BORDSTEINKANTE
(CURBSIDE)

All the other participants of this Outward Bound experience had become super close by virtue of their shared experiences, and I was even further on the outside back at school. I endured each school day buoyed by my growing friendship with Mary H. She lived on my street, and her mother had made her come over one day and introduce herself to us.

The day is so memorable to me because I answered the door, and Mary introduced herself as follows, "Hi, my name is Mary H. My mom made me come over here because she said she thought we could be friends." So, as per politeness protocol, I had to invite her in, and we played Monopoly with Laura and Jenny.

After that day, Mary and I were inseparable. We sat together on the bus ride to and from school and spent many a day after homework talking and laughing together. What a life-changing time for me to have a friend to travel through school life with each day. It was not lost on either of us how much time we had wasted by not getting to know one another earlier.

She was introverted like I was, and we introverts assume no one wants to know us. Because of her friendship, I had someone my own age to help navigate school life. It was a different bond than I had with Jenny. Mary was someone my age. Her mom let her buy *Seventeen*, and she and I pored over the pages together, reading the articles and then analyzing the photos for the hair-styles and clothing we liked and disliked.

I didn't have to travel anywhere to see her or to talk with her. We just had to walk two houses down, and we were together. She had long blond hair and blue eyes. She had an approachable beauty and ease about herself. She was more athletic than I was, and the days she had volleyball practice were the only days I had to ride the bus without her.

Mary had an older sister who had already graduated from high school and a brother in high school. I spent a good deal of time at her house and she at mine. Whenever we were at her home, we spent most of the time in her garage. She said it was quieter in there, but in retrospect, I think there was quite a bit of arguing between her mom and Mary's older sister.

Ralph, Mary's older brother, gave her a portable record player with two speakers to pass on to me. This ability to play records up in my room was glorious. Of course, I had to play them softly, as per Dad's mandate, and I lay on the floor next to the speakers so I could hear. This was such freedom to be able to close myself off in my room and listen, think, analyze lyrics, and dream.

In the solitude of my music, I began to freely entertain notions of what I thought versus what I thought others wanted me to think. I guess Dad must have noticed this change in me because he soon required me to open my door halfway. Oh, my god! Why did he have to control everything I did?

I began to question the very curriculum in school that I was being taught. In social studies, my teacher was all hyped up on the French and Indian Wars. The slant was that the Indians were massacring the French . . . but it seemed to me they had every right to protect the land they had lived on for thousands of years. So why were they being cast as villains? Although I did not ask this question aloud, the fact that I asked it at all, even internally, shifted my thinking. Who was writing these textbooks? What would the view of the Indians be if they had written them?

Dad had in his book collection several small volumes on some of the native tribes of America. I remembered them from when we lived in Rockville, although he had put them into storage when we moved to Frankfurt. They were memorable to me for the photos I had pored over many times. However, the one that stuck in my mind was of a tribe that flattened the forehead of their children with boards, for what reason I did not know but later learned was a mark of status.

I was impressed with Dad for viewing the native people of our land (the land now known as the United States) as individuals with separate cultures and wisdom. According to TV and movies, the common understanding was very cowboys and Indians. If the Indigenous people were there first, what right had the Europeans to come and steal their land?

I wanted *sooooo* badly to ask this question in class and asked Dad about it. He forbade me from doing so and said, "It would be disrespectful to disrupt the class with a question like that." Wasn't the point to disrupt thought to get to the truth? Dad told me that it was all "a matter of perception." If this was so, then what was "truth"? My mind was officially opened, and it would never close. The backdrop of Europe continued to serve as a guide for my expanded education.

NIEDERLANDE
(THE NETHERLANDS)

For spring break, Dad informed us that we were taking a family trip to see the tulips in Holland. It was going to be the Palmengarten on steroids—I just knew it. Holland in the spring. We drove there on a tour bus. The stops took us to the Keukenhof Gardens, where Dad spent hour upon hour in the drizzle and the damp cold, taking pictures of the tulips.

How many "Aren't we so lucky!" exhortations by Mom could we endure, and how many photos of tulips could one man take? Thousands upon thousands of both. I kept obsessing over my hair. The humidity of the Dutch air was causing my long locks to frizz up. April took every opportunity to share her observations on this phenomenon with me.

So, as we stood among the rows and rows of these open and opening bulbs, I tried unsuccessfully to smooth down my hair. This was so sad. If I had been two years younger like Laura, I would have been taking joy in skipping down the paths, my hair poufy with humidity, and not caring one bit.

I missed what I did not know to cherish in my "What will others think about my hair?" mindset. Once I was bitten by the "What would a cute guy think?" bug, I was chained to how I looked on the outside. It occurs to me that in menopause, we are given back the gift of being self. But on that

Holland-in-the-spring trip, I was infected with such an outer-affecting inner construct that I could not parse out what was truly important.

Mom was mesmerized by the visual floral experience, but I'm embarrassed to say that we three girls kept wondering (unfortunately, aloud), "What's next?" We had to go to a wax museum to see "Holland's Greatest Hits of Humans." Weird. Totally underwhelming to see lifelike representations of people. What was the purpose?

As much as I was getting into art from my near-obsessive poring over album covers, I could not see the waxy hominids' artistic significance. It was too much like taxidermy for people. Mom kept the air filled with, "Oh, my! How lifelike!" *Great. What's next?*

Next was a visit to the miniature city of Madurodam. I should have been in awe of the sculpted detail of "Honey, I Shrunk Holland" but instead felt like I was living in *Gulliver's Travels*. Only in my telling of this classic tale, it was the awkward teenage girl travel version.

Mom quickly picked up on April's and my flippant attitudes and informed us, "Parents built this little, magnificent city as a tribute to their son who was killed in World War II. The proceeds are going to various charities."

Ouch. Now that I knew that, I tried to walk the tiny streets less as Gulliver and more as Mom. She really had a way of shifting my thinking and feeling. She did it so quietly. There was no yelling, just statements of fact.

Mom was the consummate diplomat. Where did she learn this skill? I certainly did not possess it. I asked her one of the most life-changing questions I have ever asked: "Mom, how did you know what Ape and I were thinking? We hadn't said anything!"

Her answer was, "Body language."

What? What was body language? She did not want to go into it on the trip and said so. She promised we would talk more about it at home. She wanted to enjoy where we were, as there was little likelihood that we would ever return. Mom wanted to savor every moment.

I couldn't stop thinking about what she had said and began to watch people in a different manner than ever before. I observed the way they stood both alone and with others. I had no framework for these observations but drew some hasty conclusions just the same. I started with a guiding question to help me focus. "Who looks bored?" was one of them, as I was well-acquainted internally with that state of being.

When I ran out of bored people, I was on to the next guiding question: "Who looks thrilled?" Again, analyzing people in terms of opposites seemed like a good way to start this focused study of body language.

This quest was helped greatly by the fact that I had no idea what people were saying in their various verbal languages. Their only common language was the one Mom had let me in on, body language. I was obsessed. It made so much sense to me, and it had the double delight of also taking my mind off how separate I felt from other people.

If I am actively observing the posturing of others, I have a purpose. Prior to that realization, I felt utterly alone in a crowd. Now I had my analysis to keep me company. This was not the only breakthrough I experienced in Holland. The other involved the chinking of April's armor.

The first thing my family thinks of about that trip is not the breathtaking rows of tulips or the picturesque windmills. Instead, our first family vocal chorus when reminiscing about this Netherlands adventure is April's feet.

We spent only one night in Holland, to my recollection. We three girls shared a room, and at one point, we were nasally assaulted by an odor akin to a chemical spill. The source turned out to be April's track shoes. Or rather, her feet that had been encased in the three-stripe classic Adidas . . . plus the shoes themselves. It was the first and only time that April's body had betrayed her, and I was delighted! Finally, a horrible bodily occurrence that was not emanating from me! The trip was looking up.

Mom came to check on us and our rude, raucous laughter. Why didn't we just tell her what we were laughing about? She was moving toward the bag holding April's toxic shoes and socks with us yelling in classic movie slow motion, "*Noooo!*" Too late. She opened the bag, and the stench hit the air, followed by the very rare Sylvia McKnight, "Oh, dear *god*!"

April was not perfect. The truth was out. More importantly, I now knew the truth. I could use this information and lord it over her as she had done to me, but I decided instead to treat her like I would have wanted her to treat me all those years. That decision just felt better inside me than the evil thought of spreading the news of April's stinky feet around school upon our return.

I told her I had read in *Seventeen* that cornstarch could be used to absorb odor. Her response should have been, "Thanks, Mare!" but it wasn't. Instead, it was, "Well, that would only be helpful if we had cornstarch here!" Oh, my god! She was going to try my patience for sure.

The following morning, down we all went to breakfast. April was forced to wear wet shoes, as Mom had scrubbed them the night before, attempting to do toxic cleanup Slovak style. She had asked one of the maids for the Dutch version of Clorox. The offending shoes were scrubbed and set out on the balcony to dry. The only flaw in that plan was the weather. Spring in Holland included a fine mist and a nip in the air. Hence the wet shoes. I was secretly glad.

At breakfast that morning, we girls were starving. We quickly consumed the contents of the continental breakfast bread basket, leaving us hungry for more calories. Our waiter spoke in broken English, "They are, how do you say, hungry still? Wait." He came back with an enormous platter of lunch meat and cheese. We probably looked like the plague of locusts to the other guests, who were quietly dining on one hard roll and strong coffee.

The shoes did not dry, and April had to wear them "damp" for the trip home. She did not dare go stocking-feet stench on the bus, as it was a contained environment.

Back at home, Mom was true to her word and began the discussion of body language. So off we went to the post library to check out a book on the subject. She never did say how she learned about this. I don't think I asked either, as my focus was on acquiring as much information as I could on the subject. I didn't have any end goal in mind. It just fascinated me to be able to understand people's unspoken bodily manifestations of feelings and thoughts.

This newfound interest and knowledge allowed me to finish the school year with a softening internal dialogue, no longer focusing so much on "me." It did not completely quiet my anxiety, but it gave me a break from its constancy. I was now an observer of people. *Great, I have a skill now, and to top it off, one that April does not have. So now how do I make a career of that?*

FALLEN (FALLING)

On the last day of junior high, our principal played "School's Out" by Alice Cooper over the speakers. I don't imagine that song with the lyric, "School's been blown to pieces," is a popular tune anymore in schools. But it was the kind of moment that John Hughes would characterize in his eighties films with the entire school singing along, boys with air guitars and hair flying everywhere. Girls and boys with long hair and massive Afros catching the breeze skipped out the doors with a freedom we were sure would bring a memorable summer. I would not be disappointed.

During the school year, Colonel Rhodes and his family had moved in across the street from us. They had an eighteen-year-old son, Alan . . . my first love, unrequited though it was. He was such a nice guy, not at all standoffish, despite our four-year age difference. Perhaps it was the military-family influence that required politeness on his part, but I was hoping it was more than that.

I hadn't really noticed him during the winter, as the damp, gray German skies had necessitated indoor activities. But then the first blush of spring brought with it my awareness of his aura. He floated in a cerebral air far above my earthly ineptitude. I so wanted to speak to him, but what would I say?

Not much at first. I just sat on the curb in front of my house with whomever would join me. When no one came, a book was my companion. Generally, it was *Leaves of Grass* by Walt Whitman, a collection of writings so thick that Alan would surely inquire. He did. It is hard to talk when your breath is taken by the force of a first love.

"What are you reading so intently?" he inquired, sitting beside me with his tall, lanky body and unruly, wavy dark hair.

"*Leaves of Grass.* Walt Whitman," was all I could say. I wanted to ask if he'd read it, but the silence after my words was quickly and politely filled with his admiration of my choice of author.

"Ahh ... Whitman. He writes with an understanding of the need for solitude and the ache for companionship."

Although I understood Alan's words, I was utterly unaccustomed to anyone besides Mom taking the time to engage me in intellectual repartee.

"Yes, I feel at home when I read his writing," I replied. Oh, was it enough to keep Alan sitting with me? It must have been because he remained there, asking me about various authors I had never heard of, and recommending that I "check them out." He did not tell me to read these authors. He simply suggested that, given my love of Whitman, I might enjoy the works of other authors he either was currently reading or had read.

If he was reading it, I was interested. As I revisit this time in my life, I realize what a muse he was for bringing me such glimmers of self-knowledge beyond my faults and frailties. How expansive to be in the company of someone who thought that I might enjoy these literary heroes of his!

Alan periodically hung out with me curbside, along with Vanessa, who lived at the end of our street and was, like Alan, a senior in high school. When it was just Alan and me, I learned about Richard Adams's *Watership Down*. Whatever he read, I read. To read *Tropic of Cancer* and *Tropic of Capricorn* by Henry Miller, I would go running up to the post library and check out his recommendations.

It wasn't just literature he shared with me; it was music too. He lent me his records, most memorably Judy Collins's *Judith*. To just hold his possessions in my hands, even prior to listening, was such a privilege for me. He believed I would handle the vinyl on the edges, place the stereo needle so as not to scratch, and return the albums in a timely fashion. I did. I wore huge 1970s earphones plugged into the living room stereo to create a world all my own. (My own record player needed a new needle, and I didn't want to sully his records.) Judy Collins, with her angelic voice, her songs filled with depth and cloudy emotions—they sank deep inside me. Thanks to Alan's generosity, I listened until I knew all the words. I still know all the words.

VON DER LIEBE
ZERQUETSCHT
(CRUSHED BY LOVE)

I sn't it easy to love someone when they expect nothing from you, and everything they do surpasses any experience you have ever had before? Mary H. often kept me company on the curb. She had a crush on Alan, but my emotions were deeper than that—they were love. He took photographs with his single-lens reflex camera (SLR) and rode his bike everywhere. He was perfect. He was my first love, and April informed me that she had told him.

She justified her actions by claiming that she did it to "save me from unrealistic expectations." I knew she was just jealous that he was paying attention to me and not to her. I finally had someone who thought I was important (besides Mom), and she could not stand it! I was sure of this. Her revelation to him did not deter him.

Mary H. and I sat on the curb in front of my house that summer of 1975, just waiting for Alan to come out of his house. Even in the frequent dull, dark, impending rains, Mary and I were curbside, just waiting for an "Alan sighting." We were all the while talking, laughing, and trying to figure out where we wanted to go in our lives. We had each picked out a picture in a magazine to represent what we wanted to look like—our ideal selves—to show each other.

I think Mary's was a Breck Shampoo girl with long, straight blond hair, perfect features, and ideal body proportions. Mine was from an Herbal Essences ad of a girl with hair so long it wove under her armpits. I think she may have been nude, riding a horse. I concentrated only on her hair—the nudity and underarm hair were not what I was going for.

As we shared our "reveal," a pigeon swooped over us, which sent us into paroxysms of laughter until it smacked into the big single-pane picture window of my house and landed on the ground beneath it, which then sent us into screams of horror.

Dad came outside and said he would take care of it. Somehow, I took that to mean that he would get a box for it, feed it with an eye-dropper, and bring it back to health. But I couldn't figure out why Dad had a wooden board. Was he going to fashion some type of splint?

The board smashing on the pigeon's head, accompanied by the squish of guts was not at *all* what I had thought he would do. Dad coolly said, "Now it's out of its misery." Mary and I were crying and screaming. I guess the neighborhood was used to that type of emotional outburst from us because no one came outside to see what was happening. There would be no Alan sighting that day.

Perhaps he was off on the streets of Frankfurt on his bike. To increase the likelihood of interacting with him, I needed to get off the curb and onto a bike. But first, I had to get a bike, which required money. As I had no marketable skill set, I capitalized on my comfort with young children and did some house-sitting for various people on our block when they went on vacation.

During one of those house-sits for neighbors at the end of our block, I was to feed their cat and water their indoor and outdoor plants. They were to be gone a week, and I would be paid handsomely. This was easy work for me, and I had Mary accompany me on some of the days. She suggested that, in their absence, we could use the Ping-Pong table in their basement. This seemed reasonable, as they were gone, and it was just sitting there.

This was a marvelous activity, and for much of the week, after I had fed and played with their cat and watered every plant possible, we played match after match. This was grand until they came home a day early and found us playing. This was not good.

They were not pleased. Their body language, mostly the wife's downturned mouth and the two lines creased heavily between her eyes, let me know that in fact, playing on their Ping-Pong table without their permission was not what they had in mind when they hired me.

They said nothing but, "Come upstairs and we'll pay you for services rendered." Yikes! Oh, this was going to bring dishonor to my family. Were they going to tell Dad? Should I tell Dad preemptively? Had I made enough money to buy a bike? I was not questioning how easily I had followed Mary's suggestion. Instead, I was consumed with how the outcome of Colonel and Mrs. Ping-Pong Table's early arrival would affect my life.

I decided I had better tell. But I also decided that I could only reveal my error in judgment to Mom. Mom was not happy. She had the same downturned mouth and two-line crease between the eyes as Mrs. Ping-Pong. She told me, "I hope you have learned your lesson. You need to go back over there and apologize to them."

What? I had to go back over there? Yes, I had to go back over there. Their house was just two houses down from ours, but the walk that day felt like some sort of moral death march to me. My head hurt, my heart hurt, and I was sure I would never err like I had again. I never wanted to feel the heaviness I felt with every step forward.

The knock, knock on their door was met with quick footsteps and then me facing Mrs. Ping-Pong. "I am so very sorry . . . I should not have taken advantage of your trust in me. I hope you can forgive me, but I understand if you can't." And then I just burst out crying. I really tried not to, as I was sure that I wasn't supposed to show anything but active remorse.

Mrs. Ping-Pong hugged me and said, "Don't worry. We have all done things we shouldn't have. You took excellent care of our cat and our plants." Then she said other things, but I was too busy trying to stop crying to really comprehend anything.

I walked back to my house with a lightness in my step and my heart. It wasn't my apology that had caused this shift in spirit; it was Mrs. Ping-Pong's response. Note to self: Always forgive others in their errors of judgment when they have shown remorse.

Mom asked me how it had gone, and I explained. Then she said the magic words, "We don't have to tell your father. He wouldn't understand. You have done the right thing and learned your lesson." Oh, thank god! We didn't have to tell Dad! I wouldn't have to listen to how I had shamed our family, put a dark mark on his career, and any number of other awful things I probably did as the result of a few games of Ping-Pong.

Being able to dodge the Disappointed Dad bullet was great enough, but the best part was that with that last house-sit, I had enough money to buy my bike.

NUN, ICH WERDE VERDAMMT SEIN (WELL, I'LL BE DAMNED)

I went to the PX and purchased a Raleigh bike for $126—a *crazy* amount of money in 1975. I was not a good bike rider because I had little or no sense of direction and short legs. My determination to be bike-ready for Alan fueled my ambition to overcome my deficits and practice. Dad liked to go on frequent bike rides, so I asked if I could accompany him.

Dad agreed to take me on ungodly long bike rides to increase my skill and stamina. I did not share with Dad that my enthusiasm and willingness to suffer via "no pain, no gain" was all fueled by young love. I know Dad took secret pleasure in dragging me up the highest hills Germany had to offer.

The more I struggled and complained, the faster Dad got, always accompanied by his shit-eating grin. I wish I could say that this silent competition fueled me to greatness, but instead, it just made me feel like giving up. Why couldn't we ride side by side, talking, laughing, and taking in the sights? Competition is not my fuel; cooperation is.

I dared not ride by myself for the gut-wrenching fear and strong probability of getting lost. I was sure that if I sat on the curb, bike outside at the ready, Alan would come out and invite me to ride with him. He never did.

I don't know what I thought was going to happen with my curbside plan. What I did get was an education. I owe so much of my intellectual and artistic knowledge to Alan Rhodes. Before his record selections, I had no active knowledge of current female singers. The first chords of the Joan Baez song "Diamonds and Rust" still send me back to that summer of '75.

That whole album opened me to her wondrous storytelling through song. I could not help but wonder if his album choices were his singing to me or if he just thought I would like the music. Dad came home one day as I was listening to that album and said, "That singer sounds like a cat screaming."

What? How could he think that? This was handpicked for me by Alan! This was a beautiful voice, a beautiful singer, and Alan had lent it to me! But of course, I said none of that; I picked up the needle carefully from the album and turned the stereo off.

Dad must've been tired of seeing me waste my time sitting on the curb and felt it important to share his observation. I was sitting, staring out the window at Alan's house since it was pouring rain. Dad entered the room, looked me in the eye, and unequivocally said, "You're wasting your time. I think he's attached."

Now, the fact that Dad knew that was weird enough, but for him to say it out loud in 1975 was mortifying!

CHEERIO

Perhaps to free me from the spell of Alan Rhodes, Mom and Dad agreed I could go on a trip to London, England, with Father Ketchersid's visiting niece and the niece's female travel companion named Cici.

Just before the trip, I was also gifted with a mouth full of metal: railroad-track braces. The installation was performed by two Army dentists in uniform, pounding away on my teeth, wrapping each in cold metal in an hours-long procedure.

For the month before binding my mouth in metal, they had prepared my teeth for acceptance of the bands with rubber "spacers." But unfortunately, those just made it look like I had boogers caught between each of my teeth.

The walk along the street to the orthodontist's complex was a fear fest. I inevitably went past the Turks who leered and said things like, "Where are you going, pretty girl?" I told Mom about this, hoping she would walk with me on future trips or drive me. Instead, she insisted I walk by myself and said their behavior was "a cultural thing," but that did not stop me from feeling like I was going to throw up every time it happened.

She assured me they were "harmless," but their individual and collective undressing of me made me certain she was wrong. I was instructed to ignore them and to walk confidently. I guess this was another character-building exercise for me, but all it did was sharpen my internal panic response. There is nothing "harmless" about verbal and visual assault.

My orthodontic care was free, which was the only redeeming thing about the whole experience, as far as I could tell. While in Germany, we were under the care of the socialist system of medicine that the US military community provided. Dad reminded me that it was not, in fact, "free," as "it is paid for by my putting my life on the line in the protection of our country." Yeah, yeah . . . free, not free; it still hurt like hell and brought me to the point of tears with each pound of the hammer.

After each tooth was encased in a band, they were all wired together and then collectively tightened. Finally, I was sent on my way home with a container of pain pills. These pills enabled me to have an anxiety-free London vacation. I have no idea what sort of narcotic they gave me, and I did not care because, compliments of the brain-altering pills, I was free of worry, free of panic, and ready to go see and experience Great Britain.

JUST A TOURIST

We flew British Airlines, and British-proper it was. We each received a boxed meal during the flight. Because I had no worries, I was hungry and opened the box with gusto. After picking up the sandwich, I quickly noted that it had what looked like grass sticking out of it.

This "grass" wasn't just a little greenery—it was loads of blades of something greenish white. In 1975, Americans were not eating sprouts, but the Brits were. It was an interesting and time-consuming experience to try and pick all the wedged-in sprouts out of my railroad-track braces.

We arrived at Gatwick Airport and were transported via classic English taxi to a hovel of a hotel. It was my first experience with a public shared bathroom, known as the WC (water closet). I tried to hold my "business" so as not to have to go hang out in line with gangly British men in robes too short to cover their skinny, hairy legs, but inevitably, nature called.

I wasn't sure if I was to make pleasant conversation while in line, so I didn't. It might have been a great time to hone my skills in body language, but my embarrassment weighed in, and I just stared at the floor. No one else was talking, so I assumed silence was de rigueur.

I mentioned my quandary to Cici, and she decided that we three traveling companions should always accompany each other to the bathroom. This was a comfort. Wow. By speaking aloud my question and my fear, I got an answer. Those pain pills apparently lowered my defense mechanisms. (I had read about defense mechanisms in the book on body language.)

Our days were spent visiting Trafalgar Square, riding a double-decker bus for a city tour, and searching for a decent hamburger. I just marveled at the accents and had the greatest trouble understanding the locals. They did not sound at all like the few Brits I had seen in movies, like Angela Lansbury in *Bedknobs and Broomsticks*.

We hit all the major tourist attractions, including the Changing of the Guard at Buckingham Palace. I was hoping to catch a glance of Prince Andrew (this was when he was young and not mired in scandal). Yes, this is what I was thinking about while surrounded by a history I had only previously read about in books.

With no HRH Prince Andrew in sight, I had to settle for being awed by the grandeur of Westminster Abbey. Tomb after tomb of historic eminences of literature and science dotted the interior of this grand building. Seeing the gravestones of historic figures was surreal, but I was preoccupied with all the elaborate carvings and sculptures on the walls.

Somehow, people carved in stone were not as creepy to me as people rendered in wax. How did the artists manage the detail with nothing but a chisel and hammer? Without my constant companion, anxiety, I was free to be in the moment. We spent hours in Westminster Abbey. I read each plaque, each description, and each name, all the while also taking time to observe body language.

People of various ethnicities traveled in groups around the Abbey. Some traveled close together, almost touching, while other groups were clearly together but seemed to have an agreed-upon distance of personal separation. I did not know it then, but I was observing cultural differences. I knew there were differences between the group interactions but did not know what questions to ask myself to guide my thinking. My only question was, "Why?"

I was not prepared for the cold and damp that is London. As we walked to church, I shivered in my polyester miniskirt and stockings. I knew church was not going to be optional, as Father Ketchersid had arranged the vacation. The Mass was in Latin. I spent the whole time marveling at not being in a state of panic.

This was what life was like for most people. It was sublime. I began to wonder, if I were to lose my anxiety permanently, would I also lose other parts I cherish about myself? It seemed like it might be worth it at the time, but I did not want to jinx anything, being in church and all.

I suppose the notion of "jinx" is not very Catholic, but I was not going to take any chances. On the other hand, I had to be careful if there was spiritual magic in the air. April had said, "God has a plan for you and for everyone." I didn't believe that was true, but if it was, I doubted I was supposed to wish away anything!

Going up to Communion was a ritual I had done many times before, but somehow, hopped up on painkillers, I became aware of how gross it was to have the priest's hands all over the eucharistic wafer he was going to place on my tongue. And of course, those were the very same hands that had gone near or perhaps accidentally touched the tongue of all the people before me!

What really surprised me was the lack of internal panic reaction at my awareness. No wonder people who don't suffer from anxiety believe in their hearts and brains that breathing deeply to bring awareness will help. Awareness is quite amazing, but when you are anxious, you cannot take yourself out of yourself to experience it.

The whole trip was filled with my new cognizance of sights, sounds, and experiences not laced with an anticipatory "What if?" I didn't worry about getting lost, I wasn't homesick, and I looked forward to eating. In short, I got to have a dread-free vacation. I hope I was outwardly grateful to both my parents for the opportunity of this trip, but I doubt it was enough. My familiar apprehensive state had time to resume soon enough; shortly after we returned home, the pain meds were gone with no refills.

Upon my return from my London getaway, April quickly informed me that Alan had acquired a girlfriend named Liz. What? How did this happen? How did April know? Where did she come from? What did it matter anyway? It's not like I was on some "girlfriend short list." I was just a dumb kid, hanging on his every word. Who wouldn't like that? My heart was feeling like a cat toy, drawn in close and then bitten and scratched to shreds. Would he still share books and music with me?

WIE KÖNNTE ER?
(HOW COULD HE?)

Shortly after I returned from my successful London jaunt, Alan and his insta-girlfriend pedaled across Europe. Prior to leaving, he told me about their plans, and I listened with a face that looked like I was happy for him. I wanted to be happy for him. Or perhaps more honestly, I felt I *should* be happy for him, as he was my friend. I was devastated.

The only sign of growth in myself was that I did not regret going to London. Even to this day, calling that city to mind and heart fills me with a solidness that was and remains absent of fear. Is my perception of that trip colored by whatever narcotic I was taking because of my mouthful of metal? Probably. I was still too immature to stay with the memories of my trip and instead just counted the days until Alan's return.

Perhaps he and Liz would argue and fight in the little tent they were bringing. One tiny tent could be stifling . . . couldn't it? But no, it was going to be thoroughly romantic, with bike rides and baguettes in the moonlight. Was Liz from Texas? When was she leaving for college? Maybe they were just bicycle partners. Yeah, right. She was taking the one person in my life who didn't make me feel like a child.

Mom must've been tired of seeing me mope around because she expressed her concern at "the inappropriateness of the two of them traveling together." *Get with it, Mom. It's 1975. These things happen. Marriage is just a piece of paper, a construct set up by men to control women.* Uh-oh, by my argument, Liz was a liberated woman. How could I admire her and hate her at the same time? I was crushed that he had found someone to share literature, music, and who knows what tawdry activities in my short absence.

TEIL DES PLANS
(PART OF THE PLAN)

In his absence, I hatched a plan to allow for more Alan Rhodes time. We hosted a block party in our backyard. I pitched the idea to Mom, probably under the ruse that it was a good way to "hail and farewell" the neighbors in the Hansa Allee officers' quarters.

Mary H. and I planned the whole thing and went door-to-door to our neighbors, some of whom knew us, and some of whom did not. We asked them to sign up for food, beverage, or paper goods. It was quite gutsy and brave, all in the silent name of "love." Apparently, love could conquer my fear of speaking to others.

We finished the party preparations just in time for Alan's return. He was gloriously tan, summertime tan, golden tan . . . He was a god. I was determined not to go out to the curb. He had shown that I had been replaced, and I was not going to come groveling back. That stance lasted about half a day. I came groveling back. He regaled me with stories of castles, pastoral settings, simple food acquired while traipsing across Germany and France.

I asked no questions; I just listened. He told me how impressed he was that I had organized the upcoming block party. This was good. He was impressed with me! I should have been impressed with me, but I was more concerned that he would arrive with Liz and thwart my efforts to have it be "Alan Rhodes Fest '75."

The day of the party provided one of the few comfortable temperatures of the summer. So we held it in our backyard. Each family brought their own lawn chairs, and of course, being military families, everyone arrived at the same designated time. This allowed for a smooth setup and perfectly cooked hamburgers and hot dogs.

Alan came with his mother and father. No Liz. Good, as she was not part of my plan. I sat on the lawn at Alan's feet and listened to more of his European bicycling vacation tales. This was not what I had imagined our time together would be like. I had just assumed that he would have new books for me to read, but it was not like he had toured libraries on his European sojourn.

The comradery, laughter, food, and drink went on late into the night. Alan stayed, ate, laughed with Vanessa Burns, his end-of-the-street same-age friend, and smiled at me. I could barely eat in his presence. He asked me a couple of questions about London, and after the party, I ran my insipid answers over in my mind, chastising myself for my ineptitude. Love will do that to you.

SIE HATTE IMMER RECHT
(SHE WAS ALWAYS RIGHT)

"You know, any plans you are hatching to have Alan fall in love with you are not going to work. You're too young for him, and he is way too old for you." April shared this older-sister insight with a frequency that induced both cringe and heartache in me.

She was right, of course. She was always right. Everything worked out for her as far as I could tell. She seemed so comfortable operating in this world. How could that be? I was sure I was adopted—I had so many deficits that we surely could not be related!

She noted that my face was beginning to break out in periodic pimples and informed me, "That is probably punishment from God for your vanity." Could that be? She had perfect skin. I wanted perfect skin. Why would a Supreme Being spend his or her time creating red, pus-filled bumps for a fourteen-year-old who simply wanted to fit in?

I just couldn't grasp or accept this whole male-god construct. But if I didn't, was I going to hell? Was there a hell? From my earliest memory, I had always thought of myself as a good person who cared about others. In fourth grade, I had started a Helping Hands Club in my neighborhood. I, along with my neighborhood friends, went around and did good deeds for others for free. I loved this so much. It filled my heart with such joy to see their smiling faces after we raked their yard, watched their babies while they did housework, and organized a newspaper recycling program. With Dad's help, we would take the newspapers to the dump since curbside recycling did not exist yet.

Really? Vanity was my sin? It's not like it had any payoff value for me. As far as I could see in the mirror, things were getting worse, not better. Was April correct? If she was, how long was this punishment going to last? When was this god going to move on to someone else?

Alan told me he was an agnostic. I had no idea what that meant and had to look it up in the dictionary. How cool. He was not constrained by the artifice of organized religion. His face was clear. He was not being punished for not being a devout person. Perhaps April was wrong? Maybe I could work up the courage to tell him my beliefs and ask him what he thought. Unfortunately, I did not muster up the intestinal fortitude in time.

He left at the beginning of August for Texas. It was where his parents were from, and he still had family there to help him get settled into Texas Tech for his freshman year. A whole year without him. What would I do?

Mary H's dad had gotten orders to transfer back to the States, so she was gone too. I was going to start ninth grade. Big whoop. Ninth grade with the same bunch of immature, lackluster boys.

Mom told me that a new hairdo always perked her up. She helped me put my long hair into pin curls the night before the first day of school. That morning, I tied a bright red bandanna around my head and let the curls cascade, just like Rhoda did on *The Mary Tyler Moore Show*.

Standing at the bus stop, I now had Laura and Jenny. Suddenly, I did not feel alone. Could it be that this year was going to be better than the last one? Had hanging out with Alan changed me into an interesting person? Was I pretty? Uh-oh, this was vanity and I did not want more pimples.

Without April, who was off across the street in high school now, I had an opportunity to try to be myself for the first time in my school life. Only . . . who was that?

EIN WEITERES JAHR
(ANOTHER YEAR)

Ninth grade at FAJHS already felt hopeful with so many people complimenting me on my hair. This had never happened before. It turned out I was not invisible. But did that mean I had to wear my hair like this every day to maintain a you-are-noticed status? What was the expectation for me now? I had to figure all that out later because now I had to focus on finding my locker.

Lockers were at a premium at FAJHS, so my little sister and I had to share one. Ours was on the top, with the one below belonging to some long-forgotten person.

Laura was messy, and our locker reflected that. She and I stuffed our bulky down jackets into our assigned small storage crevice along with our textbooks for the second half of the day. Laura was charged with holding everything in while I slammed the locker shut. That meant we had to time it just perfectly so that her hand did not get smashed.

Me, giving the countdown: "One, two, three, *go!*"

Laura, in response, after swiftly getting her hands out of the way: "You barely missed my fingers!"

"Well, if you didn't have so much junk, we wouldn't have such a problem! You don't need every paper you have ever completed. You could take some of them home."

"No, what if I need them for class? I must be ready! But you wouldn't know about that because you are a slacker! April said so. She said you have potential, but you squander it away by obsessing about your looks when you could be studying."

Ouch! What do you say to that? Nothing.

Then we said, "See you at break," and went on about our day like nothing had happened. Laura's words did not sting as April's did. Of course, Laura had a temper, and when it flared, you wanted to stand far away from it, but most of the time, she was easygoing and pleasant to be around. I admired that she spoke her mind and let the proverbial chips fall where they may. How did she manage to come out of our family able to do that?

I have no idea, really. She moved in and out of social groups with ease, as far as I could see. FAJHS was the first time I was able to witness her in a school setting. Prior to that, we were sequestered in separate classrooms in different grade hallways in whatever school we attended. Laura was a leader. People naturally gravitated toward her, and she toward them.

The upside for me in all this was that I was brought into her groups during our one year together at school, and her friends all looked up to me. It was strangely enchanting and mystifying, as my own peer group had not done this with me. Maybe it was my newfound curly hair.

I needed to put effort into my classes because I knew Laura would. So how was I sandwiched in between two sisters with such drive and belief in their abilities? Perhaps the more enlightening question was, how was I such a self-imposed procrastinator, and what was I hoping to gain by choosing to be so?

Laura was like Yoda before there was a Yoda with her breakthrough insights about me. "Mare, so much you could be behind this mask of insecurity and self-doubt, but you hide. Hmm."

How did she know all this at age twelve? Where was she getting her information? The bigger question for me was, how could I get out from behind this supposed mask? Insecurity and self-doubt were the sewn-in lining of my personality fabric. I must have been adopted. That was the only reasonable answer to my being so drastically different than my two sisters.

With that thought sealed in my mind as a possibility, I did not need to confront my mantle of insecurity and self-doubt for many years.

Laura and I met in the cafeteria during our break each day and shared a Long John pastry. While noshing on our calorie-laden midday snack, we made quiet, disparaging remarks about the "popular people" who all sat together around a beautiful ninth grader, Ernie Ramirez. I was not in that crowd. I was in no crowd, really. I was emo before it was stylish to be so.

TAPFER SEIN
(BEING BRAVE)

My tortured, artistic self finally found a home in school with my ninth-grade English teacher, Miss McKinnon. She was beautiful—everything I wanted to be but felt I wasn't. She was a natural, petite brunette beauty, and I spent hours on her assignments. I sat in the same classroom seat all year and wished my time with her would continue forever.

She opened my heart to prose and finally gave me a place to belong in school. She did this with such ease, and when she looked at me, I believe she may have seen herself at a younger age. I certainly would not have thought that while in her class; I just knew that her eyes smiled and revealed the way that I could begin to find and redefine "Mary."

Miss McKinnon had us read excerpts from *Walden* by Henry David Thoreau. "If a man does not keep pace with his companions, perhaps it is because he hears a different drummer. Let him step to the music which he hears, however measured or far away."[11] Oh yes, that was me. I was dancing to a different drummer. Well, I was dancing in my head and heart and was working on revealing that to others.

Thoreau's literary compadre, Ralph Waldo Emerson, spoke words that I had felt at the sensory level but had previously not known how to piece together in cerebral form. "It's not the destination. It's the journey." I have returned to these words and this wisdom many times in my life thus far. In that ninth-grade classroom, with Thoreau and Emerson by my side as written witnesses to the value of my existence, I knew to the core of me that I was home. But unfortunately, that home was with dead male transcendentalist writers of the nineteenth century. This did me little or no good in the mid-twentieth century, but rather made me feel more like an intruder in this life than a participant. Were there other transcendentalists my age? I was certain there were not.

Miss McKinnon was the first person ever to tell me that I was a writer. I listened to her with great skepticism, as I believed to my core that April was a much better writer. April could spell, apply grammar principles, and never make typing mistakes. My preconceived notions about the box of skills one needed to possess to be a writer constricted me for the better part of forty years.

I wrote poems that did not rhyme. Miss McKinnon called it "prose." April had said that that writing style was for the "lazy poet" and that "talented writers took the time necessary to rhyme." But I had an ally in Miss McKinnon and E.E. Cummings. *Ha! So there, April!*

One of our English class assignments was to find a news article in *Stars and Stripes* and write a literary story to go with it. We were to turn the who, what, when, where, why, and how of it into something compelling, something lasting, something that inspired.

I pored over the pages of the fold-down-the-middle format of *Stars and Stripes* in search of something that moved me. The tales of the woes throughout the world—fighting, standoffs, the Cold War—did not interest me. I was searching for a story that was poetic in its reach.

The article I finally chose was about a Pinta Island tortoise on the Galapagos island of the same name, named by his discoverer "Lonesome George." George was still alive at the writing of the article, as the last member of his species. The sadness of his solitude spoke to my angsty teenage heart.

Of course, I, along with the researchers, was anthropomorphizing George. I wonder if the researchers served their own needs by shuttling George to their research center on Santa Cruz Island. They claimed that they were able to take care of him and help him by letting him live with other tortoises, although none were of his exact species.

Maybe George had been super happy living on Pinta Island and not in a research center—was that ever considered? What if when the researchers found him, he was only on a stopover from his actual home on some other remote island? Was that ever considered? I owe those expansive thoughts to Germany and to the travel we were doing while there. That, and Mom's near-constant thinking aloud during the travel.

When we only see things from our vantage point and experiential background, we are potentially viewing them incorrectly. This was my take on Lonesome George. I wrote that if he was "lonely" before the humans arrived, he was lonelier when they moved him with the misguided notion of "helping" him. I was taking a real chance by inserting my opinions. I was veering off the path of the expected, of the lemming mentality.

I felt so vulnerable producing something so unexpected. I wrote another "within the lines" version, containing the requisite "Poor George, all alone in this world" country-song vibe, and then promptly threw it out. It sickened me to conform in my writing. I turned in my original assignment written in my Truth Voice.

A few days later, prior to receiving our papers back with grades attached, Miss McKinnon decided that we should each read them out loud to the class. *What?!* If I had known that ahead of time, I would have turned in the "within the lines" version. Now my classmates were going to witness my honest voice, and I had no protection against their potential laughter and derision.

"Who wants to go first?" was Miss McKinnon's opening question. In a moment of unbridled fear mixed with resolution, I quickly answered, "I will." An audible and visible sigh of relief wove throughout the classroom as all the others knew they could wait to read theirs.

She passed the paper back to me, and there at the top of the page, in large red print, was an A+ with "Stunning" written next to it in bold letters. I was dumbfounded but still sure that my classmates would not understand or accept my literary take on this depressed reptile.

I stood to the side of my chair and held my paper up high so that it hid my face while still allowing me to see it to read. "Mary," Miss McKinnon said, "lower your paper a bit so you can still see it but we can see you." Great, she knew what I was doing and was undoing my protective mantle. Or perhaps she knew that with my writing I had already dropped a layer of protection and was ready to begin to be myself in front of others.

Whatever the reason or revelation, I began, "My article is on George, a Pinta Island tortoise, originally discovered by scientists visiting the Galapagos Islands. He has been nicknamed Lonesome George because he is believed to be the last of his species on the planet."

A collective sigh of "Aww" settled over the class. I continued, "It would be easy to feel sorry for him, but the bigger sorrow is that people decided his fate by removing him from his island and putting their human narrative on him. My story is told from the vantage point of George."

When I finished reading my one-page assignment, the room was silent. *Oh shit. Now here comes the laughter, the giggling, the whispers of, "What a weirdo."* I searched for the one face I knew would meet my eyes and reassure me that my voice and writing were important. Miss McKinnon's eyes were holding tears at the cusp, making me gulp the swallow of thanks and "Please don't let me cry in front of my classmates." Then they, the very people I had assumed would try to put me back into what I was sure were their boxes of beliefs, erupted in unified applause.

From that day forth, I wish I had banished my internal censor and written and spoken the questions and ponderings rolling around in my mind and heart, but I didn't. The censor lived large in me and was not freed for good that day, only set aside as it would be from time to time.

That assignment was thrown away long ago, but I saw as an adult that someone had written a children's book about George some years later. The only difference between that author and me was that they believed in themselves enough to write the book. How was I going to find this courage in myself? It was right there . . . when I put the censor aside, I had my courage. But I did not yet know that to my core. I only saw my ninth-grade Lonesome George assignment and the reaction of my classmates as, "Oh, I guess I did a good job on that homework." But it was so, so much more than that. It was a pivotal moment for me that I chose to shelve until I could no longer put off myself and my worth.

NASSE GUMMIBÄRCHEN
(WET GUMMY BEARS)

The physical time in Miss McKinnon's class was just ten months, but the effect of her tutelage and encouragement has lasted to this day. Other teachers that year were influential in other ways.

Frau Steiff was my German teacher. After day one, when we were subjected to a lecture on the dos and don'ts of her classroom, I knew that there would be no deviating from the assigned German textbook. She was German-born and ran our classroom straight by said textbook. There was no freedom in that class unless she left the room. When she did, the rowdy boys in our class threw sharpened pencils up into the dropped-ceiling panels, as well as propelling spit-moistened gummy bears skyward.

The good Frau was unaware of the ceiling adornment until the gummy bears dried sufficiently and fell from the ceiling with a ceremonious *plop*. This was always followed by a shrill yell of "Tony!" Any German I learned that year was limited by my own disinterest in home study.

Frau Steiff made it clear that her goal was for us to understand German as we understood English. She was hell-bent on teaching us to diagram German sentences. Why wasn't she teaching us how to converse with each other? Hmmm ... she looked to be a bit older than my parents, which meant ... Dare

I think it? Could she have been a Nazi? Had she been a Hitler Youth? April had told me about the Hitler Youth. Whatever the reason, Frau Steiff seemed more interested in German discipline than in German conversation.

I did not take opportunities to practice my German on the Economy, which would have surely increased my skill and confidence. I was too afraid. There were German people who worked at the PX. What if I had said to one of them (in English), "I want to learn how to speak German. Can I practice with you while I'm here?"

If I had had the courage to do this, I feel certain that it would have been met with openness and willingness. But I didn't. April had laughed at my German accent the first time she heard me practicing aloud in my room. My fragile ego was in charge and shut me down behind my walls built from fear and missed opportunities. I was experiencing my own internal Cold War and had built this wall to keep me "in" where my ego could stay safe and unchallenged.

ANFENGEN! (BEGIN!)

I had a small circle of friends that I had met the year before in school. With Mary H. gone, I spent more time talking with them. There was Laura L., whose father worked for the Army but was German; Delores, whose mother was French; and Denise, whose father was an Army dentist. It was a very nice, innocent group of girls. None of us were in the "popular" group, but together, we had our own group. Once I had this small clan of fellow innocents, I gained temporary confidence in taking up the space I did in the school world.

We four met at lunch and talked, laughed, and shared various classroom goings-on. These were not the deep friendships I had had with Mary and still had with Jenny. Their presence in my life that year and the next gave me a framework to navigate school with less trepidation. Because there were three of them, if one was sick, I still had two others to associate with in the halls and at lunch.

It was challenging to figure all these people into my life. Luckily for me, there was no expectation of communicating outside of school via phone. With only one phone line in each of our houses, they needed to be kept clear for our fathers to receive work-related calls. Phew! That meant that when I was home, I could hang out with Jenny. I liked this compartmentalization of relationships.

Laura L. was taking a new class on computers and was learning about punch cards. I couldn't imagine what possessed her to study something that seemed so useless to me at the time.

I, instead, took a typing class with a teacher we were all afraid of in ninth grade, Miss Williams. She was two hundred pounds of intimidation. She had taught at that school for so many years. On the left side of her classroom were the manual typewriters, which is where I was to begin the year. Miss Williams shouted out the sequence of letters we beginners were to practice, "A S D F!" and right before we were to begin, she cracked her ruler on her Army-issue wooden teacher's desk.

The kids on the right were on electric typewriters. They were typing from stands that contained paragraphs to practice typing without looking at the keys. Then, halfway through the year, she shouted, "McKnight! Olivetti!" Olivetti was the name of the electric typewriter, and I quickly gathered my things and nervously posted myself in front of the upgraded technology.

I had never touched an electric typewriter before. Mom's old manual Underwood from her college days was all we had at home. One stroke on the Olivetti and I had created at least fifteen lowercase letter *a*'s on the page. Not quite the start I had imagined for myself. She yelled at me to *"use a lighter touch!"*

She was always bellowing, but if you've never experienced a room full of people wildly typing on typewriters, you have no concept of the din it makes. These are sounds and experiences my daughter will never have.

I owe my ability to easily type out this book to Miss Williams. She lived in the BOQ behind us. I saw her amble down the street and wondered about her life outside of school. My mom called her a spinster—not to call her a "name" but just to label her life choice, I guess. I do not know what happened to her. She seemed already ancient in 1976.

When I look back on her now, I so admire her life. There she was, a single woman who had decided to teach for DOD schools overseas. She had more freedom than I had, and yet at the time, I viewed her with sorrow because she was single and overweight. She would never "get a man," and that seemed tragic. It *wasn't*. She was free.

PRÄPARATION
(DISSECTION)

Dissecting fetal pigs was the capstone project in my biology class. My science teacher that year was Mrs. Crain, who was also my next-door neighbor. We carved into "Babe," all in the name of science. I sat with a girl named Sherry, who had been a peripheral friend in eighth grade. She turned wild midway through ninth grade and began hanging out with the smoking crowd.

There was a designated smoking area outside the main school building, and there she stood with the other beautiful people. They all seemed so confident with their smoke rings, perfect skin, and laughter. I was thankful that Sherry wanted to be my lab partner.

Seated behind us in class were two lustful boys. They had no shame in asking us our bra size. How did Mrs. Crain not notice my look of complete discomfort in their presence? I probably put on an "unfazed" look so as not to appear inexperienced in the eyes of the boys.

What was that all about? Why did I care what they thought and how they felt more than I cared about how *I* thought and felt about what they were saying to us? I just knew that the social expectation for girls was to stay silent in the face of "boys will be boys." Their behavior was meant to silence us. It was meant to control, and control it did.

Back to the pig, which I suppose could equally reference the boy asking my bra size. Mrs. Crain had big plastic buckets filled with (I guess) formaldehyde. Each pair of students had a large metal tray, dissecting tools that probably hadn't been sharpened since the school opened after World War II—and no gloves or masks. The piglet—bright pink with closed eyes—was plopped onto our tray, and we were instructed to "cut down the middle."

I recall the room turning black and then taking a big breath to regain my sight, which was important as I was the one with the scalpel. This exercise ensured I was not going into medicine as a career. I can't pretend it wasn't fascinating to hold the various organs in my hands because it was. Everything fit tight up against everything else and, once removed, would not fit back in. I did not express my inward interest, as the consensus of the extroverted students was that this was "gross."

It's not that I wanted to be like my peers; I just didn't want to be ostracized by them. The curious thing, in looking back, was that there was no outward cruelty toward anyone at FAJHS. The rejection construct was one I had composed internally. I was sure I was wired differently than my peers, and that difference carried with it a solitude that lacked any possible poetic nature.

REISEMÖGLICHKEITEN
(TRAVEL OPPORTUNITIES)

Although ninth grade was going better socially for me than eighth grade had, I was always glad for the weekends and even more glad for any travel opportunities over vacations throughout the school year. Mom had planned a trip for us at Thanksgiving to the village of Berchtesgaden in Bavaria. All we each had to do was pack for it, be awake at an ungodly hour for the road trip, hold any pee during the trip until Dad felt the need to pull over according to his travel plan, and keep the complaints in the back seat to a minimum.

By the time we got to the designated "rest area," I had held my bodily needs beyond the point of comfort. I could barely climb out of the car as I was doubled over in abdominal pain. After I finally inserted the pfennigs in the slot to open the bathroom stall, I sat down and was unable to loosen my muscles to let urine out. Of course, it did not help that April was chiding me with unhelpful commentary like, "Come on! You're holding us up! How hard is it to pee? Just relax your muscles! Think about water."

After a successful voiding sometime later, off we went for the last leg of the trip down south. I had no idea what to expect or to anticipate. When I was with my family, my anxiety level was at bay. It didn't mean I wasn't worrying; it was just that I wasn't panicking. There is a huge difference! I could still enjoy myself and worry; panic mode shut down all pleasure.

We stayed at the General Walker Hotel contained in the Armed Forces Recreation Center. Back when the Nazis owned it, it was called the Platterhof. It was where high-ranking Nazis and German officers went to schmooze with Hitler. This history was not discussed at any point during our vacation. I only learned of the area's sordid past many years later upon viewing Dad's slides as we all sipped German riesling and pondered our days overseas.

While in the Obersalzberg Mountains, we spent our days sightseeing. Our responsibilities were to get up, get dressed, brush our teeth in the one sink shared among the three of us, keep the arguing to a minimum, and make it down to breakfast at a given time. Lateness was not an option, ever!

Mom had chapels and cathedrals on her list of must-dos, and Dad had castles. First on the schloss list: Neuschwanstein.

We had seen other castles on Rhine River cruises, and they were cool and all, but I was unprepared for the staggering beauty and the ornate opulence that Mad King Ludwig's domicile provided. The exterior, the interior—where did one fix their attention? It reminded me of the mythical King Midas's castle—everything encrusted in gold and glitz.

I decided in that moment that no matter what life handed me, I was going to have enough money to make *my* dreams come true. I did not know at the time exactly what those dreams were. It just seemed like I needed gobs of money, regardless.

Throughout the interior tour of the castle, Mom kept warning us not to touch anything. There was no danger that we were going to do so. We had been schooled since we were toddlers not to touch anything that wasn't ours. So why did she think we would suddenly break ranks and sully the trip by touching things?

If the tour guide explained how the king went mad, I wasn't listening. Perhaps King Ludwig was just a guy who liked pretty things and decided to surround himself with them. Dad commented, "It would be tremendously expensive to heat in the winter." Who could think of such banal things while in the presence of genius expressed in architecture and decor? Not me.

As a child, I had loved fairy tales, and this castle was the embodiment of every legend ever told. I went from room to room along with our tour group and soaked up a stardust that lives with me still. It was the energy of potential. Perhaps it was better to express oneself and risk being called mad than to remain in a self-imposed state of "the follower" or, as I call it, the lemming effect.

HINEINFALLEN
(FALLING IN)

Each day in Berchtesgaden was an eye- and art-opening experience. The visuals of the staggeringly stunning Linderhof, King Ludwig's other schloss, had me snapping away with a Kodak Instamatic 44 in hand and no thought of preserving film. I don't think the sky had ever looked bluer on the day we toured his country estate. I had on my stupid purple down jacket, Ali MacGraw/*Love Story* hat and long scarf, pants with extenders, hiking boots, and the desire to preserve the memories forever.

The garden paths had been plowed to seven-foot walls of ice and snow. I was backing up to get a full view of the majesty of the back of the palace. I was backing up, backing up . . . and then off the edge I went, *splat* into the frozen swimming pool. Ape ran over and collapsed with laughter. Mom and Dad came running over but not because they were worried about me. It was to stop April's rude laughter. When they arrived, the entire family erupted into laughter, with me still lying in a "snow angel" position.

There was no actual danger of falling through the ice, as the frigid temperature in Bavaria rendered it safe. However, the climb out was treacherous and shed light on my weak muscles—hindered by my laughter and that of April, who was trying to pull me out. This was most likely not at all what the mad king had in mind when he created his masterpiece.

No one checked me for broken bones or a concussion. It was just assumed that I was "fine" and that, hopefully, I had learned to keep a closer watch on my surroundings. My elbows were killing me, as I had initially used them to keep my head from smacking the ice. However, I could still bend them even with the throbbing. This "maintain an even strain" behavior by my family is so military Brat. "Do you have a headache?" "Suck it up. No one ever died from that." "Is your leg a little gimpy after falling?" "Shake it off." And the list goes on. I remember calling home when I went to Syracuse University for my sophomore year of college with a 104-degree fever. Mom figured I had the flu and closed our conversation that day with, "You'll be fine. No one ever died from that." I quickly countered with, "Mom! The 1918 flu epidemic! People have died from the flu."

Mom's reply: "Well, that was a long time ago."

With my 1975 jammed elbows and a bum leg, it was on to Wieskirche, a chapel so rife with gold and detailed decor that it was overwhelming to look at and endless in its awe. I was only relating to it on a level of beauty. Mom was feeling something else and relayed the following story: "The locals say that the wooden statue of Christ in chains actually wept tears. The people built this church around it to honor that miracle."

This seemed highly unlikely to me. Why would a statue weep? How easy would it have been for someone to manufacture this? What if someone had simply been washing the statue, stepped away for a moment to attend to something else, and in their absence, someone else walked up, saw the moisture on the figure, and assumed it was weeping? I did not share my musings aloud, as Dad would have leveled me with a stinging rebuke to protect Mom's feelings associated with her strong religious beliefs.

Dad was Protestant, and Mom was Catholic. When they were married, Dad had to sign something that said we would be raised Catholic. The priest who married them was not allowed to wear official robes as Dad was not "of the faith." Weird. What was with all the religious division? This all made no sense to me. Despite my deep skepticism, I was afraid not to believe all this stuff for fear of going to hell. I kept Doubting Thomas to myself.

Everywhere we looked was an abundance of encrusted gold, elaborate frescoes, and tall windows letting the warm sunlight stream in and bounce off to momentary blindness. We sisters started snapping away with our Instamatics until Mom came running over—horrified that we were treating this sanctuary as a tourist spot and not the House of God that it was.

Poor Mom—such a devout Catholic, forced to endure the irreverence of her three teenagers. My two sisters, later in life, embraced this Catholic dogma. I hope I have not been a disappointment, as I did not join in the embracing.

Back at the General Walker later that day, Thanksgiving dinner was held and celebrated at the B-Garden O' Club. Laughter and the clinking of glasses as officers, their wives, and their children all shared in this most American tradition, so far from "home." We entered the large dining room decorated with local greenery, cornucopias overflowing with produce, and tables festooned with china and crystal.

Mom and Dad had taken us to fancy restaurants before, so I felt comfortable. Despite the familiarity, Mom was compelled to remind us quietly, "If you are not sure which fork to use, just unobtrusively observe others and follow suit." What if the others were using the wrong forks? I did not ask this. I had remembered Dad's tutelage of cutlery being used from the outside in.

As we walked to our table, decked out in our Sunday best and Dad in his uniform, we strode past other families similarly adorned. Even when we had Thanksgiving at home, we always had to "dress" for the occasion. This seemed stupid to me. *It's just food, people.*

One of the families we passed on the way to our reserved table was that of Bruce Fye—the quarterback of our Frankfurt American High School football team. Bruce was tall, classically good-looking with perfect sandy blond, 1970s young-man hair, a square jaw, friendly eyes with long lashes . . . and yet he was out of his home element, just as we were out of ours. As we walked by their table, April said, "Great catch at last week's game."

She could speak to him because she was a cheerleader at Frankfurt High. He looked like he had no idea who she was and smiled with a grin that looked more like someone stifling a burp. He said a quick "Thank you," brought on by his mother, who had elbowed him in the ribs. This cringe-worthy exchange made us *sooo* uncomfortable. So what did I do as a good sister? Mock April mercilessly for *years* afterward, of course. It wasn't every day that the perfect April provided me with the opportunity to do so.

"Oh, that was awkward!" I made sure to say aloud once out of earshot of the handsome quarterback. "He has no idea who you are, Ape!" I said these things with all the glee possible. Mom shot me a look of "This is not the time or place," and I stopped. I felt kind of bad inside that Ape looked crushed. I knew only too well what it felt like to be forgotten. Still, I did take many an opportunity throughout the years to retell this story of their uncomfortable exchange. I guess I must not have felt too badly.

Once we were back at our family table, enjoying the traditional Thanksgiving foods, a gagging gasp filled the air. We all grew silent when a guest began choking. I don't remember who helped him (this was before the Heimlich maneuver), but someone did. Some man slammed him on the back until the offending small piece of meat went flying across his table. That was it for me and the meal. Who could eat after that?

VERSAGEN (FAILING)

It was time for some post-dinner recon. We three kids went down to the basement of the O' Club after dinner so that Mom and Dad could stay in the dining room and enjoy a digestif of brandy in peace. We toddled over to the grand piano, where April sat down with self-assurance. Apparently, her Bruce Fye gaffe had not paralyzed her as it would have me.

She played music she had memorized, and together we belted out Elton John's "Tiny Dancer" without a care in the world. Yes, she was my nemesis, but she was also my sister. We had a bond, even in our sibling caste system, with April at the top.

She was such a confident piano player. She could make a mistake sound like something purposeful. Sitting there next to her on the piano bench, I wished I had not given up on the piano. I had ended my lessons after the Recital Debacle back in the States.

Mom had determined that we three needed musical training. Our teacher had been Peabody Institute–trained Miss Fauteux. She had a beautiful round face that radiated every kindness one could imagine.

Each week, we were to have annotated our assigned sheet music to assist with the understanding and reading of it. Unfortunately, when I did it, it was usually wrong. Miss Fauteux patiently erased my incorrect annotations at the piano with me . . . patient, patient, loving, and kind . . . while I cried silently.

Large tears plopped onto my lap; I was careful not to get them on her piano.

It was mortifying to have tried so hard and failed over and over and over. I just could not permanently absorb this musical notation. She would extend loving comfort with, "Don't worry. It will come. It's just one element of the music. Your heart is the place where you feel it, and that is where you can play from."

I loved Miss Fauteux. Yes, I could play from my heart. Miss Fauteux never let on that she knew I was playing by ear and not reading the music. She assigned me some Hungarian rhapsody for the recital—a complicated piece with many pages of complex chording and a rolling beat, to perhaps satisfy my desire to learn to play modern music.

Having not slept the night before the recital due to spiraling thoughts of panic, I met the morning on the cusp of vomit-stomach, sweaty pits, dry mouth, and the desire for the whole experience to be over. I knew that Hungarian piece backward, forward, and in between. Mom brought the new portable cassette player to the recital to tape it to send to Dad, who was already living in Frankfurt.

It was my turn to play. The event was held in an un-air-conditioned auditorium on a hot, humid Maryland day. I was wearing the orange polyester, long-sleeved dress we had purchased for Dad's promotion party a few months earlier, nylon stockings bagging at my knobby knees, and suede shoes with one-inch heels that clattered across the wooden stage.

There was silence as I sat on the black bench and placed my hands in my lap . . . I flew them up to the eighty-eights and began. Everything was going fine, I was rolling along, and then I got to a note and could not remember the rest of the song.

The heat climbed up and out of the neck of my polyester dress; the sweat adhered to the stockings, to my legs, and then to the piano bench, surely leaving me with a butt-sweat stain. I was sure I could hear the blood pulsing in my ears.

The audience was silent. I started back on the piece, hoping to remember, pleading internally to do this with all Miss Fauteux's training. She'd had me practice for the recital by starting at various points in the music and playing from there.

I started and stopped four different times on that stage, trying to remember the song, and finally, the tears I had been holding back began to fall, large and blinding. I sat up there, crumpled over, trying and trying, and then finally broke through the black spot in my mind and played. The crowd erupted into deafening applause. After finishing the piece and standing by the bench as required, I looked up to see Miss Fauteux crying the same tears, only hers were joyful. The applause went on for some time. I just wanted to get the hell off the stage.

That was it for me and my piano career. As for the cassette recording, Mom played it right before we sent it off to Dad in Germany. April laughed while listening to my grand error, which I'm sure was not Mom's intent. Knowing Mom's good heart, she was probably trying to show me the triumph of my perseverance, but all I felt was the pointed sting of embarrassment and failure. I couldn't see past it. I never played the piano again.

We completed our Thanksgiving trip and returned home. I left with visions provided by the wonders of German architecture, art, and engineering. I now had more in my mental repertoire.

DIE WAND (THE WALL)

Mom always had a travel plan up her sleeve, or so it seemed. She had decided that we should visit the city of Berlin, which in 1975 was divided into West Berlin (the "good" Berlin) and East Berlin (the "bad" Berlin). That's all I knew. We would be going to Good Berlin but would have to pass through Bad Berlin to do so.

It was beyond me why we planned this trip. I thought we had already seen "The Wall" when we visited Fulda and the Fulda Gap.[12] Wasn't the Berlin Wall the same one we had already seen on that family day trip to Fulda?

Fulda had provided a gale-force windy day, and my long hair whipped my face to the point of numbness. Our guide had told us all while still on the tour bus—very sternly—"Do not make big movements or noises. Do not look directly at the German soldiers on the other side. Do not call any attention to yourself."

What were we going to do there? Just stand? Yep. That's what we did. We got out of the tour bus, lined up silently, and stood. The East German soldiers stared at us, and we at them. This was anticlimactic. The guide had storied us with people trying to escape East Germany and getting shot. This whole scene of that gray, windy day was very visually pastoral, so why would anyone try to escape? Ohhhh, because the West was good and the East was bad.

Again, not knowing any history of life behind The Wall besides what our guide had shared, I was rather bored at the time, wondering why we had to go see a stupid wall. Besides, it really wasn't a "wall" at Fulda so much as a thick barbed-wire fence. I guess calling it "The Fence" wouldn't strike enough fear into the hearts of people. My face stung from being hair-slapped. I wanted to get back on the bus.

Shortly after that Fulda day trip, I decided it was time to get my hair cut to spare my face any more hair-whipping incidents. I had been babysitting a little girl whose parents lived on the Economy. The mother had recommended a German beauty salon close to their house. The mother's hair was beautiful, so it seemed like a good idea.

April made a hair appointment too, and off we went, walking the distance to get beautiful. I had seen a few photos in *Seventeen* that demonstrated the look I wanted. But, as I was not allowed by Mom to purchase that magazine, I didn't have any photos. So how did I think I was going to communicate my hair vision to the German hairdresser? I hadn't thought that out.

It's important to note again the highly limited amount of German I could speak. April was no help either, as she spoke French.

The highly stylish, young, and hip hairstylist greeted me, "Hello! You have good hair. What do you see?" I had no idea what she meant, but April, upon seeing my dumbfounded look, added with an irritated snipe, "She wants to know what hairstyle you want!" I began to talk in broken English, gesticulating wildly with my hands.

"The hair shorter," I said, chopping my hands at my shoulders, "and sweeping right," I added, swooping my hands upward like a salute gone bad. The end product of my limited German exchange with the über-stylish hairdresser and her understanding and vision for me resulted in cantilevered bangs and hair sprayed into a shellacked wing hovering over my forehead. She looked so pleased with the end result. "You like this, yes?"

I looked down at all my hair on the floor and instantly missed my lengths. April had been waiting for me in the lounge portion of the salon and came up to my chair in time to witness my tress transformation.

She took one look at my new "do" and collapsed in heaves of laughter on the floor of the salon. It was laugh or cry for me, and I chose laughter. So as not to embarrass myself or make my hairstylist feel bad, I suppressed my laughter, which only precipitated shoulders shaking and tears streaming. It was comical to gaze upon the heavily hair-sprayed winglike bangs that now shielded my forehead like the bill of a baseball cap.

This gravity-defying bang style was not a good look for anyone, and I was sure it was German revenge at Americans occupying their soil. April was next and, having opted against leaving anything to chance, had sketched a drawing of what she wanted. Great. Now April was an artist on top of all her other talents and achievements. She got her ends trimmed and looked great, whereas my hairdo enabled me to take flight if a stiff wind came along.

After we walked home, Mom took one look at me and struggled for a positive statement. "Oh . . . how, how . . . *different!*" Yes, this was different. This was so different that I went up to my bathroom, leaned over the tub, rewashed my hair, and tried to dry it into something less objectionable.

Word must have gotten back to the family who had referred me to the salon in the first place because they never called me to babysit again. So I guess April's fall on the floor in laughter sealed our fate as Ugly Americans.

WEINEN (CRYING)

L osing that babysitting job stung, as I liked the little girl and the apartment where the family lived, but others had heard of me, perhaps through the Officers' Wives' Club. I walked to my jobs and had one in the apartment complex in HiCog. The foundation of the complex had been built from Frankfurt's World War II building bomb rubble.

The baby boy with fire-engine-red hair provided me with a night I have never forgotten. The dad opened the door with saddlebags where his eyes should have been. "Oh, are we glad to see you! Right on time. My wife will go over the instructions for Red."

The wife had equal-sized eye bags and quickly went over the baby's evening routine. What they managed to leave out of their oh-so-not-helpful care instructions was that he screamed at the top of his lungs and fought sleep for hours. I found this out for myself quite soon after their departure.

The evening consisted of Baby Boy with Flaming Hair scream-crying from seven till midnight. This left me in tears and calling Mom for advice. She told me, "Hold the baby close, make a *shhh* sound, and gently bounce up and down with him." With the amount of *shhh*-ing I had to do, I just sounded like a slowly deflating tire.

At around 11:30 p.m., the neighbor across the hall knocked on the door. Well, I hoped it was the neighbor, because when I asked, "Who is it?" that's who she said she was. I doubted a

196 ● OUT OF PLACE

robber would have entered Colic Town, so I was pretty sure I was safe opening the door. She was the one who said that the baby cried like that every evening.

I guess the poor little fellow finally tired himself out because, at midnight, he fell asleep in the neighbor's arms. She gingerly placed him in his crib and tiptoed out the door. I was beyond relieved that the parents were to return home in half an hour. They didn't. They didn't call me either. They just arrived three hours late, looking very pleased with themselves.

I never babysat for them again. At least with my hard-earned babysitting pay, I now had spending money, as well as shorter hair for this West Berlin trip. Dad was less than thrilled when Mom told him of the travel plan.

BEWEGUNGSBEFEHLE (MOVEMENT ORDERS)

"**I**f you kids are kidnapped while on this ill-conceived trip to West Berlin, I want you to know in no uncertain terms that I will not negotiate with terrorists. I will not divulge military secrets to secure your release." We four stood in silence as Colonel Dad barked out his cold, harsh truth. Apparently, there actually was a Cold War. Dad filled us with images of undetected ne'er-do-wells hanging on to the bottoms of trains with plans of capturing young dependents of Army officers. If captured, our release would then be contingent upon Dad divulging military intelligence.

I don't imagine it would have gone over well if I had suggested to Dad that we could preemptively wear T-shirts emblazoned with "Don't bother kidnapping us. Our dad doesn't negotiate with terrorists."

It was impossible for me to believe that Dad held any secrets anyway. He was a civil engineer who had built and rebuilt bridges during the Vietnam War a few years earlier. In Frankfurt, I thought that he was working for the quartermaster.

The only thing I knew about the quartermaster was that their division had provided our military family with basic furniture during our three-year tour in Germany. So as far as I knew, Dad was just a glorified furniture-procurement guy. I couldn't understand what terrorists would want with us. Perhaps they were woefully under-furnished, as it was the days before Ikea and Wayfair. Clearly, there was more to Dad than I knew, and that was just the way he wanted it.

A few days after we received our traveling papers for Berlin, I got sick, and we ended up not going. I'm sure Dad was relieved, but I felt so awful, so responsible for Mom not seeing Berlin. It was my fault. I told her to take April and Laura and go, but she stayed home to take care of me. I loved that, and I hated it. I did not want to be the cause of Mom's travel deprivation.

We would never get to West Berlin, but Mom, ever the intrepid traveler, took us three girls to Munich that same school year.

WARUM SIND WIR HIER?
(WHY ARE WE HERE?)

knew Munich as the site of the 1972 Olympics. We watched them when we lived in Rockville. Before boarding the train to Munich, Mom warned us, "No one is to discuss the horror of the Israeli team being murdered by the terrorists during that Olympics."

Not that I would have, but what would have happened if we had? I think it was all that pervasive dogma that, wherever we traveled, we represented our family and our country—and we were not to dishonor either. I was sure we were the only people on the planet operating under these conditions. So off the four of us went via German train. Mom never let us in on why she wanted to go to Munich, and we didn't ask. She had all the details. All we needed to do was remember our passports, military ID cards, clothing, and manners.

We found our hotel, which was close to the train station and centrally located downtown. The first stop post-hotel check-in would be some museum. I had a stomachache. Oh no, I was about to ruin another trip for Mom. She would be so devastated. I wouldn't tell her! Yeah, right, what was I going to do, throw up in every trash can as we viewed antiquities? Great plan.

I told her my stomach hurt, and she surmised it was "lady cramps." What a stupid name for my insides gripped in a tightness, coupled with waves of nausea, and capped off by a pounding headache. Mom decided that since I wasn't "really sick," they would go on to the museum, and I would be left alone in the hotel room.

While I was so glad I hadn't spoiled the trip, I was not glad to be all alone with no way to contact anyone who would be of any help to me! What if the three of them got in an accident and were killed? How would I know? What would I do if they did not come back? I was getting hungry—well, hungry for chocolate. When would they return? Would they have food for me? What if they never came back? Oh, my god! I barely spoke German and was pretty sure that even if I attempted English with the hotel staff, I would barf. I hated Munich.

They did return some hours later and had brought food for me. And April . . . April had gotten me a Toblerone bar. She threw it on the bed where I was lying and said, "I thought this might help." Tears welled in my eyes. She had thought of me, thought about what I was going through, and had done something to help me. I choked out a "Thanks."

Laura was all a-chatter with the things they had seen at the museums at Königsplatz, and was most proud that she had gotten the three of them on the right Strasse, headed the right way to our hotel. "Mom was going to have us go the wrong way, but I told her the right way!" Laura announced in all her twelve-year-old wisdom.

April quickly corrected the narrative with, "Oh, you should have been there. Laura said to Mom, 'Dad's not here, so someone has to tell you what to do.' Burn!"

Mom did not look at all pleased with this story. She did not seem angry as one would have thought; her face just fell. Her eyes looked lost, and that scared me. She told me in later years that it had been a real turning point for her. In the moment that Laura spoke this "truth," Mom felt she had set a bad example for us—she had been "the submissive woman."

We were only in Munich for a couple of days, but the rest of the trip left Mom's voice devoid of the usual lightheartedness we were so accustomed to from her. This seriousness of spirit reached all four of us when we got to the real reason for our visit.

LASS UNS NIEMALS VERGESSEN (LET US NEVER FORGET)

We were to take a tour of Dachau, the site of a former Nazi concentration camp. Dachau had been liberated only thirty years earlier by Allied troops. Mom had warned us on the bus ride over, "There will be no shenanigans, no laughing, no picture-taking . . . I want you all to remember all of the people who were senselessly murdered here. Just listen." And listen we did. For the tourists there, it was hauntingly silent.

We walked silently through the camp, entering reconstructed housing barracks and reading the captions below the black-and-white photos. These photos showed living skeletons of people who had been forced into the small, dank spaces lined with wooden racks. No mattresses, no pillows, no sheets . . . just people wearing the same striped, tattered uniforms. Each face had hollow eyes, a shaved head, and a look of hopelessness even at their liberation.

A suffocation of deep sadness and a quiet that made my hair stand on end filled my lungs. Each tour group, in complete silence, followed the guide.

Although I was voiceless on the outside, plenty was going on in my brain. How could people be so cruel? Why would a group of people hate another group? What had the Jews done to deserve this kind of treatment? Why would the German people be complicit in this atrocity? Why didn't the Jews just get out of Dodge when they saw what was happening? Not all the Germans had to be so awful, so why didn't the good ones stand up for the rights of the Jews?

Cruelty toward others was something I had never understood. I was a champion of the underdog and had been since my earliest memory. Were there no champions in Germany? But the German people seemed so nice. I had experienced nothing but orderly kindness since being in Germany. But, as this atrocity was only thirty years ago, surely we were living among former Nazis. At the war's end, did they just abandon their hate and choose to reform?

I sifted through all the small aggressions toward me that loomed so large in my psyche. For example, in the first grade, when we had just started school in Fort Leavenworth, a girl named Akasha punched me in the stomach at recess and said, "No one wants you here." In the fifth grade, out of nowhere, my best friend group stopped speaking to me, started talking behind my back, refused to play with me at recess, and rendered me one of the outcasts. If those times still wounded me, what did the Dachau experience of torture, having family members torn apart from one another, disease, and starvation do to someone's soul? These questions of mine went unasked and, therefore, unanswered.

The ovens were still there. Nazis had cremated the bodies after they had gassed the people to death. Our guide voiced this part. He looked each of us in the eyes as he spoke the words, "These are the ovens. Jews were forced to place the dead bodies of their brethren inside to char their bodies into ash. Their remains are scattered on this land. We stand where they stood, forced to do the unthinkable. We stand where the death lay heavy in the air, turned to smoke. We must never forget."

I never did. I needed to know more. I needed to try to understand how this could happen to keep it from ever happening again. Shortly after we returned home, I went to the post library and checked out *The Diary of Anne Frank*. Mom had recommended it to me. She must have seen in my eyes and felt from my heart that I needed answers.

After I'd read the book, she asked me what I thought.

"Mom, I don't understand the hate of others just because they look different from me or have a different religion. What difference should that make? Why would someone hate someone else because of skin color?"

Mom must have known these were going to be my questions because she quickly replied, "People fear what they do not understand. They are taught this fear and hate and then pass this on as 'truth.' The truth is that we are all human. That should unite us, not divide us. It is up to each of us to be a beacon of hope and of kindness. Mare, do you remember back in Rockville when Mrs. Rosenstein came into our Girl Scout meeting?"

LEHRE MICH (TEACH ME)

om had been our Girl Scout leader in Rockville.
During the Christmas season of 1973, we were practicing our Christmas carols together in preparation
for our neighborhood caroling. Mrs. Rosenstein had a daughter
named Cathy in our troop, and when that mother came bust-
ing in through the door yelling at Mom, I was so scared and
confused.

"Why aren't you teaching them Hanukkah songs? Have
you forgotten? Why are you neglecting the Jewish people?"
Mrs. Rosenstein's face was twisted and filled with rage. Mom
looked so sorrowful. I couldn't understand what was going on.

In her honest, kind way, Mom responded with tear-filled
eyes, "I don't know any. I don't know about Hanukkah, but if
you would teach me about it and some songs, we would be
proud to sing them."

Mrs. Rosenstein's eyes softened. Her whole self softened.
What was happening? At that moment, I came to understand—my mom had shown me the path to peace. It was the
most powerful thing I had ever witnessed in my life. Mom could
have yelled back. She could have listened and then ignored, but
my mom had listened and heard with her heart. She had then
responded with her heart and her mind. My mother, my sup-
pressed-by-men mother, held the keys to world peace.

In that formative coming-of-age year of 1976, Mom must
have thought I was ready for "the keys" because she said, "I want

you to read *Black Like Me*. It's about a white man who makes his skin dark to experience what Black people go through each day in our country."

So off to the post library I went to check out that book. More hate, fear, and discrimination, only this time, it was not the distant Nazis I was reading about; it was contemporary America. What? I had no idea. I had grown up with Black students, Chinese students, Filipino, Hispanic, and white students in school and hadn't thought much about it. I had played with Hector Lopez for so many days while living in Leavenworth. Why would I hate him? I didn't. I never had. If people were good, they were good, and wasn't that what was supposed to be important?

Once I finished that book, I returned to Mom with my questions. I was not silent. I did not stifle myself. The social justice door had been opened, and I boldly walked through it because others needed me. They needed me to be their ally. That was it. I needed to learn how to speak up in defense of others.

Mom recommended one more book to me about the culture of poverty. I do not remember the title, but the growth in my understanding of individual choice being influenced by government policy was eye-opening, to say the least. By reading it, I came to the beginnings of my perception and discernment of social policy in the United States and its impact on the individual and the family. This reading led me to a lifelong quest to be a part of the solution.

It was like Mom was some celestial do-gooder who had passed on the fairy dust of social change to me. I was now the keeper of this fire. I kept it to myself and stoked it. This quest continued with book learning and was eventually put into action years later when I taught young children in the public schools. And it all started with Mom.

ER IST WIEDER DA
(HE'S BACK)

It would be so great if I were able to say that with my newfound awareness of my social justice superpower that I went right to work as a change maker, but it was summer. And when Mom reported excitedly that Alan was coming home from his freshman year in college, he was all I could think about.

My anticipation was made a forever moment connected to my transistor radio, its dial on the AFN network. Barry Manilow's "Could It Be Magic" forever connect me to an emotion I carry to this day. Only now, somehow, the song catches me off guard and makes me cry.

But that beautiful early summer day in 1976, I met the day of Alan's return with all the excitement my almost-fifteen-year-old heart could handle. I waited breathlessly at my little sister's window until I saw him amble out his door. He was tall and lean, wearing leather sandals with a toe ring, tanned and gorgeous as ever, now with a mustache that sealed my love of facial hair forever. I thought of some lame reason to go outside. He had to know.

That smile, oh, that smile that I had waited a year to see, was everything. "There she is," he said, smiling broadly.

I wanted to say something wonderfully deep and meaningful, but I was dumbstruck. I let out a goofy laugh and said,

"It's good to see you." Oh, my god! That's what you say to the grocery clerk who is back from her vacation, not what you say to the love of your life.

"Wow, you cut your hair!" Alan remarked.

He hates it. I should never have cut it. That's it; I'm growing it out, starting today.

"It looks great," he continued. "Really frames your pretty face."

Oh, he loves it! I'm never growing it again! He thinks I'm pretty?

"Thank you. I was just ready for a change. I like your mustache." *Really,* I thought, *that's it: 'I like your mustache'?* I loved his mustache! I loved his face with this mustache. I almost fainted, I loved it so much. At that moment, I was functioning on some sort of deep-sea-diver-level breath work, as I knew I was not taking in any new oxygen.

I have no other remembrance of what we said at that moment. I think I was so flooded with dopamine that I was higher than anyone had the right to be. Mom came rushing outside with her camera to mark the occasion. *Oh, my god! Mom!*

"Alan, how handsome you look with your new mustache," Mom said with the benefit of full breath. "Here, you two—sit down, and I'll take your picture." I was mortified and inwardly thankful to her, all at the same time.

We sat near one another, each of us with our ankles crossed and our arms loosely wrapped around our legs. I don't know who looked more awkward, but the difference was that he still looked gorgeous. I looked like I was holding back vomit behind my tight-lipped smile. When I look at that photograph of him now, I am fifteen again. He was everything.

A year older, college-wise, he had new books, new music, new ideas, and he shared them with me. Mary H. had moved, and Jenny thought Alan was "too much like a girl" in his interest in books, so I sat alone on the curb that summer. He was evolved, unlike most immature, insipid boys.

On rainy days, I posted myself by our stereo and played Alan's records in a stack. Dad said that the singer I was playing (Carly Simon) sounded like a cat in pain. What? This was magic. This was a change-my-life soundtrack. Dad did not understand.

Why was Alan so nice to me? Why would he bother with me? I had nothing new, nothing life-altering. No new books, no music I felt brave enough to share. I was sure that he had already read the books Mom recommended to me.

What did I share with Alan? Not my newfound understanding of social justice and discrimination. My plucked eyebrows. That is what I shared—my plucked eyebrows.

The day that I let April shape my caterpillar eyebrows, she first used Erase, a product designed to eliminate the look of under-eye circles, to outline the area she would deforest.

Each pluck brought me tears and a runny nose, but once the first eyebrow was thin and shapely, there was no turning back. It was atypical of April to offer to help me, but I think it was not motivated by kindness but by a drive to keep me from embarrassing her.

She was a cheerleader, after all. I imagine that she was also enjoying inflicting the physical pain that accompanied each individual hair being tweezed from my virgin hair follicles.

Now, what was I going to do with those new thin brows? Well, of course, go knock on Alan's door and show him! What a sweet boy. He noticed right away, or maybe he saw the beefy, swollen red area beneath the new slim-brow look.

He said I looked beautiful. I clung to those words forever. What nineteen-year-old boy would be so kind? Alan Rhodes . . . oh, how I loved him. I would have only a few summer months with him, and then he would fly back to the States for his sophomore year at Texas Tech.

CAMPING UND BESCHWERDEN (CAMPING AND COMPLAINING)

D espite my desire to optimize my time with Alan, Mom wanted us to take advantage of our travel opportunities while living in Europe. She, along with Dad, planned a road trip through France. As I am typing this now, I am thinking, *Oh, so cool!* but in 1976, all I could think of was getting back to Alan.

Our auto expedition coincided with the hottest European summer in a hundred years, and our car had no air-conditioning. So off the McKnights went in our new Peugeot. The VW Squareback had bitten the dust shortly after we got to Germany.

We experienced every scorching degree while crammed thigh to thigh, three across, in the back seat. With all the car windows down, Laura complained about my hair blowing and slapping her face the entire trip.

Vanity kept me from tying it back. I had carefully arranged my sideswept bangs and long bob. Any efforts by anyone to alter this were just not going to happen. This was my look, and I was sticking with it. Ahhh . . . teenage flexibility.

Dad had always expressed a love for France, having been stationed in Tours in the 1950s as a young Army officer. While there, he had lived the bachelor life with a French family and had nothing but fond memories. I just knew that this sentimental journey we were on was going to be rife with his stories. Who cared about the past? This was 1976. *Get with the times, Dad.*

Mom gave her constant sunny commentary detailing the occurrence of every cow, duck, tree, flower, and building for the entire 820 kilometers. *Great, Mom. We've seen cows.*

Our foray into European camping started in Lausanne, Switzerland, at Camping de Vidy. Many tents of varying size and quality were dotted throughout the bucolic landscape. We drove around a bit until Dad decided on the place to "pitch tent." Prior to our European bivouac, he had purchased a family-size tent at the PX. When he had said it was "family-size," I had mistakenly assumed there would be various "rooms" separated by fabric. No, this was the colonial version of "family" with us all in one room.

Where were we supposed to get dressed? Where were we supposed to have alone time? These were not items that Dad had considered. Or perhaps he anticipated them and just didn't give a damn.

While Mom and Dad set up the tent, April, Laura, and I went off in search of the bathroom. Dad had assured us, pre-trip, that we would not need to dig our own latrine.

Apparently, someone had made off with the toilet because there was only a hole in the middle of the bathroom-stall floor. I returned to our home base and informed Dad, to which he laughed heartily and said, "The hole carved into the porcelain tray is the toilet."

This European anomaly required me to squat down and work very hard to squirt the pee downward. Being a female and not having any experience with small-space aiming, I learned the necessity for muscle control only after I had allowed the natural flow and covered my legs in dribbly urine. As if that weren't bad enough, when I flushed, a fast-moving wash of water began to cleanse the tray. I tried to quickly yank up my sweat-soaked white cotton shorts before the swill that was mine washed over my sandaled feet.

I knew, right then and there that, if the hole-in-the-ground toilets were our only option for "taking care of business," I was going to be constipated the entire two weeks.

Not everything was so primitive while at Camping de Vidy (pronounced "Videe"), as there was a cafeteria. Spaghetti with very little sauce was on the menu. It did not sit well in Mom's stomach, and it produced one of the rare evenings in my young life when Mom was ill. Mom had only been sick once before, and that was at least seven years ago when she'd returned from her ten-year-anniversary vacation with Dad in Hawaii.

While Dad was stationed in Vietnam in 1968, he was given a week's leave to meet Mom in Kauai. We sisters stayed with our adult cousin Pat in Illinois in her absence. We had never been away from Mom, and when she returned, she lay on Pat's couch for a week with what we kids were told was the flu. Many years later, Mom said that she had been sick with grief over leaving Dad, missing him, and worrying for his safety as he returned to the war.

Now, here we were all together in what was called a family tent, squished five across with no ventilation beyond two little netted windows. The condensation from our breath collected on the ceiling and dripped down the walls. I know this because I was awake most of the night.

Mom slept silently. Dad snored in the tone and decibel of a chain saw. April kept saying, "Geez, MaCrow!" in response to his vociferous vocalizations, and Laura blessed us all with this highly annoying dry cough. At one point, I recall threatening to strangle Laura in her sleep if she didn't stop. This was met with firm rebuke from my father: "Under no circumstances are you to strangle Laura." Dad's 1970s love of hiking and camping was probably not played out in the constant complaining of his three daughters. Mom felt better in the morning, and we continued our road trip.

AH, LA RIVIERA
(AH, THE RIVIERA)

My goal for this trip was to get a tan. Yep, that was it. This was going to be possible, I was sure of it, on the Riviera. Dad had described it as the playground of the rich, famous, and insufferable, but worth seeing for the breathtaking scenery. Dad was spot-on in his description. The water of the Mediterranean Sea was a blue green that looked fake in its color and clarity.

The narrow windy roads that Dad seemed quite adept at revealed jagged rocky outcroppings, giving way to views of the immense yachts docked at the water's edge. Oh yeah, now this was living! This was a landscape I could get used to quickly.

The biggest surprise for us all was when Dad pulled up to the Hotel Le Dauphin in Menton and said, "This is where we'll stay." A hotel! This was going to be epic. I looked forward to a shower and defecating on a real toilet. We would not have to breathe the same family air as we were forced to in the tent. April and I shared a room that had a bathroom containing what we thought were two toilets.

We kept asking Mom what the second "toilet" was for, but she just turned red and said it was for "hygiene." What sort of hygiene? It turns out it was a bidet for power-washing your hindquarters after defecating.

When it was just April and me in our room, she showed what I considered to be her best self. She was talkative, funny, and less judgmental of me. It was moments like those that gave me hope for her. And it was moments like when I put on my bathing suit that reminded me of what an a-hole she was.

Before our trip, I had purchased a two-piece tan bathing suit at the PX. Mom had approved it for its coverage to maintain decency.

"Oh my gosh! The color of your bathing suit is exactly like your skin. It looks like you aren't wearing anything!" April felt compelled to share just prior to my first Riviera sunbath.

I didn't give a rat's ass what she thought at that moment. Dad had said that the afternoon was ours, and I was going to soak in that glorious sun and turn my skin into a golden wonder. However, my enthusiasm was somewhat dampened by all the boulders and stones that pretended to be a beach.

Why was this such a popular sunning spot? Was the whole coastline like this? Mom came out with me, as did Laura, but they stayed in the shade for fear of burning. Mom kept coming to me to make me put on suntan lotion and admonish, "You better not burn, or your father will be very angry. He has really been looking forward to this trip, and you don't want to spoil it."

What about *my* good time? Why did we always have to keep *him* calm? By day's end, you could barely tell I had been out in the sun at all. This was not good.

We were still in search of sundresses, and the Monaco and Nice boutiques had those and more. Mom was horrified at the "skimpy bathing suits" and "streetwalker ware." All I saw were super-cute outfits that she was not going to buy. How could we come all the way to such a fashion-driven area and clunk around in our American duds?

I was enamored of the women in their resort-wear: wide-brimmed hats, oversized sunglasses, white capri pants, tube tops, and high-heeled sandals. So chic, so effortlessly chic. I tried to talk Mom into buying me some white capri pants, but she said white pants were hard to keep clean. I didn't even attempt to ask for a tube top. Even if one had fit me, Mom would not have purchased it because "People will see that you're not wearing a bra." I was quite sure even if that were true, no one would have noticed.

RÈGLES DE LA RESTAURATION (THE RULES OF DINING)

All McKnight family travel required historical sight-seeing, which meant walking Monaco's streets. The Prince's Palace of Monaco, in its pale yellow, trimmed in a bright white, was brilliant against the crystal blue sky.

Unfortunately, our hopes of touring the fortress were dashed, as it was closed due to the extreme temperatures. Mom, ever the intrepid and chipper traveler, shared a piece of her own history instead. "When Grace Kelly married Prince Rainier, Grandma was supposed to wake me to watch it on TV. She did not, and I was devastated. At the time, Grace's style was one I admired but could never afford. So I turned my devastation into time spent becoming a skilled seamstress."

I really should have been motivated by her story, but all I heard was, "We were poor, and my mother did not wake me to watch an event I had long looked forward to." This was most likely her only opportunity to visit Monaco, and she marveled at seeing a few of the palace guards!

Was she really that upbeat inside, or was it all a cover to never show devastation or sadness? I was just aggravated that our palace tour plans had been dashed. Couldn't there some-times *not* be a silver lining? Couldn't a person just be miserable for a while?

As Dad suggested lunch at a chichi restaurant overlooking the Mediterranean, all was not lost. The crisp white tablecloth, white cloth napkins, and white table setting induced a "How elegant!" gasp from Mom. The waiter in his crisp black-and-white suit soon came to our table and offered us rolls served with silver tongs.

The *clunk* on the plate should have been the first indicator that the crustiness factor was high. I made the grand faux pas of picking the roll up in my hand and starting to take a bite. Dad cautioned, "Stop! Put that down!"

What? Was there a bug in it? Nope, no bug. "At this type of restaurant, you break a piece of the roll off and butter it. Then you consume it." Rules, compliments of Dad.

How was it possible that there were more rules to follow? Wasn't I already following every damned rule ever imagined by mankind? I began breaking off pieces and then got another rebuke from Dad.

"No! Break off one piece, butter it, and then eat it!"

Oh, my god! I was starving, cranky from the heat, and ready to just put the whole damn thing in my mouth! But, one piece at a time, I ate what was possibly the best roll I had ever tasted in my life. To this day, whenever I'm faced with a roll, I break off one piece at a time, apply butter, and then consume it. It really enables me to savor, rather than shovel, the food.

According to Dad, salade Niçoise, a classic French salad, was the special of the day. This was a perfect blend of crisp green lettuce combined with tuna that didn't stink, hard-boiled eggs that did not reek of sulfur, boiled red potatoes, the most flavor-filled chopped tomatoes, thin slices of red onion, and (Dad had to explain these) capers, all perfectly marinated in a light vinaigrette.

The dessert was a crystal goblet filled with a mélange of summer berries, topped with a lightly sweetened heavy cream.

Yes, this was living! This was living the good life. I carry to this day the memory of this Mediterranean meal. Every bite, and everything, was perfect: the ambiance, everyone talking in soft tones, waiters moving in and out without words, refilling beverages, anticipating our needs, and afterward, using a "crumber" to clean off our table.

After the meal, a stroll down on the sand where the blue-green waters met the shore, gazing out onto the elite yachts of the rich and famous, was the perfect way to end the afternoon. *Let's never leave! Oh, but wait, what about Alan? On second thought, let's keep the vacation moving in a homeward-bound direction.* So, with the Riviera under our belt, it was off to Lyon as a pit stop on the way to Tours.

PÂTE FEUILLETÉE
(FLAKY PASTRY)

When I am hungry, I start sweating, shaking, and then top it off with a little blackout when I go from standing to sitting. But the blackness passes if I fill my lungs with a deep breath. When we arrived in Lyon, I was starving and on the verge of a blackout. Our first meal of the day was long past the time I should have eaten to maintain proper blood sugar.

The small bakery we stopped at in the countryside was my first experience with a croissant. The first bite was a flaky, buttery wonder, and the rich apricot filling made the moment a gastronomic high. Dad and Mom had theirs with coffee, and we had ours with hot chocolate.

This was no Swiss Miss instant hot chocolate. This was fresh cream and deep chocolate that made all other cups of hot chocolate in my life dull by comparison. Unfortunately, the sugar in my depleted state made me feel like I was going to throw up.

"What's the matter, Mare? French food too rich for you?" said Dad, noticing my sour green pallor.

"No. I just need some water," I countered quickly. I could not be weak. I had to find a way to compensate for my biology to be able to push through. This Army Brat mentality was part of my DNA, and I have called on it time and time again to enable me to handle crises of varying degrees throughout my life—sometimes to my own detriment but often to my triumph.

With a little warm water, I was able to balance my blood sugar and finish the croissant by which all others throughout the rest of my life were compared. Did anything else happen in Lyon? If it did, the croissant and the memory of its lightly salted, buttery goodness shield it from memory. Or perhaps I did black out, and they just loaded me in the car and kept on driving. Either scenario is possible.

I was so proud that I was able to endure the semi-faint state! Go, me! Years later, when I was thirty-nine and went into six-week-premature labor, I drove myself to the hospital to stay mentally strong for my baby. If I had called for help, I would have dissolved in a puddle of worry. Being able to power through kept me mentally prepared to handle whatever that early birth would bring. It was my finest Army Brat training moment.

I have also suffered because of this mentality by staying in toxic relationships, gutting it out while they were psychologically disemboweling me. But right now, let's get back to France in '76.

MAINTENANT C'EST
UN CHÂTEAU
(NOW THAT'S A CASTLE)

Lyon was simply a stopover on the way to our next destination, the Loire Valley. The city of Tours, where Dad had been stationed in the mid-1950s, was a must-see. I figured Dad's enthusiasm for Tours was because it enabled him to say the one word in French he could produce with an actual French accent, *Loire*.

Once we got to the Loire Valley, I was visually knocked on my keister by the beauty of the countryside. I was present in my surroundings and out of my head. Rolling hills of green, small country cottages dotted with colorful gardens—Château de Chenonceaux dwarfed all.

The beauty of this castle was in every twist and turn on the land and over the water. Dad was yammering on about the "engineering marvel" to Mom, who looked like she was hanging on his every word. I suspect it was a look she had cultivated while entertaining her own thoughts and reactions.

The one thing he said that I have retained was that this was the castle Walt Disney had used as the basis for Sleeping Beauty's castle in the Disney movie. I do not know whether this is true or not, but it seemed reasonable.

The way the castle was situated, the sun pouring through the windows on one side and spilling out on the other, was a marvel. I suppose this was by design. The architect was someone who understood nature. Chenonceaux was to me as organically beautiful as the trees in the Taunus Mountains. The majesty of this wondrous chateau took me, for a brief time, outside of myself and my petty concerns about my hair.

Dad drove the streets as though he had never left. He narrated as he drove, pointing out the various stores where he had shopped, places people had lived, and other trivia that filled the oppressive, steamy summer air.

He took us to his old French neighborhood and up to the gate of the home where he had lived. Then, wonder of wonders, we met his former neighbor, Madame DuPont, who must have been a hundred years old and remarkably remembered the "young American." A gracious, elegant lady, she went on and on about her positive experiences with Dad. Apparently, having children had caused him to become a hard-ass because she painted him as a fun-loving fellow.

She gave us the address of the home for the aged where his former host, Madame DeLise, lived, and off we went to the French older people's home. What the hell would anyone say to each other? Why weren't we going to spend our time clothes shopping in Tours? No, we had to go visit a woman who was at least 110 years old whom Dad hadn't seen for over twenty years.

Madame remembered him! Dad spoke broken French, and she spoke French with an attendant interpreting for us. I kept waiting for Dad to make April use some of her French, but he didn't! So why had I been commanded at Mespelbrunn to have a tête-à-tête with the violin guy, but April wasn't made to speak the French she always bragged about?

Life was just not fair. I had thought that April was going to be humiliated as I had been, but she wasn't! She was a golden girl. What was I missing in the DNA pool of our family? By entertaining these thoughts, I then felt so guilty that I had done so. Oh yeah, if there was a hell, I was probably going there.

Mom ensured that we went to some clothing stores in Tours, searching for sundresses. These were cotton, printed midi dresses with thin straps. Mom assured us that we needed them. Mom was stylish, so I assumed she knew what she was talking about.

We had never had a shopping experience with the clothing out on the sidewalks, but we did in Tours. I was sure I was going to come out of this with at least one dress, but Mom was appalled at the "spaghetti straps" that would not allow bras. No bra, no go, no dress for me. Oh, my god! It was like shopping with the Propriety Police. *The Army Wife* strikes again.

I cannot recall the hotel's name in Tours, but I know we stayed at one. In typical young teen memory, I do recall the look on April's face when she ordered a dessert at the chic hotel restaurant.

Dad had remembered that this hotel was known for their *oeufs à la Neige*, or eggs in the snow. Okay, nice memory, Dad, but did you have to embarrass us all by recalling your time in France with our waiter, who probably couldn't give a damn? "Pardon, monsieur, *oeufs à la Neige* still?"

"Oui, oui, the eggs of the snow are still here."

Oh, my god, our waiter was cute. And that accent!

April ordered the dessert, but the idea of eating eggs at dessert sounded gross to me. I kept picturing deviled eggs topped with sugar. No thanks. I ordered the pear tarte tatin, and it did not disappoint. Mary, for the dessert score!

When April's dessert showed up with its meringue made to look like actual eggs floating in what was custard but looked like thick, yellow urine, Laura and I could not contain our laughter.

Yes, we two burst out laughing, and then the universe cracked. Dad—serious, hard-assed, rule-driven Dad—began to laugh.

Wow! That had never happened! He quickly composed himself and told the confused waiter that we were all "joyful." Oh yeah, we were joyful, especially me looking forward to April eating her "eggs in urine." The following day, we started on our journey up north.

CRO-MAGNON A PARCOURU CES ROUTES (CRO-MAGNON WALKED THESE ROADS)

The lack of fresh air in our family tent on the way to northern France renders the nights as one long blur for me. The sensory input left from each place we visited while in France remains. I have measured so many other experiences in my life against it. How incredible when La Grotte de Font-de-Gaume and Les Combarelles Cro-Magnon caves are what I have as a reference point for an underground cave experience.

There wasn't much to prepare me for witnessing these caves besides past viewings of *The Flintstones*. I set eyes on the walls filled with artistic renderings created by someone around 17,000 BC. Their daily existence was survival of the fittest, and still they had to have their art.

This was the way I felt in my writing. The big difference for the BC folk was that potentially a saber-toothed tiger could be lurking around the corner as some ancient woman or man smeared their fingers with paint made from rocks and flowers. My metaphoric tiger was usually April or the critical voice I had carefully crafted in my head.

Did the early human Cro-Magnon individual stand back and say, "Is this good enough?" Clearly, from the sheer volume of work on the cave walls, someone felt driven to continue producing these colorful renderings. April's commentary—"I don't see what's so special. These are like stick figures"—was an analysis formed by someone who had the luxury of time, safety, and narrow-mindedness on her side.

I was struck by the colors of the paints and pondered how they had been produced from plants and rocks. When the materials were sourced and gathered, there could not have been any room for self-doubt in the hearts of these ancient artists.

Had this been a secret cave when the paintings were made? Was this where the artists lived? Did they have to sneak off and tell their cave-dwelling families, "Hey, I'm going to go out and search for berries. See you in a bit." Did they live alone? Were they ostracized from their group as someone "not contributing in a meaningful way" to the group's welfare?

I kept all my questions to myself while reading the information plaques installed along the path. It really bugged me that, in the modern renderings on the plaques, the artists were always referred to as male. This meant that even way back in ancient times, women were toiling away making dinner, but men had time to express their souls. Oh, my god! Was that never going to change?

Mom interrupted my internal dialogue—always the cheerful rock for all of us—with her pithy statement: "Imagine! Cro-Magnon man walked these very roads." At which point, we three teens felt compelled, with tear-splashing laughter, to correct her, as there were no actual *roads* at that point in history.

Many times during our French vacation, I vacillated between deep philosophical thought and teenage hubris. Perhaps that is the gift of teenagerhood: the time and the willingness to do both. But then there was my hair . . . The hottest summer in a hundred years was frizzing my hair.

Yes, I was concerned with how my hair was going to look in our photos. Mom must have had enough at one point and said to me pre-photo, hanging out in front of the caves, "Your hair looks fine. Just be happy you're not bald." Of course, that was no comfort to me then, but recalling her saying that to me back then makes me smile now.

The caves were such a respite from the oppressive heat. Mom forced us to stay hydrated by drinking Pschitt, a French soda that came in lemon and orange flavors. In 1976, any bottled water was carbonated (think Perrier), which was super hard to guzzle when thirsty. Mom would not let us drink tap water for fear of dysentery.

We couldn't figure out the big deal, as we drank tap water in Germany. Were the artificial borders of Germany and France enough to keep the gut bugs out? It wasn't worth asking, and I just drank Pschitt and giggled with April and Laura about the name. We never missed an opportunity to say, "May I have some more Pschitt?" Or, "Haven't had my daily allotment of Pschitt." With glass bottles of Pschitt in hand, off we continued for the north of France.

JOUR J (D-DAY)

The next destination was to be Normandy and Omaha Beaches. Dad provided a quick history lesson. This was helpful as I had thought we were going to two beaches to sunbathe. After Dad's lesson on D-Day, I knew that we were not.

Dad's encapsulated lesson consisted of, "We are headed up to the places where the United States and Allies launched the D-Day invasion. This was pivotal because it gave the Americans a stronghold from which to destroy the Nazis. Many soldiers died that day. Back in the 1950s, when I was stationed in France, you could still see shrapnel washing up on the beaches. We are here to learn about history, not to lie in the sun."

Ugh. This was going to be torture . . . just walking along a beach and seeing nothing. It was not. Dad described the boatloads of US soldiers emptying out into the ocean, being gunned down by the Nazis who had built cement bunkers. He emphasized how young many of the soldiers were: eighteen and nineteen, just three or four years older than me.

How do you walk into a war zone? How do you come out when the war is done? I still couldn't figure out what caused someone to convince others they should take over the world. What was with the drive for domination? As I pondered this, the crystal blue sky, warm summer sun, and sandy beaches begged to be enjoyed.

This was not to be. Then came the American graveyard, with the lines and lines of endless crosses. It was such a perfect day when we visited, not a cloud in the sky . . . people walking in absolute silence around the grounds.

Had this land healed yet? What became of the blood spilled? I began to understand, in that time on the north coast of France, how we all carry scars on the inside. We must. How could any of those soldiers on either side have lived unaffected by what they had seen, heard, smelled, and done?

And what became of the French people whose families had lived along those beaches? I was just a walking question. Mom said very little during our day on those beaches. What she did say has stayed with me: "Your uncle Tony [one of Mom's older brothers] fought in World War II. When he came back, he had changed. He drank from sunup till sundown. I'm certain it was to keep from reexperiencing the horror. He fought in the Pacific."

We did not ask any questions. It didn't feel like she was really talking to us so much as talking aloud to herself . . . processing, working to understand . . . and yet Dad went to Vietnam and came back just the same as always.

I have read about people who have the cultivated ability to compartmentalize their lives and the associated emotions. I suppose that that ability allows them to "move on," but I think the cells hold memory. Somewhere inside Dad lives the Vietnam War. Was he thinking about it as we walked the beaches of Normandy and Omaha?

NOUS AVONS RI JUSQU'À CE QUE NOUS AYONS PLEURÉ (WE LAUGHED TILL WE CRIED)

Our final evening in France was to be a magical, romantic evening for Mom and Dad. They were to visit a five-star restaurant while my sisters and I dined at a local café. April had taken every opportunity to lord her French-speaking abilities over us, so we depended on her to order. Our requests were "safe" with two hot dogs and a hamburger.

When our food arrived, we three erupted into the most raucous laughter I have ever experienced in my life. Our two hot dogs were stuffed into two loaves of French bread, just the tips of the hot dogs sticking out on either end, and Laura's hamburger had a fried egg on top. Nothing could have prepared us for our heat-induced giddiness.

About an hour later, Mom and Dad showed up, and we could tell Mom had been crying. Her red nose, separated eyelashes, and sunken posture caused my insides to knot up because Mom never cried. Or, to clarify, she never let us see her cry. The restaurant Mom had been dreaming of, planning for, and looking forward to was closed.

It was supposed to be their long-anticipated romantic anniversary celebration, and now they were in a little café with their three children, eating hamburgers and hot dogs. I now understand that Dad's curtness with the three of us that afternoon had nothing to do with us. He had wanted to provide Mom with this once-in-a-lifetime gourmet meal, and it was out of his power to do so.

All of Mom's anticipation was for naught, and she was hot and starving. I imagine she ate the fried egg that Laura had scraped off her hamburger—I don't remember. I was glad the waiter didn't tell my parents how rude we had been with our laughter. We did not confess it until we were all well into our thirties.

During the drive home from France, it was about five hundred degrees. We were wearing clothes that needed to be washed, drinking more Pschitt than a body should have, with Dad and Mom verbally recapping our adventures, and me only wanting to get home. Home to the curb to see Alan. When I told my own daughter this France story and my Alan Anticipation, she said, "Mommy, you were a stalker!"

I recently viewed the two maps Dad had used throughout France, and we traveled a total of 2,840 miles. He had highlighted our route, and when I traced it recently with my finger, my eyes and my heart cherished each of the experiences we had had on that trip.

MEIN HAAR UMDREHEN (FLIPPING MY HAIR)

I t was right back to the curb for me upon our return from France. The hottest European summer in a hundred years felt better outdoors anyway, with no air-conditioning or fans in our house. Well, that's what I'm telling myself now as a reason for kicking back curbside, but I know it was just to see Alan.

The beauty and the secret of all my new inner life, compliments of the French countryside, was something I pushed aside to return to the familiar. If he had only pummeled me with questions about the trip, maybe I would have taken the time to process the magnitude of what I had just experienced. But he didn't ask, and I didn't process.

He kept recommending books to me, and I kept reading. I did not know that I could have changed this dynamic with input of my own. Or perhaps I was afraid that if I inserted myself, he might lose interest if I wasn't hanging on his every word. I was not willing to risk this happening.

I hung around that summer with his same-age friend, Claire, sometimes with Alan and sometimes without him. She was brash, funny, and seemed so self-assured. She was physically much taller, of robust stature, and cut an imposing figure wherever she went. At their senior high prom, which had been held at Kronberg Castle, Claire had jumped into the water feature there, fully decked out in her prom gown.

I knew I did not have that type of drive in me, but I admired her brass just the same. Her dad was Colonel Vanguard, and when he sneezed, you could hear it through closed windows, even though we were four houses apart. I always found this highly amusing. Our family still refers to loud sneezing as a "a Colonel Vanguard."

Claire admired my shorter haircut and inquired where I'd gotten it done. Her waist-length sandy blond hair was just begging for some change before she, too, headed off for college in the fall.

I accompanied her to the German salon where April had publicly shamed our family with her laughter. With my fractured German and Claire's magazine cutouts, the transformation began. Her crying became visually and audibly apparent as soon as the scissors came near her hair. I should have said, "Hey, I don't think you're ready for this," but I was only fifteen to her nearly nineteen and kept silent.

Once her straight locks were shoulder-length, the hairstylist pulled up a cart with a massive quantity of multicolored plastic rollers with elastic bands. Unfortunately, the permanent-wave outcome was less appealing than we both had hoped it would be. She bawled the entire walk home and slammed the door when we got to her house, at which point I finally could not hold back the flood of my remorse.

I fled up to my room, flung myself on my bed, feeling the weight and responsibility for Claire's despondency, and sobbed into my pillow. Shortly after I had worked up a boogery lather, there was a knock at my door. The door opened . . . and it was Alan! Boys were not ever allowed on the second floor! Mom was home, so she must have granted him entrance into our hall of virgins.

He sat on the edge of my bed. Where was I going to wipe my snot? With a quick turn of my head to the right, pulling the pillowcase out for some slack, I wiped my face and hoped that it wasn't smeared all over my cheek.

He quietly explained, "Claire's reaction and her decision to have her hair cut was hers, not yours. You are not responsible, and she should not have made you feel that you were. She hides behind her hair, and now that it is shorter, she must face herself. That's what's going on. She isn't as confident as you are."

What? Me, confident? The only reason I liked my hair shorter was because Alan had liked it. If he had said nothing or had said, "Oh, I miss your long hair," I would have grown it out in a second. But still, I liked that he thought I was self-confident. I was just a good pretender. I had mastered "Fake it till you make it."

I have racked my brain trying to remember more from this tender exchange, but I am only flooded with nostalgic euphoria from Alan's beneficence. He did not stay long, as he was headed to Claire's next. After he left, Mom came upstairs and quickly advised that we would not tell Dad that Alan had been allowed entrance to my room.

"Mare, Claire defined herself by her hair, and without it, she will need to form a new self-image." I wish she had told me that the world judges us by our intellect, not our looks, but she did not. By and large, the world of men only values women for our attractiveness, our cleaning and cooking skills, and our ability to sublimate our needs to theirs.

Sweet, sweet Mom . . . I hope I thanked her for her understanding and for letting Alan up, but I don't know if I did. Right before leaving my room, she closed with the familiar, "Don't tell

your father that Alan was up here. He would not understand."
I survived the high, unbending standards by which Dad lived
(and expected us to do the same) with the loving overt empathy
from Mom.

It's not that Dad was unfeeling; I just think that he had
learned from an early age, and with additional military training,
how to compartmentalize things. In 1976, I was unaware of
how his disciplined influence saved me time and time again
as I grew into adulthood. Without him, I might have crum-
bled during many a difficult time, but I didn't. Well, I know
and believe that now at age sixty-one, but during the Frankfurt
years, I was sure that he was simply trying to keep us all in line
for his career. Perhaps both are true.

JUGENDLICHE SIND IDIOTEN (TEENAGERS ARE JERKS)

During that same summer was the family's infamous Kitty-and-Dad incident. Kitty was an indoor cat, but any chance she got, she bolted out whatever door was opened. To quell this maneuver, we put Kitty on a chain in the front or backyard of wherever we lived. She took great pride in crouching in the foundation bushes and then launching herself to the end of her tether at whatever unsuspecting soul dared to walk up to our door. She became legendary among our friends and extended family visiting us in Europe as a creature to fear and avoid.

On the day of "the incident," Kitty was battling with another cat through the glass in our front door. There were many low growls, air-cutting hisses, and fully extended claws scraping the glass door. Our door was covered with an ugly gold-and-white brocade curtain attached to metal rods bolted top and bottom to the doorframe. Kitty had figured out a way to push the curtain aside to carry on her hiss-and-paw battle.

During her afternoon display of dominance, she became entangled in the curtain, and Dad was attempting to help her detangle when she turned, chomped down on his thumb, and did not let go. He strangled her with his free hand and *threw* her up the stairs.

In true teenage fashion, my sisters and I screamed, "Is Kitty all right?!" Dad was not pleased. My father never cursed in front of us, ever . . . until that moment.

"Goddamn it!" my father yelled. "I am bleeding, and all you kids care about is the cat!"

Off he went to the hospital to get stitches and, most likely, a tetanus shot, returning with a very fat bandage around his thumb. He wasn't wrong in his reaction to us. We just thought he hadn't needed to throw her across the room.

My older sister once said, when she was a mother of four teenagers, "Teenagers should have their own island and not be allowed on the mainland until they have been socialized to think of others." At the time she told me this, I had no children and thought, *What a hard-ass*, but upon reflection, perhaps she was right. Of course, I guess that was the setting for *Lord of the Flies*, and you know how that turned out!

Our response to the Kitty-and-Dad incident was selfish. Dad and Kitty avoided each other for months. If he came into a room and she was asleep, she woke and slunk away. When the standoff was finally over, she hopped into his lap. I was sure the fault was his. Teenagers have tunnel vision and tunnel emotions.

ER IST WEG (HE'S GONE)

Why did summer always pass so quickly? This one seemed even briefer than usual, as with each passing day, it brought Alan closer to leaving for college. He spent a good deal of that time with Claire and Steve, a friend of his from FAHS.

From Laura's window, I watched them gathering at Alan's doorstep, the three of them laughing and leaving. Why is it always easier to be the one doing the leaving rather than the one left behind?

The evening prior to his departure for the States, I had been playing no-boundary badminton with Laura, April, and a few of Laura's friends from our street. We were taking a break, as the amount of running necessary to keep the birdie in play was staggering with our purposeful lack of boundaries.

Alan came out of his house. The streetlights were already on, signaling both the shorter daylight hours of August and the eventual end of summer. He sat down next to me, and for the first time all evening, I was acutely aware of the sheer amount of sweat pouring off me. This was not how I had mentally planned for him to remember me.

"I'm leaving for college tomorrow," he said.

"Yes, that should be exciting for you. I wish I were going somewhere." I immediately winced at my stupid comment. It sounded so needy and whiny.

"Well, you'll be going to high school soon, and I know you'll enjoy it. The teachers at FAHS are quite an eclectic group of people." I did not know what "eclectic" meant, but he looked pleased about this, so I was too.

"Yes . . ." My voice trailed off, leaving a massively uncomfortable silence in its wake.

April chimed in with a question that I never thought she'd ask: "Hey, do you want to come inside?"

What? April had initiated an opportunity for me to spend more time with Alan? Hmmm . . . what was she up to?

"Sure."

Up we rose from the curb; Laura's friends had already gone to their houses, and once we were inside, Laura went upstairs. Alan sat on the couch, as did April. I sat in the matching olive-green chair adjacent to him.

I don't have any recollection of saying anything. I know that I was investing tremendous effort in not crying. That's what I remember. That and his sweet face, those dark brown eyes that I didn't know if I'd ever see again. That and his voice—so deep, clear, and kind—talking to April as she pummeled him with questions about college, probably so she could get an angle for her college applications.

He graciously answered them all and, around midnight, said, "Well, I'd better go since I have to get up pretty early to get to the airport." Every fiber of my inner being screamed, "Don't go!" but I just eked out a smile and said, "Have a good trip."

I walked him to the door. April stayed in the living room. *Oh, if he could just kiss me goodbye, I'd live on it forever.*

"Mare, I want you to know just how special you are to me," Alan told me. "I want you to enjoy yourself in this life and get out of April's shadow. You belong in your own light."

Oh, my tears were heavy orbs at the crest of my lower lids, and no amount of squeezing my fingernails into my palms stopped them. *Plop, plop, plop*, they fell, sliding off my cheeks and onto my navy-blue VW T-shirt. He put his hand up to my face, wiped my cheek, and said, "Now, let's have this be a happy goodbye. It isn't forever."

With that, he turned, walked down my sidewalk, out into the street, onto his sidewalk, and through his front door.

I walked up the steps, closed the door to my room, and sobbed into my pillow, touching my face where his hand had been.

The next day, devastated at my loss, I did what any fifteen-year-old in the 1970s did to show their devotion—I called the only American radio station in all of Germany during their request hour and had a song dedicated to him.

"I Need You" by America: a sappier, more sentimental song one could not hope to find. I waited by the radio, crying as they played it. Then, shortly after, there was a knock at our door. It was Alan's mother, Mrs. Rhodes, suddenly needing a cup of orange juice for a recipe.

Mom made me come downstairs to say hello. So, I dragged my boogery face down to her knowing smile. I did not understand it at the time—I thought she was laughing at me, but now as a mother myself, I believe her smile was a thanks for my admiration and young love for someone so dear to her. She had heard my dedication, and so had all of Germany. It changed nothing. He was gone. I felt a sadness that had no words and a loss that kept me searching for many years to recreate his aura with others. I never saw or heard from him again.

GIB MIR DIESE SCHUHE
(GIVE ME THOSE SHOES)

Life did go on, and it was important that I figure out what to wear for the first day of high school. I spent close to an hour on my hair on the morning of day one, trying to make it "wing" back, only to have it resist with every fiber. I wore the red pants and short-sleeve cotton sweater from a German store we affectionately called The Hole in the Wall.

It was tucked behind some other stores and had no name on the front. What was this place? Mom learned about it from one of her Wives' Club friends. I suspect it was some black-market clothing store, but at the time, Mom framed it as "a real bargain." This meant good quality at great prices.

All April and I cared about was acquiring clothing from somewhere other than the PX or the Kaufhof Sausage Emporium. The clothing at The Hole in the Wall was crammed tightly together on racks, and Mom instructed us on how one shops in this type of store. "You will have to search through a whole lot of ugly stuff. Pull out items that have some appeal and try them on. Things look totally different on the body than they do on the hanger."

She was right. The faded gray-and-yellow numbers looked like extras from an "I Have Cholera" collection, and the olive collarless jackets could have come from the Mao Zedong Warehouse. But in between these hideous offerings were gems such as red bell-bottoms and a short-sleeve, off-white cotton sweater with slim red-and-blue stripes on the bottom of the sleeve.

Mrs. Motsko had recently given me a pair of four-inch-high navy-blue clogs that were a half size too small for me, but I wore them anyway. They looked perfect with my new outfit for the first day of high school. I was finally able to retire my Mickey Mouse too-big-for-my-feet shoes.

I loved my new shoes, and so did April. She begged me to let her wear them, but for once in my life, I drew a line and said, "Nope. You have never let me wear your platform shoes from your trip to Rome, and I am not about to let you wear these." Right after those words left my mouth, I felt so selfish, but Mom had warned me that April would want to wear my shoes, and I was not to let her.

"You know your sister is going to ask you to borrow these shoes. I want you to remember how she has not shared her Rome shoes with you. Under no circumstances are you to agree to let her wear these shoes. She has to learn that if she is not willing to share prized possessions with others, she cannot expect others to share with her."

It was all very *Wizard of Oz* with Mom as Glinda the Good Witch: "Don't let those shoes leave your feet. She wouldn't want them if they weren't so powerful." So that made me Dorothy Gale, who twists the lovely red shoes from side to side, admiring them, and April was the Wicked Witch of the West: "I may not be able to get them here, but I'll get *you*, my pretty!" (There was no little dog in this scene.)

While I appreciated Mom's thoughts on the situation, I doubted very seriously that April was ever going to learn to share. So why couldn't Mom just preempt this all and go to April and say, "Don't even think about asking to borrow Mary's new shoes!"

Mom spent her efforts on me by saying, "Mare, you let other people walk all over you. They take advantage of your good nature. You can only be a doormat if you lay yourself down first."

"Mom, aren't I supposed to treat others like I want to be treated?"

"In theory," Mom replied, "but that was written by men to manipulate women into doing their bidding. You need to learn to read a situation for what it is. When someone shows you who they are, believe them. Your sister is selfish and needs to learn that she cannot manipulate you."

The thing I could not reconcile was how Mom knew all of this and yet remained in her "good woman behind the man" role. She seemed destined for a role so much more significant than that. Were people going to like me if I stuck up for myself and for what I wanted? Wouldn't they want to look out for me and willingly meet my needs and interests without me having to tell them? No, they would not.

I struggled with these questions for many, many years. My core nature is to do for others. The part of the equation I needed to learn was that others could do for me too, and should. I wish Mom had told me that the "warning sign" for being taken advantage of is when you feel like you are doing all the giving or when the other person only "gives" when you have something they want. In this case, it was those beautiful navy-blue leather, four-inch-high clogs. I wore those ankle crunchers all over the Frankfurt High campus.

EIN TOLLER KERL
(ONE GREAT GUY)

With my hair heavily sprayed to stay in place, my new clothes, and a new three-ring binder, I was ready to transform into a popular person. Well, I was hoping to do so. I was glad to be able to walk to school, which meant I could get up later and spend more time on my hair.

My overriding thought that first day was, *Don't get lost. Don't get lost.* So, with a map in my hand, hope in my heart, and the knowledge that I was coming home for lunch each day, I was off.

The high school complex consisted of the main building, which was one street over from where we lived, the Quonset huts, and the Annex, which was down near the IG Farben Building.

High school provided an opportunity for me to try some new courses while testing into my leveled English and math classes. One of these courses was my science class, medical biology.

It was held in the Annex, still within walking distance of our house. I think our medical biology teacher wore the same tweed sports coat to class every day. During one class, he had a black light and said that clean clothing "glowed." Unfortunately, his coat did not glow. Ever since that day, I have remembered this, and I've always been ready with clean clothing so that if someone happens to shine a black light, I will glow. No wonder I had to go on Paxil for a lifetime.

For one of our first assignments addressing bacterial cells, we needed to bring in a urine sample. When I got home to eat lunch, I filled the glass jar. I knew I could not fill the jar in the school bathroom, as I felt too embarrassed to have others hear me urinate. What a weird phobia. Every human urinates. It makes a sound. I pee, and it makes a sound.

Normally, I did not drink anything during the morning of the school day so that I did not have to pee. With my lack of liquid over the course of the many previous hours, trying to eke out a little liquid was hard that day, even though I was at home. The delay in filling meant that I needed to hurry, hurry to get to class. In my hurry, I neglected to place the jar in a bag and walked to class holding the pee jar in my hand. These were the days before American students carried backpacks to school.

And who did I run into on my way to medical bio class but Bryan Henderson, my tenth-grade crush. He was a twelfth grader who had an Afro that was positively poetic. He was my gorgeous lab partner and a very kind soul. He (I am sure) pretended as we walked and talked that I was not holding a jar of urine.

For another assignment, we needed a blood sample, and that required a finger stick. We were each to stick our own fingers and then spread the drops of blood onto glass slides. Our teacher suggested that we use our ring fingers, as they were generally the least calloused. I held that needle over my finger but just could not bring myself to plunge it in. Was there nothing I did not have a phobia about?

Bryan Henderson volunteered to help me. "That's okay. I get it. I can do it for you if you want."

Such simple words spoken with a finesse that I am still thankful for to this day. As I think back on it now, this was all accomplished with no gloves, no safety gear of any kind beyond a cotton ball soaked with alcohol. I surrendered my ring finger, and he stuck me quickly, squeezed the droplet onto the slide, and wiped my finger with alcohol. It was the Bryan Hendersons of the world who periodically renewed my faith in men.

WAS IST EINE NUTTE?
(WHAT'S A HOOKER?)

B efore high school, my school health and PE classes had been all girls. One of the required classes for tenth grade was a coed sex ed class held in a Quonset hut. This was going to be awful! It was going to be worse than Mom welcoming me to womanhood when I got my period. The ante was upped on the day we presented our "role-playing" assignment. I was to play the part of a "hooker" to dissuade kids from this type of life.

I had no idea what a hooker was, so after receiving the assignment, I quickly asked Mom for clarification. The poor woman almost passed out! She did not answer and just asked why I needed to know. So I ended up asking April who, of course, knew; how she had this knowledge, I do not know.

In this role-playing assignment, the teacher "interviewed" me, and the only question I remember was, "How many people do you have sex with in an average day?" I believe my answer was, "Upwards of forty." Knowing April, she probably gave me this number fully aware that the boys would erupt in laughter, and they did. One thing was for sure: I knew I could never choose being a hooker as a life path—not that I was in any danger of it prior to the role-playing.

Sometimes after school I walked over to Dad's office building. This solo journey was a way for me to clear my head and to recalibrate after a high school day inundated with people and expectations. I never visited Dad while he was there, as it would have been inappropriate to interrupt whatever Army stuff he was doing. I just liked hanging out by the reflecting pool, hoping to catch some rays, or going to the snack bar to get something to eat.

There was only one day I remember that Dad came home from work early (the man never missed a day of work—*ever!*). The IG Farben Building had been bombed by the Baader–Meinhof Gang, a Red Army left-wing terrorist group active in West Germany in the 1970s.[13]

Now, even though the high school Annex building was within spitting distance of where the bomb had gone off, classes went on. There was no evacuation, just business as usual. That was life as an Army Brat. Bizarre perhaps, but a very assistive ethic for me during difficult times for the rest of my life.

The part I had to figure out on my own was that, after I had stuffed down some sadness or trauma, I needed to release it in some constructive way. Instead, I bottled it up for years until it manifested as panic attacks and an autoimmune disorder. That would have been good to know!

DAS SIEHT ZWEIFELHAFT AUS (THIS LOOKS DUBIOUS)

Physical exertion can release long-held trauma. Unfortunately for me, the required class of coed PE at FAHS just added to my trauma. The only time I had interacted with boys in physical activities had been during dodgeball in elementary school. Even this had been a traumatizing event.

There wasn't a dodgeball unit in tenth-grade PE, just a harmless-sounding "trampoline." Ours was made of canvas fabric, likely constructed from World War II tents. The security system for this circus apparatus was made up of classmates instructed to stand around the perimeter of the trampoline while holding their arms up straight, fingers spread. This band of distracted teens did not look like they were on a vigilant watch. Their lack of commitment to my safety was highly concerning. If I lost my balance, could they catch me before I plummeted to the asbestos tile floor?

My shorts and the canvas trampoline just weren't a comfortable combination. Apparently, my German soccer shorts with attached net underpants did not conceal my pubic hair. So, as I "piked" away, I was exposing myself to the entire class. My good friend Dolores let me know this afterward. I had begged Mom for these shorts. We had bought them at the Sausage

251

Emporium, as the PX did not have any girls' athletic shorts that fit me and my growing hips.

The likelihood of Mom going to get me another "cool" pair of shorts was slim to none, so the choice was either to get a pair of PX old-lady shorts or continue to flash everyone. I chose the latter.

Each student was to devise "routines" on the trampoline consisting of elements, each increasing in complexity. I was all right with the beginning elements—pike at the waist to turn, bounce on knees to standing . . . but any flipping resulted in a temporary blackout. Now one might think that my awareness of this could bring a desire to tell someone. But I didn't. I was willing to risk a bad grade by blacking out and hoping that wherever I landed, it was being guarded by someone who gave a shit.

I got many a canvas burn during that unit and never mastered anything resembling a flip. I couldn't do a forward roll on the ground without getting dizzy, so doing one in the air was out of the question. I had told Mom about this happening, and she said it was just because of my "nerves."

I'm pretty sure that my nerves were not the cause of my blacking out each time I attempted a backbend or had hyper-extended my neck washing the bathroom ceiling on a ladder. There was probably some medical reason for this, but I was led to believe it was "all in my head," so I never had it checked out. I just tried to avoid situations where it might happen.

WOFÜR TRAINIEREN WIR?
(WHAT ARE WE
TRAINING FOR?)

After I had survived the trampoline unit, it was on to gymnastics. Walking into class on the unit's first day, the gym floor was reminiscent of a 1950s East German Olympic training camp. This was not going to be good for so many reasons. The mats under each piece of scuffed and scarred metal equipment appeared totally devoid of any bounce or insulating quality.

Each apparatus had its own place in the gym: the uneven parallel bars, the pommel horse, the parallel bars, the floor routine mats, and then the gender-specific stations of the balance beam (girls) and parallel rings (boys). What was the goal here? When was I ever going to have to use the skills required to master this equipment?

Yes, this sport was super fun to watch on the Olympics, and Hitler Youth had probably used this very equipment to train for the invasion of Paris. But in 1976, was there really a need for students to be able to flip, twist, and pivot on anything to gain economic success or to ensure world safety? Was this a secret recruiting station for the CIA?

I avoided the uneven bars beyond swinging with my legs extended from the waist on the lower bar. I feigned many a muscle cramp during my week assigned to that contraption. I was the official "spotter" as my classmates forward rolled and easily transferred from the low to high bar. What was I going to do if they released from the high bar too soon and came flying at me? With my arms held high, my fingers spread, one leg in front of the other, I was willing to take the chance of being knocked out this way rather than having to perform stunts myself.

The pommel horse requirements were minimal for girls, as it was assumed that we lacked the upper body strength to attempt the static hold-the-bars that the boys had to do. We just had to run from far back, jump on a wooden springboard, grab the bars with our legs out in front and make it over, hopefully without face-planting in the process.

Finally, my disproportionately long arms (observation compliments of April) were helpful to me! I had no trouble learning and executing this jump and just did it over and over for the entire week. It is important to note that, apart from that week in 1976, I have never again used this skill.

We each had to pick three pieces of equipment to "master" during the unit. The culmination of the unit during the fourth week was a test on a self-selected apparatus. We were each to develop a routine for the class to observe. Why did I have to be in a class with descendants of the Flying Zambezi Brothers?

The balance beam seemed safe enough to earn a passing grade, at least, as no one else had chosen it for their routine. With no one for the teacher to assess me against, anything I did would be viewed as brave. I could balance and was very flexible. I was sure I must be good, as I seemed to draw a crowd each time I went to practice my routine. The same good friend who'd alerted me to the pubic-hair trampoline show quietly told me that with every full leg extension, more was showing than just pubic hair. I had to change my whole routine to maintain my feminine dignity.

It was time to go outside for the track portion of PE. Most days it was cold and damp, and I talked Mom into letting me get a black-and-gold Adidas tracksuit. Unfortunately, with my freakishly long torso, the stretch stirrup pants kept riding too low, lending a visible butt crack with each warm-up bend. So I tried to solve this problem by wearing a bodysuit underneath that divided me in half right through my private parts.

I had no stamina and, worse, shin splints. But I had begged Mom for the new brown suede Adidas. She paid half, and I paid half. This was long before cushioned athletic shoes, and my shins screamed in pain with every hit to the pavement. With more suffering in silence, my answer was Bengay. That sweet minty smell meant I was working hard. It was the era of no pain, no gain. I had been living that my entire life. That was how you earned respect.

April had no shin splints, was fast, could also run long distances, and was in her second year on the track team. She said that college admittance required various activities in addition to high grades.

I wanted to join track because of the cool uniforms, but my blubbery thighs (description again compliments of April) couldn't do the uniform proud. So instead of putting in any actual work to become stronger or faster, I let her definition make my decision for me. I did not join track.

DAS IST ALSO FREIHEIT
(SO THIS IS FREEDOM)

I had tested into the honors tenth-grade English class, which meant that I had the same teacher April had, Mrs. Bates. My knee-jerk dread at this realization was to be upended by my actual experience. The Nebraska Curriculum developed by the Nebraska Curriculum Development Center and the finesse of the talented Mrs. Bates provided me with a yearlong master class in active listening, formation of opinion, and the joys of spirited debate.

I was somewhat familiar with the curriculum, as April had shared a few of the more controversial essays with us at dinners the previous year. The first essay was by Albert Einstein, called "Religion and Science." In it, he says, "One hopes to win the favor of this being by deeds and sacrifices, which, according to the tradition of the race, are supposed to appease the being or to make him well disposed to man. I call this the religion of fear. This religion is considerably stabilized—though not caused—by the formation of a priestly caste which claims to mediate between the people and the being they fear and so attains a position of power."[14]

I thought Einstein's encapsulation of formal religion sounded about right and argued for the freedom to hold an opinion other than that held by the moral majority. April was disgusted by my stance on this subject and reported my "subversive thought" to Mom and Dad. Mom, the über-Catholic, actually supported me by saying, "April, the point is not to try and talk someone out of their thoughts. Mary is expressing her opinion, not yours. I should think you might be pleased that she earned an A on her essay. Wouldn't that be more godlike?"

Burn! Wow, Mom threw it down! April was silent, with a look on her face like the Grinch when the Whos down in Whoville sang on Christmas morning, even though their presents were gone. It was a classic moment, and I felt good in my bones. But April, being who she was, could not have me feeling good, and right before we went to bed that evening she slammed me verbally with words that took me years to get over.

"Mare, I want you to know that I love you because you're my sister, but I don't like you one bit."

Those words—and the timing of those words—absolutely devastated me. I had always suspected I was not April's favorite person, but now she had spoken the words so clearly. She took the wind out of my sails and left me in the hallway, crushed.

Mom must have heard because she came upstairs and found me sobbing into my pillow. "Mare, April is jealous of you," she told me. "You have always had an easy time making friends, getting along with people, and so many other wonderful things that April must work at. She should not have said what she did to you. You go right on thinking your own thoughts and being your own person."

If I said anything in response, it was in cry-talk, and I don't remember it. All I know is that Mom hugged me tightly and believed in me. I thought she was wrong about the "easy time making friends" part, but I liked that she thought that about me. I don't know if she talked to April after leaving my room.

I continued to delve into the Nebraska Curriculum with the instructions from the guide: "If one looks at what these essays say, at the problems they pose, one will perhaps be better able to envision the possibility that men in other times have, in their diverse cultures and places, seen very different things."[15]

I had never been in a class where the students were encouraged to openly discuss and/or debate one another, with the teacher as a guide rather than a lecturer. Our English class gave me my first experience with speaking my mind as I volleyed back and forth with my classmates Eric Fox and Steve Foy.

I first felt free enough to join in their lively repartee when I read the second work in our curriculum, Simone Weil's *Waiting for God*. The line, "With the exception of God, nothing short of the universe as a whole can with complete accuracy be called beautiful," was one we were to discuss among ourselves as a class.[16] Eric and Steve began as they had during the previous essay, dominating all conversation with their ideas posed as "truth." Well, that's how it sounded to me.

"I disagree with this statement." That was all I said, and then I felt like I was going to throw up. The room was silent.

Eric spoke up. "Disagree? How can you disagree? Disagree with what? God and the universe are the ultimate beauty. Anything else dulls by comparison."

Yikes. Now what was I going to say? "It seems to me that beauty can be seen, witnessed, and expressed in varying degrees," I replied.

I was going to go on and give examples, but Steve cut me off with, "Oh, you're going with that 'beauty is in the eye of the beholder' triteness?"

"I don't see that as trite. I see it as making sense," I shot back. "Why have all our senses, thoughts, and feelings if we were not meant to find our own truth and beauty?" Oh yes, this felt so good. This was fun.

It helped that our teacher looked quite pleased and smiled at me. Now, was she smiling because she thought I had made a good point or because I had finally spoken up? I didn't know. I just knew that in tenth-grade English, I had a lot to say, and I said it.

We wrote essays frequently in that class and learned essay format and how to use text to support opinions. I fell in love with the essay. In my yearbook, Mrs. Bates wrote, "You are the only student I have ever had who loved writing essays." And I did; I loved writing and reading them, and I earned an A+ in that class.

My day of "Hey, maybe I'm not so weird after all" came when we read an excerpt from *The Wind in the Willows*. Ha! We were not reading excerpts from April's beloved *A Wrinkle in Time*; we were reading from my beloved book. I guess April had forgotten to bring that up the previous year at any of our family dinners, but you can be sure that I did!

"Oh, hey, we were reading from *The Wind in the Willows* today in English," I stated coyly.

Mom quickly brightened and said, "Oh, Mare! You loved that book!"

If ever there were a time for the childhood, "Ha, ha-ha, ha-ha!" it was then—right to April's face—but I was the good daughter, so I just said it in my head. Literature was giving me the perfect pushback to my bossy sister.

It had taken me fifteen years to stand up to her. Fifteen years of sniping comments, mean observations, and one-upping me on everything I found important—and I finally had rendered her silent. And then I felt bad for her. She looked so defeated.

Drat, my big heart. I just could not help myself. I gloated internally for a little while at my triumph and then became "me" again. It did not feel good to harbor those thoughts. I wasn't a competitive person, and just wanted her to be nice to me. Well, I just wanted everyone to be nice to me. My crafts teacher was not.

GEBROCHEN (CRUSHED)

I had purposefully signed up for crafts with my new creativity awakened by our trip to France, and I looked forward to expressing myself in various "crafty" ways.

We started with an exploration of two-dimensional design rendered in marker. (Markers in 1976 were flammable and fragrant. There were tiny letters on the side of each marker indicating they should be used "in a well-ventilated area.") We were to create our own designs using only black markers.

I worked very hard on my ideas and did not procrastinate. The day we turned in our see-through plastic binder of designs was such a happy day for me. I was sure I had aced that assignment and was crestfallen when I saw that my teacher had written in red pen on the front cover in large letters, "B- Messy." *B minus? Messy? What?* Tears rose to my eyes, but I fought them back in class. I glanced around, and everyone else at my table had earned As. I should have spoken to my dream-killing teacher after class, but I didn't. I just shoved the stupid plastic binder inside one of my textbooks for the walk home. I didn't dare let April see, as she would probably say that it was divine punishment for my internally "Ha-ha, ha-ha-ing" her.

I planned to prove myself to my teacher on the next assignment. We were to each choose a craft tool to work with from his table. There were two tabletop looms, and I chose one of them. He had explained that whoever chose the loom was in for a real challenge and that should impress him. That's what I needed to do—impress him.

Mrs. Crain was in her front yard when I came home carrying the loom and mentioned that she knew how to weave! This was good because it came with no instructions. I had planned on going to the post library to find some, but with Mrs. Crain's help, I didn't need to do this. I chose heavy orange thread for the warp and forest green for the weft. In retrospect, that sounds really ugly, but I liked the color combo back then.

She and I attached the warp threads at her house since she was sure Kitty would make a mess of it at ours. When we finished hours later, she neatly tied the overhanging warp threads into a loose knot. She then demonstrated how to move the wooden machinery to lift one row of threads at a time to be able to insert the wooden piece with the weft thread.

There was something so delightfully repetitive about the whole weaving process, and in short order, I had woven a table runner. It was so artful, and we finished it off with tassels at the end. I had put so much good time and effort into this project and was looking forward to doing more weaving after turning it in.

On the day of grading, Mr. "I Have a Beard and Look Like A Hippie, However I'm a Narrow-Minded Asshole" came over to me and said, "I didn't expect much from you, but this project was so inventive. Your use of different fibers was brilliant. Excellent job."

Then he handed me a project that was not mine. It was beautiful in its brown, white, and blackness. It looked more like a wall hanging than something useful like mine was. My face dropped, and I said, "That is not mine."

"Oh . . . yours is the other one. You completed the project and tried a piece of equipment new to you, and I applaud you for that. Other than that, your product is ordinary."

"Ordinary." My project was "ordinary," and I had earned a B+. It was ordinary, and I was ordinary. I was ordinary and messy. I wasn't creative after all. I had thought I was, but clearly, this teacher did not think so. No one should ever have to feel so dismissed as I did. I vowed then and there that I would never underestimate anyone. It's not that I thought I would, but my personal experience with someone doing it to me made me vigilant. I understand that in the current grading system, one is evaluated, but the point of this should be to work with the student to identify specific ways to grow as a learner. It should not be a "value of person" judgment.

I was not a competitive person by nature. It made no sense to me to pit one person against another in any way. It seemed to me that competition was the root of all greed and long-held social caste systems. I was interested in living in a world, a society, a life where people developed skills not to be better than someone else but in a quest for a personal best that benefited the individual and hence the collective. This would never happen . . . sigh.

ΜΑΡΜΑΡΑ ΤΟΥ ΕΛΓΙΝ
(ELGIN MARBLES)

In my efforts to define myself beyond April's and my crafts teacher's narrow opinions of me, I decided to take a humanities course with Mr. Martin. Perhaps if I knew about the origins of art, I could become better than "B+ Ordinary." Mr. Martin was such a charismatic speaker, knowledgeable, engagingly funny, self-deprecating, and often sarcastic. His wit was most evident in his description of the British acquisition of Elgin Marbles. He put his foot up on a chair, leaned forward, asked someone to turn the lights down, and clicked on the first slide of the day.

"Lord Elgin, aka Thomas Bruce, the seventh earl of Elgin, the British ambassador to the Ottoman Empire, traveled in Athens, Greece, in the very early 1800s. The Ottomans were the occupiers of Greece at that time and, as such, conducted themselves with a 'spoils of war' mentality. He was a great admirer of the Parthenon and took it upon himself to ship many ancient marble statues back to Britain. His claim to these was that a sultan gave him permission to do so. Do we have a name for this sultan? We do not. Do we have a signed document professing such permission? We do not. You can currently view Elgin Marbles at the British Museum."

He put his foot on the floor and began walking slowly in between the aisles of desks and continued. "Now, one asks oneself . . . did the sultan, whoever he was, actually have the authority as a non-Grecian to grant the good Sir Elgin permission to remove these pieces of antiquity? That is not for us to decide, but it does beg the question: Should all museum pieces be returned to the . . . let's say, the Indigenous people, the country of origin? Or is it a greater good to humanity to have them spread to the winds for greater viewing and thus an expanded appreciation and understanding of world cultures?"

I have never forgotten this lecture. (I have recounted it to the best of my memory.) It has informed my view of usurped lands (like the land on which I currently live, which was initially the Susquehannocks') and my firm belief that greed rules the world. I also never forgot the engaging teaching style of Mr. Martin and emulated this in my own teaching career. He presented information and did not tell us how or what to think. He posed questions for us to ponder and to make up our own minds.

He had a vast collection of slides he had taken on his travels and projected these onto a small screen as he spoke. He had a very articulate speech pattern and enunciated the word "Etruscan" as "*Eeee*-truscan." When teaching about the statuary of Egypt, he pointed out the prevalence and significance of the "stylized archaic smile." His pronunciation of the word—"*sty-oh-lized*"—is one I hear in my mind to this day.

We sat in rows by last-name alphabetical order. The kid behind me used to put his feet on the metal book-holder shelf below my desk and bounce his legs rapidly. Unfortunately, this meant that I, too, bounced rapidly. It was most unpleasant, but I could not muster the courage (or whatever it was that I did not have) to ask him to stop.

Mr. Martin's class assignments were about memorization of dates, facts, time lines, pieces of art and architecture, and their significance to human societies. I spent loads of time outside of class committing his teachings to memory.

I am sure that his teachings were further solidified in my heart and mind by our family trip to Greece for Thanksgiving in the fall of 1976.

ΕΔΩ ΕΙΝΑΙ ΟΙ
ΩΤΟΑΣΠΙΔΕΣ ΣΑΣ
(HERE ARE YOUR
EARPLUGS)

The adventure began with Space-A travel status. *Space-A* stands for "space available," which meant hours of waiting in the Rhine–Main Air Force Base airport for five spaces to open for a trek to Athens, Greece. After one long morning and most of the afternoon, we were finally granted boarding passes. This enabled us to have the unique experience of traveling by Army-cargo-plane-converted-to-passenger-plane.

After we sat down in our rickety seats, a GI passed us earplugs. He was going to be our stand-in flight attendant. I had no idea what these earplugs were for and did not put them in immediately. Dad did not offer up any unsolicited advice on their purpose but put them in his ears, as did the rest of the family. I shoved mine deep down into my carry-on bag, bucking the conformity.

This sad little display on my part of "I can do what I want" abruptly ended right after the engines started up. With no insulated walls, the jet engines—propellers or whatever the hell—reverberated throughout the cabin. This deafening sound and my scramble to find my assigned earplugs sent Dad into deep laughter at my expense. I located them and quickly shoved them into each ear canal. Unfortunately, the devices muffled but did not mute the noise.

After a layover at Aviano Air Base in Italy for refueling, we were back on course to the ancient city. By the time we reached Athens, I was anticipating that, given the primitive conditions of this flight, we'd depart via parachutes. One horribly choppy landing later, we landed at the US Air Base in Hellenikon, no parachute required.

We stayed in an American hotel, the details of which are lost to me. That is not surprising, given the depth and breadth of the surrounding landscape and architecture. However, my newfound acquisition of historical background information via Mr. Martin heightened my awareness.

For the first time since landing in Europe in 1974, I had no interest in anything American. I wanted to soak in the sun and glory of Greece, both historical and current. The garbage on the Athenian streets was a real disappointment and wonderment to me. I had just assumed that everything would be pristine, in keeping with the Grecian discipline of yore.

Dad and Mom were quick to whisk us off base and up to the Acropolis. It really was the city on the hill, as it had been in Mr. Martin's slides. The closer we got to the top, the easier it was to forget the noise and pollution down below. But, as with all trips, we were instructed by Dad, "No shenanigans. We are guests of the Grecian people, and as such, you will conduct yourselves accordingly."

There it was . . . the Parthenon . . . framed by the cloudless blue sky, standing where it had witnessed so much human history, built from limestone formed during the time of dinosaurs . . . and I was about to walk the steps. We did not know it then, but soon after our trip, the steps and the interior of the

Parthenon were forever closed to visitors. We were some of the last people to ever walk in the footsteps of its past.

Dad and Mom hung together, along with Dad's five-thousand-pound camera bag, while April, Laura, and I quickly scampered up the steps to the inside. Since this was architecture as opposed to a museum, we felt it was all right to touch the columns, and we did. I wondered who before me in ancient times had stood where I was standing. What were their lives like?

My eyes cast upward to imagine the rooftop, long gone. Lord Elgin had certainly passed this way on his grab-bag adventure. I noted divots in the floor and pictured the white-robed individuals whose feet had begun to create them. Now my presence was minutely carving away a bit more of this floor.

I vacillated between my awe at where I was and my annoyance at the fact that my mother had made us all wear those matching London Fog trench coats. How could I look "cool" in an outfit custom-made for a flasher? Every slide we have shows me with a smirk, tugging at that stupid taupe-colored coat.

What was *taupe* anyway? Mom always had a ginormous vocabulary, and taupe was one of her words. As far as I could tell, it was not quite brown, not quite gray, mixed with a Hi-I've-got-Bubonic-plague blend.

Dad was quick to ask me questions about the architecture and history. "Mare, why don't you tell us about what we are seeing." I was not used to being the go-to person for anything of intellectual value. That was April's domain, and the fact that I was about to usurp her as unofficial tour guide did not please her. She was quick to point out, "Jackie Kennedy married rich Grecian tycoon Aristotle Onassis." Great, thank you, *Entertainment Tonight* reporter. And now, on to the important historical information I contributed.

"Pericles built the Parthenon in the fifth century BC. The Venetians damaged it in the sixteen hundreds during the Morean War. There had been gunpowder stored in here, and when a cannonball hit, there was an explosion."

After every few of my sentences, April interjected her knowledge of Greek mythology and Greek gods. "Yes, and it was built as a temple for the Goddess Athena. The Greek people were polytheistic, meaning they believed in many gods."

It was clear that she was not willing to give up her throne as "Queen of Knowledge." I am talking about April, not Athena. The anger inside me boiled, as it was my time to shine, and she just couldn't let me do it. The temptation to just huff my way into silence and retreat was great, but the desire to impart my new ancient knowledge was greater. I shared the stage with April.

Mom understood my sacrifice and took it upon herself to whisper in my ear as we walked the grounds of the Acropolis, "Well done, Mare. You could have lost your cool with your sister, but you kept calm." I guess this was good. It was one of those classic win-win scenarios, but I really wanted it to be win-lose, with me as the winner. When was it going to be my turn to win?

Η ΟΜΟΡΦΙΑ ΤΗΣ ΕΛΛΑΔΑΣ (THE BEAUTY OF GREECE)

t's not that I wanted to crush anyone—I just wanted to be beyond B+ ordinary. The beauty of Greece took me away from my self-obsession. So it was off to Corinth on a Hellenikon Air Base–sponsored day trip. Thank god we were on a timetable; otherwise, we would have spent the entire trip at the Isthmus of Corinth. Dad, being a civil engineer, took the requisite five thousand photographs of the man-made link between the Ionian and Aegean Seas.

Corinth, the site of the Apostle Paul's Corinthians Bible verses, based on his preaching to the people of Corinth, was in Mom's wheelhouse. I imagine he had quite a task, trying to convince them to believe in one god as opposed to many. This is still super weird to me—to try and talk others out of their beliefs. They believed in many gods. What was the big whoop? It seemed to me that a Supreme Intelligence had to allow for many belief systems.

April must have sensed my blasphemous thoughts and swept in with, "If you don't follow the teachings of Christ, you will not be saved. You will not be among the chosen."

She was going to be among the chosen? She who would not let me have the goddamned spotlight for even a little bit of time? This seemed highly unlikely. The more she preached at me, the more irritated I got.

I finally got fed up with her holier-than-thou attitude as we walked ancient Corinth. "You know, I've had it up to *here* with your phony religious fervor. Stop preaching at me!" Apparently, the architectural acoustics are quite good in ancient Corinth, as I heard my voice echo throughout, which of course caused Dad and Mom to whiplash head-turn our way.

April's face had dropped . . . I had hurt her feelings. I'd wanted to hurt her feelings. I wanted her to feel what I had been feeling all those years from her near-constant suppression and critical analysis of me. But then . . . I didn't. I really didn't want to hurt anyone's feelings. So I apologized for yelling at her and blamed it on my period, though I don't even know if I was having one at the time.

Besides, there was the Doric Temple of Apollo! Nothing like a phenomenal piece of ancient architecture to take my mind off sisterly squabbles and to delay the pivotal moment in which I could stop being a metaphoric doormat.

I was too swept up in the way the sun poured through the columns. Dad had given me his old Pentax SLR camera, and I was off searching for the perfect angle for my shots. This was quite an upgrade from my Instamatic, and I was not going to waste any film on bad angles.

I still have that beautiful camera, and it was not lost on me that Dad had given only me one of his old cameras. Not April or Laura. Maybe he did like me. Maybe I wasn't the disappointment I had decided he thought I was.

The Archaeological Museum of Ancient Corinth provided many opportunities for me to test my knowledge of light speed and aperture. Around my neck, I wore the portable light meter that Dad had also given me, which I used prior to each series of shots. The natural lighting in the museum removed the need for a flash. Mom reminded me, "Remember to be where you are and not get too caught up in trying to capture everything on film. You will miss the experience of just being here."

But I didn't want to ever forget this! The archaic smiles on the statues, the mosaic floors, the hand-painted pottery . . . she was right. Mom was right, although I did not figure this out until I had my daughter. I have very few photos of my girl because when I am with her, I just want to view the world through her eyes and through my heart. My eyes and heart in 1976 were still turned inward a great deal, working hard to expand and explore.

The Treasury of Atreus completed our trip that day. By the time we arrived, the cloud cover had welcomed stiff winds, and I was truly thankful for my London Fog flasher coat. Our tour guide confirmed what I already knew: "The Tomb of Agamemnon was constructed during the Bronze Age. The entrance to the Treasury is an excellent example of the power of the post-and-lintel building style."

Walking through the Lion Gate, he continued, "We are now entering the citadel of Mycenae. The Late Mycenaean period was one of great prosperity for the Peloponnesian people." From there, we climbed rock after ancient rock, with me attempting to get good camera shots. I quickly learned that without a visual focal point, my photos were just going to look like piles of rubble. This was not what I was after.

Mom suggested that I include people in my photos "for interest and perspective." How did she know so much about photography? I suspected that Mom knew a whole lot but had been born at a time when her vast knowledge was not valued or encouraged. Consequently, I have a lot of photos of April, Laura, and Mom smiling on piles of ancient rocks. The gloomy sky was not inspiring. Apparently, the light was necessary for interesting angles and shadows.

ΠΟΥ ΕΙΝΑΙ Η ΣΟΦΙΑ ΜΟΥ
(WHERE IS MY WISDOM?)

The next day, the Grecian sky was once again an azure blue, and we were off via tour bus to the Oracle of Delphi, estimated travel time of two hours. All of us military families in search of the wonders of primordial greatness had to get up at O-dark-hundred. It's a wonder that I didn't incur a concussion with my head leaned against the bus window, banging hard as we trekked along corduroy roads on the way to Delphi.

I was hoping that whatever vapor spirits used to visit the ancient peoples might do so for me. The High Priestess of Delphi (I thought it was super cool that it was a woman) was the earpiece to the gods. Without her, the likelihood of my receiving any smoky wisdom was slim to none. I was certainly glad that I had the historical background already in place because the temple was underwhelming visually.

This could be because it blended in so well with the rocky outcropping of the surrounding landscape. I stood over where the High Priestess used to receive her intel, but found no visible vapor. No messages for me. No "You will move beyond your 'ordinary status' and be shown your real purpose in this world." Rats. I was really hoping for some clarity.

The Theatre of Epidaurus was phenomenal, carved out of the hillside in a perfect semicircle. Our tour guide encouraged us to sit at various levels of the theater, and for April and me, that meant running to the top. She got there first, of course. As we sat, the guide dropped different American coins onto the ground. Because they were American, I knew the sounds associated with their hitting the ground. How was it possible that we could detect a penny from a quarter? But we did! Oh no . . . this meant that Dad was going to give us a follow-up lecture on "the wonders of acoustics via engineering." To his credit, he held off on this lecture until dinner that evening.

Prior to that meal, we were able to visit the Archaeological Museum of Delphi. Dad was totally into the Byzantine mosaics, but I was eager for a viewing of the *Charioteer of Delphi*. I had learned in humanities class that it was "one of the finest examples of bronze sculpture," and I made sure to tell my family this before we arrived at his feet so I had a jump on April reading the description below it.

What I had not shared out of embarrassment was that it was odd that the statue was not nude, as athletes of that era competed without clothing. I thought Mom might not appreciate this little tidbit. I did whisper it to April, who burst out laughing. Mom tossed us a "You're being Ugly Americans" look, and we silenced ourselves.

The dinner of moussaka and stuffed grape leaves served alfresco was sublime. I had no idea what I was eating, but the rice filling of the grape leaves reminded me of Mom's stuffed cabbage and the moussaka of spaghetti sauce. Laura was still in her picky-eater stage and consumed only plain bread. We were served olive oil, and none of us knew what that was all about. Mom took a quick look around to see what others were doing with the shallow saucer of oil and then dipped a piece of her chunky bread in and instructed us quietly to do the same. Oh . . . no butter here, only olive oil. I have been a fan of thick, hearty bread dipped in olive oil ever since. Mom reminded Laura quietly, "Chew thoroughly and take small bites. You don't want to vomit."

Poor Laura. I know Mom meant well. Yacking at a public meal wouldn't really cast us as savvy travelers. Laura had a fear of vomiting for years and years. I had a fear of her vomiting for years and years. The only thing that broke this thought was having our own children; there is no time to think about yourself when you are loving and taking care of young children.

ΜΕΓΑΛΕΣ ΠΟΝΤΙΣΕΙΣ
(GREAT PONTIFICATIONS)

We were scheduled to take a tour of some islands off the coast of Athens and had a day in between. On that beautiful day, we started with a viewing of the Artemision Bronze—the god of the sea statue of Poseidon at the National Archaeological Museum of Athens. Well, Mr. Martin had described the controversy as to whether it was Poseidon or Zeus.

"Depending on to which camp you surrender your artistic wanderings, this statue is either the head honcho of the sea, Poseidon, or that great god of the heavens, Zeus. Great pontifications have been made analyzing the position of the thrower's hand and whether the lost item is a trident or a bolt of lightning. No matter who it is, the wonder is in the detail of the statue in totality. Take note of the generous beard and hair details."

And take note, I did. I had begun to relay the artistic point-counterpoint arguments when April swooped in, "It's all conjecture. I don't see why it has to be naked." *Thank you, Puritan Princess, for your in-depth analysis and totally mind-numbing commentary on that about which you know nothing!*

People have bodies. Why are we so ashamed of them? Why does a naked body have to represent sex? Why can't someone just be naked? When did we start covering up? I was convinced the answer to all my questions was the desire of some (spread by many) to influence and, therefore, control. *Just let me enjoy the damn museum!*

The Mask of Agamemnon meant so much after just walking the grounds of Mycenae. I couldn't help but ponder the right and wrong of digging up someone's burial site, all in the name of art, architecture, and anthropology. My ponderings led me later that school year to take a course in anthropology, which I will go into a bit later.

While I was in the National Archaeological Museum of Athens, there was much to see. I had my Pentax SLR with a new roll of color slide film all loaded, the sun was streaming through the almost floor-to-ceiling windows, and I got the shots of a lifetime.

The Jockey of Artemision, a large Hellenistic statue cast in bronze, provided the perfect study for three of my shots. I had composed them based on the emphasis Mr. Martin had placed on these three characteristics: the image of the goddess Nike on the right thigh, the features of the boy's face, and a photo of the entire statue.

The decision-making was fueled by the expense of color film and color development. Slide development cost less than prints. The only drawback to this was having to ask Dad to set up the slide projector to view them. This was a process and a half, according to him, because he had to allot time for the setup of the white screen as well as the projector itself. Although carousel-style slide viewers had been invented, Dad still had the vertically-load-one-set-of-slides-at-a-time projector he had purchased in his bachelor days in France.

I believe this artistic choice honed my skills as a photographer. It required patience for the correct natural light—moving just far enough away to allow for the type of lens I had (and I only had one), and it developed my steady hand in working without a tripod. With a manual SLR camera and the need to understand light and aperture, I felt like a "real" photographer. It was an internal boost for my self-esteem, and in that museum, I was going to soak in every endorphin-producing moment of it.

On the city bus trip back to our hotel for lunch, crammed in tightly with people on both sides, I had time to witness all the Greek men playing with these beads around their wrists. What was that all about? Mom had rosary beads she prayed on, but apparently Vatican II had eliminated the emphasis on beaded prayer. As a product of the Vatican II wave myself, I did not know what Mom did with her beads and had even less of an understanding of the grown men fingering theirs.

Mom took it upon herself to ask the receptionist at our hotel about the beads. She was never shy to talk to people. I guess she figured that the young woman with jet-black hair must be a native of Greece, despite working on an American air base. She was right, and the receptionist's face brightened when Mom said, "Good afternoon. We couldn't help noticing the beads around the wrists of people throughout the city. Are they connected with the religion of this area?"

Even though I was interested to hear the answer, I was teen-wincing inside that we probably looked stupid at not knowing. That strikes me as so amusing now. How could we have known? The receptionist went on to answer with her perfect face and her perfect olive skin, "Oh, these are worry beads. Mostly older men carry and use them to dispel the concerns of the day." *Hmm . . . worry beads.* I needed to acquire some of these prior to leaving Greece. If there was anything I needed, it was a way to "dispel the concerns of the day."

Our receptionist had on the most lovely, airy blouse with billowing sleeves and simple embroidery at the neckline. Mom inquired about her "stylish garb," to which the receptionist responded, "This is a Greek peasant shirt. It is made from cotton and is traditional among our people." Oh, I needed one of those before leaving Greece too.

Mom did not stop there. Did she ever? "Your skin is pristine. Would it be too personal to inquire about your skincare routine?"

Mom! Oh, my god! Was there nothing this woman would not ask a stranger? Hmm . . . what *was* this goddess's skincare regime? Whatever it was, I wanted to start doing it because apparently what I was currently doing was causing my complexion to resemble a bad pizza.

"Olive oil," she replied with smile. "We wash with local olive oil." Oil? Wasn't this just the thing I was trying to eliminate from my face? Wasn't that the cause of all my pore-filled problems? All the products I was currently using were intended to strip the oil off my face so as not to clog my pores. I figured she knew something because her face was luminescent, and mine was not. But April did not wash with olive oil, and her skin was perfect. Oh, that's right, God was punishing me for my vanity. I forgot.

After lunch, it was off to romp in the Aegean Sea and hopefully catch a few rays to disguise my pimpled skin with darkness. We rolled up our jeans and stepped into the warm, sublime waters of the Aegean. The sand was soft and gently warm between my toes. The color of the water was a bluish green I did not see again until I visited Moraine Lake in Banff National Park in Canada many, many years later. Note that the Canadian water was not warm like the Grecian Aegean.

Wet jeans do not feel sublime. Jeans in 1976 were all cotton, and rolled-up bell-bottoms did not stay rolled up. I had two choices—attempt to keep them dry and miss out on the most beautiful day I had ever encountered in my life, or let them get wet and deal with it later. I chose the former. I cannot believe I chose the former, but that was me at age fifteen. I had to pay vigilant attention to what I looked like in case . . . in case a boy paid me some attention. What was I readying myself for here?

The Greek men were stunning. They had dark reddish skin, heavy mustaches, and whiter teeth than anyone had a right to have in the days before teeth whitening . . . Oh yes, Greek men were gods. Oh, wait . . . what was with those teeny, tiny pieces of cloth pretending to be bathing suits? Oh, this was not good!

This was hideous! These suits looked like (as my dear friend Ellin later put it) they were trying to smuggle grapes inside them. April, Laura, and I could not quell our internal laughter created by our discomfort at witnessing this proud fashion choice. It erupted as fall-down-onto-the-sand, tears-pouring-from-our-eyes laughter.

Dad was insistent that after dinner we hurry to the Temple of Zeus. I wanted to go back to the beach, but Dad was right. He was right because the lighting at that time of the evening was a photographer's dream. The sky was playful and generous, with pinks, oranges, and gold taking turns against the crystal blue.

These colors and the sun's angle must have been considered by the architects of this temple in the sixth century BCE. How was I going to limit my shots when the photo ops were limitless? With only one lens at my disposal, I had to stand in just the right spot to capture both detail and depth. When I finally had the perfect shot of the Corinthian columns, Dad came up behind me with his camera. "Hey! This is my shot!" I yelled.

Uh-oh . . . I'd yelled at Dad. I'd yelled at Dad in a foreign country. I'd yelled at Dad, who had given me this camera. I'd yelled at Dad because this was my damn shot! I lowered my camera and began to move out of the way because it was Dad, and I had just yelled at him.

"Hey, where are you going? You took the time to find this shot; now take it!" Dad's face had a smile, but I couldn't tell if his voice was angry, irritated, proud, or perhaps a mélange of the three emotions. I took the shot, and it was amazing.

Fifteen of the temple's original columns were still standing, but I was also intrigued by those that had fallen. Dad asked me to sit on one for perspective. Yes, in 1976, you could just walk up and sit on ancient columns, and I did, all belted up in my stupid taupe London Fog all-weather coat. I think I earned Dad's respect that day by speaking up to him. I also think I was lucky as hell that my timing was right.

What made for that right timing? No one knows. It must have been some space-time continuum anomaly because it has never happened again.

ΛΙΩΝΕΙ ΣΤΟ ΣΤΟΜΑ ΣΟΥ
(MELTS IN YOUR MOUTH)

The last day of our Grecian holiday was spent touring the local islands of Poros, Hydra, and Aegina. We took a small boat and were greeted at the Poros dock by a large group of feral cats. Mom quickly reminded us, "They might have rabies, so don't get too close."

None of them were foaming at the mouth, so I wasn't sure where her paranoia was coming from. Dad assured us, "They're fine. They are part of the local flavor, just waiting for fishermen to come in with their catch." How did Dad know either of these things were true? Had he been to Greece?

The day was overcast, gray, and breezy. This did not dull the tenderness with which I soaked in this magical island. No McKnight adventure was complete without a trip to a museum. The Archaeological Museum of Poros looked unremarkable from the outside—a plain two-story building in keeping with the surrounding architecture.

The inside did not disappoint. How did the Greeks manage to build structures flooded with light? The collections of artifacts were arranged closely together, and it was too easy to walk past something thousands of years old in search of something else thousands of years old.

Mom was totally into Minoan pottery and marveled at the intricacy. At some point in our Poros tour, she purchased a modern vase modeled on the Minoan decorative arts. She still has it. It is matte black with decor painted in harvest gold, accentuated by a thin black line. Mom must have been acutely aware of how incredible it was for her to be in Greece, on the island of Poros, as a daughter of poor Slovak American immigrants.

I was hungry, as we had gotten up early to make the boat to the islands. One Grecian café later, and I had tasted my first gyro and my first baklava. Had I known that the melt-in-your-mouth meat on the gyro was lamb, I might not have ordered it out of a preconceived repulsion. Luckily for my taste buds, I didn't realize this, and I enjoyed bite after bite of the shaved lamb meat, lightly coated with a white sauce, feta cheese, tomatoes, and shredded lettuce, all wrapped in fried pita bread.

The only familiar ingredients were lettuce and tomato. Then there was the baklava. *Oh, sweet, savory layer after layer of pastry so flaky with infused butter, drizzled with local honey, and crunchy with fresh walnuts—may I taste you again someday!*

On the island of Hydra, I purchased my Greek peasant shirt. It was made of stretchy cotton with intricate lacework around the circular neckline. Oh yes, this was the shirt that defined my style for life. Mom called it "Bohemian queen," but wouldn't that mean we'd have to be in Hungary?

I wore that shirt all the way through my thirties when it finally gave out from all the wear and washings. I also purchased my worry beads—simple black beads on a leather cord. I must not have learned the proper method for alleviating anxiety with them because I wore them all throughout my fear-ridden college years.

I left Greece knowing my fashion style and having a more refined flavor palate. I left Greece wanting to go back. And I left Greece hoping never to see a man in a teeny-weeny bathing suit ever again.

KEIN VORSPRECHEN ERFORDERLICH (NO AUDITION REQUIRED)

U pon our return to Frankfurt from Greece, it was soon time for my second semester of high school. I was finished with humanities, and because of the trip to Greece, had decided to take anthropology. I was driven by the questions of why people create art and architecture and why people then wage war against one another and destroy everything that was created. I did not understand group mentality, and I wanted to.

My anthropology class was a mixed-age class, as most classes at FAHS were, other than English. One of my classmates was Awilda Rios. She was a senior and originally from Puerto Rico. She sat beside me on the first day and spoke to me. Awilda was stunning with her golden skin tone and shining jet-black hair . . . Why was she talking to me?

She noticed my worry beads and asked me about them. On the other side of me was Tim. He was a freshman like me and quite talkative as well. I got the feeling that his interest in conversing with me had a motive. It turned out he knew that cheerleader April was my sister and wanted me to introduce him to her.

Why should I? Why should I help April in any way? I decided I should because I kept hoping that if I treated April in a kind manner, she'd reciprocate. After fifteen years of her not doing so, I don't know why I thought she would change now.

As luck had it, I was talking with Tim one day after class, and April happened to walk up. Yes, I introduced them, and shortly after that, they were boyfriend and girlfriend. It was sort of weird that Tim was a year younger than April. That dynamic was not one you saw too often. Mom and Dad liked him because he was "a respectable young man." He was. He and I volleyed verbally during anthropology class. I couldn't help but wonder why there weren't any guys interested in me.

Mom suggested that I involve myself in some activities at school to try something new. There was an upcoming talent show to showcase the thirty-year anniversary of FAHS. The casting call for singers and dancers was to provide entertainment throughout the show between acts. This seemed like something I could do. All I needed to do to be a member was to show up on the first day of practice. There was no audition required.

REFLEXIONEN EINES ADLERS (REFLECTIONS OF AN EAGLE)

Mr. Mecham, an English teacher and the head of the drama department, was the faculty advisor for the show. He was an outwardly dramatic fellow. Both his facial expression and his body movements looked and felt over the top for the situation. It made me feel like I did not belong.

Despite my gut screaming, "You don't belong!" I stayed. Initially, my friend group and I were planning on doing an act for the show in addition to my being part of the chorus. Too many disagreements over the choreography, mostly by my attempting to lead the group and dissolving into, "Why the hell can't you do this right?" ended our act.

It was up to me to tell Mr. Mecham, and I knew he'd voice his displeasure at having to rework the timing of the entire show because of our exit. "Uhh . . . I'm so sorry, but I have to bow out of our act. It's just not coming together as we had hoped, but I still want to be part of the chorus if that's all right. If it isn't, I understand, and I am soooo sorry. It's all my fault. I'm not a good leader and—"

"Enough!" he interrupted. "Stop putting yourself under my feet. Just spit it out and leave me to deal with it. Jesus, grow a pair!"

I had no idea what "pair" I was supposed to grow; what was he talking about? Was he mad at me for quitting? Was he just mad all the time? What was I supposed do now?

"Are you still in the chorus, or is that too much for you too?"

Oh, I wanted to leave this situation so badly. But if I left, if I quit the show, then I'd have to face Mom and Dad and tell them. Their likely disappointment at my failure to see a commitment through till the end was my deterrent and my motivation.

"No, I mean, yes . . . yes to still being in the chorus, and no, it is not too much for me."

Daily rehearsals meant learning songs I had never heard of, like our opening tune, "Everything's Coming Up Roses." Mr. Mecham wanted it to be a very Ethel Merman and Old Hollywood performance, complete with dramatic hand movements with our fingers spread wide and large smiles while singing.

"More drama, more smiling—you are excited to be here, now show it!" he screamed. During each act, we, the chorus, were to sit on the stage steps, gazing intently and then clapping wildly afterward. Our direction from Mr. M. was, "Think *Bye Bye Birdie*–level adoration." What the hell was *Bye Bye Birdie*? I had to ask Mom. With no Internet back then for instant reference, visual or auditory, I had to make do with Mom's explanation.

"Mare, think adoration, hanging on his every word like you do with Alan!"

Oh, now I had it. *That* I could channel.

Our closing song was to be the original Frankfurt American High School song. This song sounded more like a battle cry for Vikings, with its "conquer and prevail," rather than a school song. I suppose when it was composed in 1946, battle was still fresh in the minds of the creators.

"Hail to thee, our alma mater. Herald to the sky." At the word "herald," we were to gaze upward, our right arms raised high above our heads, our fingers close together but not saluting. Oh, my god! So many details. It's not like this was going to be a hit Broadway show. It was going to be one night only, captured on Instamatic cameras and Dad's SLR.

I was not friends with any of the other chorus members, but I now shared the experience of the thirtieth-anniversary show, entitled *Reflections of an Eagle*, with them. Many of the chorus members were also in the drama club and looked like they were always acting. People broke out into mime and had dialogues with one another in subpar British accents. Weird.

Was this acting? Did I have to constantly be "acting" to act? Wasn't it supposed to be subtle? I looked forward to the night of the show so this whole experience would be over. The entire family was in attendance, of course. The auditorium was packed with students and families.

As a chorus member, my costume was to be a long-sleeved black leotard, solid-color A-line skirt, black tights, and black shoes. I had none of these items in my possession, so off Mom and I went to the PX, into the "Dance" section, small as it was, for the leotard and tights. We sewed the skirt—a bright orange polyester blend with a zipper in the back.

The shoes, oh those beautiful shoes, were purchased at the German shoe store next to The Hole in the Wall. They were black suede, with a rounded toe and four-inch-high chunky heels, and I loved them. When I wore them, I felt as close to a Barbie doll as I was ever going to get.

I wore them to school each day to break them in before the show. The walk from the main building to the Annex and the Quonset huts made the pain in the balls of my feet excruciating.

290 ● OUT OF PLACE

I did not care. These shoes were the most beautiful thing I had ever owned. When I took them off at the school day's end, my feet retained the Barbie-doll shape for at least ten minutes. After that time, I could wiggle the muscles back into use and step on my flat feet again.

Dad took photos of me during the show and printed them in black and white. Unfortunately, because of my railroad-track braces and the stage lights, it looks like I have missing teeth. April was quick to point that out. Thank you, April; it is still all I see when I look at those photos.

At least I had one activity to add to my college applications in the future. I also had the acting bug but could not figure out how I was going to satisfy that and be among the thespians who were in perpetual pretend mode.

As a side note, actress Julianne Moore went to FAHS and was in the drama club. She was Julie Smith back then. I did not know her because she arrived the summer my family moved back to the States. Clearly, the acting thing worked for her. I used my drama skills in the classroom with young children and got paid a hell of a lot less than Julianne Moore.

DER UNGLÄUBIGE
(THE INFIDEL)

This small foray onto the stage had me wondering if acting was "my path." Our church catechism classes kept
speaking of "God's plan." I did not buy into this idea
wholeheartedly but was also at a loss as to what was moving the
universe in favor of some at the expense of others.

How could some people be "blessed" and others "cursed"?
We were living on a land where the Jewish people—God's chosen people—had almost been wiped off the face of the earth
during the Holocaust. Was this part of God's plan?

Mom shared that the notion of "God's plan" was a product of Vatican II. "I was schooled in the idea of free will," she
explained. "People are flawed, Mare. We can only do what we
can do."

What was that supposed to mean? Who was going to
answer all these questions for me?

April took it upon herself to "enlighten" me as often as
possible. She was a force, and Mom had decided that her influence was one I could use. This force was made stronger by her
involvement in a school group called Agape.

April explained that *agape* meant "friendship love." *Hmmm
. . . why do we need a group for this?* I soon understood that a
major requirement of the members was to go out and recruit
others.

I guess I fit the bill as someone who was worth saving, as Mom was totally on board with my investing some time with them. I did not particularly gravitate toward those people at school, or in April's case, at home, so what made anyone think I would benefit from spending more time with them outside of school?

An Agape-sponsored ski trip to Davos, Switzerland, seemed like the perfect compromise. I had never been skiing and was pretty sure there could be no time for holy rolling.

In preparation for the trip, Mom suggested that we borrow ski goggles from the Motsko boys, who were heavy into skiing. This seemed like a marvelous reason to go to their house. I volunteered to go over and get the requisite goggles.

Nick showed up at the door, goggles in hand, and said, "Don't crash into any trees," his wry, fabulous smile punctuated by a bushy brown mustache.

"I'll try not to." That was it. That was all I said. Why was I so tongue-tied around boys? I didn't have time to debate this with myself, as I had a ski trip to prepare for. April had a stylish, waist-length ski jacket. I had my bulky, butt-covering, purple down jacket. One of us looked *très chic*, and the other like the Michelin Man.

With no ski helmets back then, the topper for my head was a scratchy wool hat that elongated my head even more than it already was. April wore a wool beanie that fit her head perfectly. She gave me strict instructions for how I was to behave on this trip.

"Although we will be skiing, we are joining in fellowship to celebrate the love of Christ. You are not there to scope out boys. You are there to learn and live the word of God."

Yeah, right. You go ahead and tell yourself that. How is a ski trip learning and living the word of God? I really didn't care and was just glad to be going somewhere in the middle of winter.

Enter the snow-covered Swiss Alps, wooden chalets, quaint streets dotted with cafés, and the trip was looking up for me. Our group stayed in a small mountainside cottage where April and I shared a teeny-tiny bedroom. I was just glad I didn't have to sleep with people I hardly knew. April was irritating but a known irritant. I could deal with that for a day and a night.

Mom had packed us a classic Sylvia McKnight lunch with gobs of food and drink lest we get hungry. It was only a two-night trip, at least in terms of actual time. The hand-holding prayers at the communal dining table were cringe-inducing. I did lower my head at their behest but peered around at the others as they babbled on in thanks for the food, the trip, the mountains, and the chairs . . . Oh, my god, the food was getting cold!

One night down, and it was skiing day. First came the fittings for boots and skis. I was given K2s, which I guess were good because the other God people were oohing and aahing. It was only because I had big feet and short legs that I was assigned these special boots and skis.

After I was all geared up, it was off to my first lesson on the Swiss equivalent of the bunny slope. I have never been too coordinated, and skiing just reinforced that. But being a McKnight with one ski lesson complete, I was convinced I could go to a higher part of the mountain and ski down. I had watched the Winter Olympics before, and it looked like something I could do.

I had to take the ski lift to get up said mountain. I had imagined it was a chairlift like the classic winter scene skiing postcards from the 1950s. Not so—it was a J-bar. April briefly instructed me on the procedure, but about halfway up, my legs were getting tired from putting all my weight on them. My thigh muscles were shaking, I was sweating from every pore, and I needed a break.

I soon learned that you do not sit on a J-bar. Upon doing so, I promptly plummeted over backward, tumbled down the mountain (remember, this is the Swiss Alps—not some dinky manufactured hill), and finally stopped with one ski planted straight up in front of me and one ski planted straight up in back—my feet still in the bindings. Small Swiss children without ski poles whizzed by me, laughing hysterically. My own sister came skiing by me, laughing with equal hysteria. They had to stop the entire ski lift to disengage me from the skis. A ski patrol guy helped me out. "Bad luck for you. Next time, don't sit." Thank you, Swiss Patrol Guy.

He encouraged me to go up the rest of the mountain and ski down. So, with my wounded ego and bruised and battered body, I got back on the now-functioning ski lift and arrived at the top where I met April, who was ready for another run.

I was feeling a bit more confident, snowplowing pigeon-toed down the mountain and suddenly gaining speed I was not ready for when I came to a bump (a mogul, unbeknownst to me) that sent me flying into yet another sprawl. The same damn Swiss kids were laughing at me again. The only reason my sister wasn't laughing was because she was too far ahead of me.

Another ski patrol guy dislodged me and told me to "watch for the moguls." I had no idea what he was talking about, thinking he was referencing wealthy oil barons. I nodded my head and smiled my best smile.

Down the mountain I went again. I encountered yet another "bump," only this time, as I was tumbling, everything turned *white*! I could not see four inches ahead of me. This was not the relaxing *swish-swish* down the mountain I had imagined.

People kept on skiing. I figured they were endowed with Swiss sonar that I was not privy to. Finally, April said, "Oh, watch out for the moguls."

"What the hell is a *mogul*?!" Once the whiteout cleared, I made it down the mountain, avoiding the bumps and the jeering Swiss kids, to spend the rest of the day in the lodge.

That night, I slept as deeply as I had ever slept—exhausted physically and mentally. I did manage to escape the Bible meeting that night, as I was limping and bruised from head to toe. I'm sure they prayed for the "bumbling heathen" as I slept. I have not been skiing since. I wasn't any more "saved" than I had been before the Agape ski trip, but I was certainly ready for more adventure.

ICH VERSUCHE MICH ZU BEKEHREN (TRYING TO CONVERT ME)

Following Nick's instructions, I hadn't hit any trees while skiing. I had just shut down the entire lift operation, bringing the Davos resort to a halt while they extricated me from my skis and from the packed snow beneath the lift. I was glad that Mom chose April to return the ski goggles to the Motskos. I did not want to have to fess up to my total ineptitude as a skier to Nick or Greg. It was exhausting to care what they thought. Why did I care what any boy thought? It's not like anyone was putting any effort into figuring out what *I* thought! Was I supposed to think, or was I supposed to make men comfortable? It seemed like they were only comfortable if they were driving the conversation.

As boy crazy as I was, I vacillated between wanting to be asked out and wanting *not* to be asked out. April had had a few boyfriends already and was rather derisive of my inability to get a date.

Unbeknownst to me, she had arranged for me to go out with the best friend of her then-boyfriend Charles. The guy's name was Chip, and he carried a Bible under his arm everywhere! April had invited me to go with her and Charles to see the Diana Ross movie *Mahogany* at the Idle Hour Theatre, two streets over from our house.

It sounded like fun, so I agreed to go. While we were standing in line, up came Chip, Bible at the ready. I am a highly empathetic soul, and as he got closer—his sweat stains lengthening rapidly—I caught on to the ruse. She had set me up with Chip-the-Bible-Toting-Guy! What was she thinking?

He gripped the Bible with both hands during the entire movie. Perhaps he was hoping to share a passage with me afterward, as the others suggested that we get a bite to eat. I declined, saying that I had already eaten, which was not true. I preferred to starve rather than endure a forced date with the three of them quoting scripture and incanting prayers to bring me to salvation.

April expressed her displeasure with me later. "You totally embarrassed me! I went to the trouble to set you up, and you did not even give him a chance!"

"Oh, thank you, Great Sister. You set me up with a robot!"

"I set you up with someone who can morally guide you! At least he was paying attention to you. Not like the great Alan Rhodes, whom you haven't heard from the entire time he's been gone!"

Oh . . . that hurt. She didn't understand. Alan was busy. He was a college man! He was otherwise occupied, deep in thought and in books, and it wasn't that he was neglecting to write me—he just had other important things to do.

It was not the only time she tried to convert me. A few years later, when she was a college sophomore at Johns Hopkins University, she invited me to attend a party there. Well, how could I resist that? The ratio of boys to girls at that time highly weighed on the boys' side!

I was attending another college in Baltimore and arrived via bus transport, all dressed up, ready to meet cute guys and share a beer. Instead, opening the door to a common area in the dorm, I came upon a sea of students all kneeling with their heads down, the room silent. Hmm . . . what sort of party was this?

I spotted April, so I knew I was in the right place. I stood motionless at the door and witnessed person after person confessing their "sins," sometimes crying openly for forgiveness.

There was a long table with food, so it had the trappings of a party, but it turned out to be some cleansing-of-the-soul gathering. There was no beer, no music, and the cute guys who were there had probably never dated someone who thought their gathering was stupid.

After the crowd had confessed their impure thoughts and expressed their disdain for nonbelievers, I entered the room. They offered me the opportunity to "unburden my soul," but I passed, more interested in the cookies than any spiritual bloodletting. No dates came from that ruse of a party.

My actual first date was in the spring of '77 while I was still in Frankfurt. It was not one I wanted to go on. Mom made me go. April had told her that Craig had asked me out. I don't know how Big Sis had acquired this intel, but she had. What was her motivation for sharing with Mom? I knew it was not going to be anything but memorable for the agony.

DAS WIRD NICHT GUT (THIS IS NOT GOING TO BE GOOD)

Craig Epps was two years older than me, a druggie, and not anyone I was interested in. The date was lunch at the Terrace Club. I wore a forest-green pantsuit I had sewn a few months earlier.

Mom insisted that I wear a blouse under the vestlike halter top for "discretion." That totally ruined the look, as it bulked me up like a linebacker. To complete the look, I wore my four-inch, navy-blue clogs.

April chimed in just minutes before my date, "You can't wear those shoes! You will be taller than Craig!"

"So what? I like these shoes, and they look great with this outfit."

"Guys don't like girls to be taller than them," April insisted. "So you have to change into flats."

"If I change into flats, my pants will drag on the ground, which will look stupid and ruin the hem of these pants."

Mom weighed in, "April is right. Men have very fragile egos. I have a pair of flats that will work with your outfit."

Fragile egos? What? They ruled the world! Why did we, as women, let them rule the world if we knew they had fragile egos? It seemed like we could use this knowledge to our advantage and take the world back. I did not have time to debate this, as it was minutes before my first date.

Mom brought down a pair of hideous mustard-yellow flats with weird brass buckles across the top. And unfortunately, Mom's shoe was a size and a half smaller than mine. So now, because of men and their fragile egos, I was cramming my feet into shoes that were too tight, like some Asian foot-binding ritual.

Craig knocked on the door, and Mom insisted on answering it to meet him and size him up. I was to come from the maid's quarters like I hadn't been sitting in the bathroom feeling like I was going to throw up.

Our big date was at the Terrace Club by the IG Farben Building.

When we got there, the hostess seated us, and this rather large, distressed-looking woman came up to our table. I just assumed she was a very attentive waitress. Yes, she was a waitress, and yes, she was attentive then and throughout the entire meal because she was his mother!

"Mom, this is Mary. I told you about her."

Mom? Our waitress is his mom? Why did she look like she was going to deck me? This was not good. After his brief introduction, she burst into tears, sobbing, "My baby! This girl is trying to take my baby away from me!"

I wanted to assure her that the sooner I could get away from her son, the better for all involved, but I knew if I said that, there'd be hell to pay at home for being rude.

"Nice to meet you, Mrs. Epps," I said, extending my hand to shake hers. She did not shake mine back. The eventual withdrawal of my hand was a slow-motion angst fest. This was not a good first date. This was a scene from a bad film.

I endured this cringe fest littered with an awkward one-sided conversation about his obsession with Crosby, Stills and Nash. I think I ate two pieces of lettuce that afternoon.

What was the hope here for him? Clearly, I was not interested or even given a chance to be interesting, as he dominated the conversation. We ran in different social circles, and the date was not going well at all. His mother came over to our table numerous times, each time asking me about my background. I was producing very little saliva, which made it immensely difficult to speak.

I passed on dessert and said that I needed to get home to do homework. If I could just get home, I knew I'd be all right. He tried to hold my hand on the walk back, but I quickly pushed my sweaty hands into my pockets. What had I done at lunch that gave him any notion that I was interested in skin contact? Knowing me, I had worked at being polite, which meant maintaining eye contact and nodding my head as though actively listening—and he had interpreted those actions as interest in him.

I wish I had had the intestinal fortitude to say "no thanks" to his lunch offer in the first place, but I was a people pleaser. This ill-fated personality trait is rooted in unhinged empathy. To be personally assertive, I had to be willing to endure the unpleasant negative vibes the other person inevitably put off—which I absorbed and experienced as my own.

I can't explain this to anyone who does not believe that certain people are empaths. I am one of them. I have since learned how to form boundaries with everyone but the people I love.

I hadn't yet learned the boundaries that warm spring afternoon, and the emotions of both Craig and his mother were kicking my emotional butt. My relief grew as I approached home, walking down Wismarer Strasse, passing Colonel and Mrs. Ping-Pong's house, passing Colonel Bracy's house, and now walking up the sidewalk to my house.

Thank goodness that, in a moment of fear laced with desperation, I had asked April before my date from hell how I could avoid the "after-date kiss." She advised me to shake his hand with the door partway open (which also involved my blocking the door so that Kitty could not go charging out into the Frankfurt streets) and then jump inside and close the door.

That's what I did, only Kitty had other plans. After I shook Craig's hand and said, "Thank you for lunch," Kitty appeared out of nowhere as she was prone to do, jumped out the door, stood up on her back legs, and hissed loudly, sending Craig packing. *Good Kitty.* We were moving stateside in a month, and I worried every remaining school day that he might ask me out again. He didn't.

MICH SELBST VERGESSEN (FORGETTING MYSELF)

om was full of post-date questions. I know she was trying to move me into young adulthood, and I wanted the same, but this was not helped any by Craig's mother's behavior. Were all mothers of boys like this? Did they all have weird attachments to their sons? Mom summed it up for me: "Men . . . are a disappointment. Your father is the exception."

Thank you, Mom. Now, what was I supposed to do with this information? I guess she felt like I needed further enlightenment because she wrapped up our conversation with, "Men are a dastardly lot." Hmmm . . . that's not what they said in *Seventeen*!

I was still intoxicated by men. I wasted way too much mental and emotional time daydreaming about the perfect man, what our ideal life together could be like (laced with an outpouring of romance, of course), and not nearly enough on my own wants and needs.

What did I want out of life? What was I good at? How was I going to separate from my family to go after my dreams? I completely neglected to define any goals for my success. I was driven by emotion and sensation. What does one do with that? Obsess over Alan the Unattainable and the lack of letters from Texas Tech.

DU BIST EIN IDIOT
(YOU ARE AN IDIOT)

Despite the mental effort I put into Alan angst, I did have enough spare brain power to put a fair bit into my studies that year. It wasn't like I had actively set any goals for myself. No matter how hard I tried to understand geometry—my tenth-grade math class—it eluded me.

What was the deal with all the proofs? Why were we proving things? Where was I going to use this information? Dad tried helping me, he really did. He was so patient with me, even when I dissolved into quiet tears.

"Dad, I just don't understand this stuff! It doesn't make any sense to me, and no matter how many times I go over it, I can't remember it!"

"Now, Mare, I see you're doing all right on your homework. We just need to build off that so you can study for your tests. It's the testing that is bringing your grade down."

It was truly amazing to me that Dad was so calm and smiling gently. It reminded me of why I loved him even though he called Joan Baez's singing "cat wailing" and insisted on keeping me under his moral authority.

The only reason I did well on homework where we had to show our proofs was that the answers were in the back of the book, and I worked the problems backward to get to the beginning. That was the only way it made the slightest bit of sense to me. But unfortunately, there were no answers to work backward from on the quizzes and tests.

I was going to earn a D in geometry. I had never earned a D in anything. I do not know how April learned about my looming D, but she did. One day after school, shortly before the school year's end, she walked home with me since there was no more cheerleading practice for the year.

"Mare," she began, "I want you to know that you don't have to worry about your math grade. I went and talked to your math teacher and begged him to give you a C. I explained how you freeze up on tests and quizzes and that you're a lot smarter than you seem to be. He agreed to give you a C."

There was an instant relief in my chest, and then I was furious that she had intruded into my life without first discussing this with me!

"Ape, I earned a D. I'm sorry that it embarrasses you to be associated with a stupid sister, but that's what I earned, and that's what I should get. You should not have gone behind my back and talked to him."

"You are so ungrateful, Mare! If you had gotten the D, you'd have had to retake geometry in eleventh grade with all the other dummies!"

Ouch, there it was . . . I was a math dummy. I already knew this, but to hear it come out of April's mouth stung like the devil. I had not handled our conversation well, that's for sure. Part of me was thankful that I didn't have to take geometry ever again because of April. But I could not get out from under her opinion of me and my lack of math skills.

I finished that year with all As and one C. April finished the year with straight As for the eleventh year in a row. Colleges would be recruiting her for sure. But unfortunately, the only ones likely to recruit me were some loser schools for math idiots with bad skin and proficiency in daydreaming.

For the record, in my sixty-one years of living, I have never had to use the shit from geometry class, and there is a part of me that is thankful that April got me that C. It looked much better on my high school transcripts than the D would have.

SÜSS UND RUHIG
(SWEET AND QUIET)

Where was I in my three-year transformation? The last days of the school year were spent getting people to sign my yearbook. The overwhelming common comment was, "You are so sweet and quiet." What a horrible moniker! Was that it? Was that all I had become in the past three years? Steve Foy wrote, "You do have the redeeming quality of humor. You need to get nasty, or you will never get anywhere in this world."

That was not at all what I had envisioned on the Boeing 747 three years earlier. Why wasn't anyone writing, "I admire your confidence and your style"? Why weren't they writing, "You are going places. Watch out, world!"?

Their written assessment of me was the oft-repeated "sweet and quiet" with the additional comment of "You look so cute now that you don't have a tin grin."

The removal of my braces, every hard yank around every single tooth in my mouth with medieval-era pliers, revealed my sparkling, straight-toothed smile. So now I was sweet, quiet, and cute. Those sounded like attributes for a Kewpie doll. I'm pretty sure this was not what I had in mind on the plane over the Atlantic.

It was time for us to wear the curtain rollers on our collars. Jenny was already gone, with her family moving back to

Georgia. Alan's family had returned to Texas. The Motskos had been transferred to Mannheim, Germany . . . What was left for me? It was time to go, and Dad was to be stationed at Fort Meade in Maryland. The intermingling of my hormones mixed with my anxiety left me in a swill of sadness.

The day we left for the States was a day filled with so many tangled emotions. My avocado-green Samsonite contained only clothing, unlike when I had packed three years ago. Nothing else seemed "necessary." In my carry-on, I had my notebook with fresh, empty pages. I had thrown out all my journals, poetry, and everything marking this time so we could meet the weight limit on our move by the Army.

I opened a box recently that had been stored in my parents' crawl space and came across a few pages I had saved from those journals. They were parts of letters I had written but never sent to both Mary H. and to Jenny. This find confirmed my memories and gave me access to the titles of so many of the books that Alan had recommended and I had read. Finding these pages meant that in June of 1977, I had snuck a little bit of my history in, despite Dad's insistence that we throw away all the "unnecessary items."

"Only five minutes before we depart for the airport," Dad warned. I headed outside one last time.

Standing on that curb, looking at Alan's old house across from ours, my heart felt the crush of woe. It lay so heavy on my chest that I thought I'd stop breathing. Could I ever have that feeling again for someone? Did he ever think of me? Why did he never write? For a moment, I thought perhaps he had, but as Dad brought the mail home from work, maybe he had never given me Alan's letters!

Yeah, right, that was it. Dad was preventing our love from happening. That must be the answer. My eyes stung from holding back tears, not wanting the new neighbors to look out and see some girl weeping . . . looking, staring, longing for what was now their home.

Turning to look at Jenny's old house, I had some hope that we'd retain our friendship, even though she was living in Georgia. How many times had I walked in and out of her front door with her mother asking, in a bright tone and southern drawl, "What are you two girls up to?" We were always headed to the PX record department or hanging out in the Snack Shop, looking, gawking, and drooling over boys.

I sat down on the curb, just for a moment, and closed my eyes. I wanted to soak everything in—the smell of summer, the laughter, dreams, love, tears, my growing and shrinking . . . everything. I sought to forever imprint those sensorial memories deep inside in a place that nothing, not even time, could touch.

But then the taxi pulled into our driveway and spoiled it all. Did I seal it deep enough inside me? Could it stay forever?

"Let's go," was Dad's directive. We were leaving, but I was taking myself with me. I would forget myself many times in the coming year. But that morning, arriving back at the Flughafen, I was surprised to see a few of my high school friends who had made the early morning trek just to see me off. April's boyfriend, Tim, had accompanied them as well. Dad's face looked totally annoyed, as he had not figured any of those people into the equation of the day.

Our entourage joined us all the way to the gate with hugs, tears, and cries of "I'll never forget you!" We boarded. I lost touch with them all, and April and Tim surrendered the end of their relationship with a few letters in the coming weeks.

ICH SEHE IMMER
NOCH PUNKTE
(STILL SEEING DOTS)

I n the three years since my last trip across the Atlantic, I had graduated to the aisle seat on the jumbo jet headed back to the States. After getting buckled in, I quickly regretted my fashion decision to wear the matching gauze skirt and top I had sewn just weeks earlier. Mom had suggested, "Bring a sweater; it's likely to be chilly onboard." I hadn't listened. I was not only chilly; I was sure that by the time we reached JFK International in New York City, I'd lose some digits to frostbite.

My hair was freshly washed and dried in wings that stayed put for the duration of the trip across the Atlantic, compliments of Aqua Net hairspray. I wore my platform espadrille sandals that squeaked when wet.

Laura was in the middle seat, squirming up against me to warm herself up, although she was wearing the Mom-suggested sweater. April was comfortably ensconced in the window seat, having found a blanket ready and waiting for her. What, was the row of seats allocated only one blanket?

Mom and Dad were in front of us, Dad in the window seat and Mom in the middle. Kitty was down in the cargo hold, probably cursing her existence but comfortably doped up on tranquilizers. The trip was in the daytime, unlike the trip over three years ago.

April was crying, missing Tim. Laura was crying, missing her friends. Mom was crying, I'm sure because of having had this amazing opportunity to live where we did and to have seen sites she had only dreamed of as a child from Dixmoor, Illinois. Dad was smiling, glad as hell to be finished with a less-than-fulfilling work experience. I was crying silently, wiping away tears that I did not shed in public.

My emotions were a complete jumble of everything fifteen-almost-sixteen. I knew we were going to stay in Pennsylvania at my grandparents' house. Grandma would not be there. That truth brought every memory cell forward into a cascade of profound grief.

My eleventh-grade year was to be at a school where I knew no one. It could not be on an Army post, as there was no available officers' housing at Fort Meade, where Dad was starting his next assignment. My soon-to-be classmates were most likely going to be civilians. Would there be any commonalities?

I had traveled all over Germany and all over Europe. Anything else was going to be horribly plebeian by comparison. But I was also torn by being ready to leave as well. My touchstones—Alan, Jenny, and the Motskos—had left before us. Without these constants, I was left with myself. And I didn't seem so great.

In my hands for reading material was Hugh Prather's *Notes to Myself*. It had become my treatise of late, given to me by a cousin who had come to visit us during the previous summer. I was only now taking time to read it, as all my Alan book recommendations were complete. "There is a part of me that wants to write, a part that wants to theorize, a part that wants to sculpt, a part that wants to teach. . . . To force myself into a single role, to decide to be just one thing in life, would kill off large parts of me."[17]

Oh, yes, those words rang true. I decided to form a life, an independent life where I could be many things and one thing too. Oh, my god, how obtuse! I was midway through my teens with skin that had decided to spend its time forming a tortured, pimpled landscape. Maybe a leper colony might accept me, but wherever we were moving to was certain not to.

I wasn't leaving the same way I had arrived. I really did have more in my back pocket than I could accept or acknowledge about myself during that long ride back to the States, but I needed distance from my Frankfurt life to gain perspective.

It was no different than the Georges Seurat painting Mr. Martin had shared during humanities class, *A Sunday on La Grande Jatte—1884*. Up close, it was all dots of seemingly random color and order. Then, as one stepped back, gaining focus, and allowing clarity, it became a masterpiece of a sunny afternoon on a day long gone by.

I was still in the view of my life in "up-close randomness."

THIS IS A HELLHOLE

During the return-to-the-States plane ride home, I had plenty of time to daydream and ponder that "going back" did not feel like "going home." I was pretty sure that spending my soon-to-be-sixteenth birthday in Podunk, USA, was going to be quite a step down from my three previous birthdays in Europe. I was not yet an adult and was sure I wasn't doing that well as a teenager. It didn't matter, as I had made the journey back across the Atlantic a little less ignorant, in the throes of adolescence, and wishing to hell I didn't have to start a school year in a few months in a school where I only knew April.

Arriving at Kennedy Airport in New York City on June 16, 1977, we were met at the baggage claim by April's old boyfriend, Charles! He had come to surprise her and to help us acclimate to the States. April seemed less than pleased to see him, which gave Laura and me much to giggle about.

Old boyfriend or not, we had a schedule to keep. One rental car later, and we were on the road headed toward Pennsylvania. It was a gray June day, and there was garbage everywhere. Well, it looked that way to us, having come from the pristine living conditions of Europe. Trash and graffiti littered the landscape. Drivers hogged the left-hand lane instead of using it solely for passing, as they did in Europe. The United States was wretched.

The car ride wasn't long in terms of time, but inside me, it was as if time stood still. We drove up the ever-steep Green

Street back to Dad's childhood home in Freemansburg, Pennsylvania. The three years of bottled-up grief over my grandmother's death began to overwhelm me. The sturdy stone wall was still there, one chair on the porch as always, but no flowers.

I kept spiraling these words through my brain and heart: *Don't make me stay here. I can't do this. I can't get out of this car. I can't face this house, this place, these memories without her.* My grandfather, always a paragon of stern face and demeanor, looked like he was going to cry upon seeing us. He and Dad shook hands. Mom hugged him deeply and dearly.

When I got out of the car, Grandpa was shaking as he hugged each of us from the side. I wanted to leave this place. It was all familiar, but my insides were a toxic brew of nostalgic pain, a sadness that had no words, a confusing desire to go back in time, and yet a pull to go forward. This was a house where nothing had moved, but everything had changed, including me.

EPILOGUE: *KLARHEIT* (CLARITY)

My idea of a goodbye consists of a "See ya," followed by having people and things drift away. It was much easier to do this when communication devices consisted only of a wall-mounted landline and airmail.

I had said, "See ya," to the Germany chapter of my life and hadn't looked back with any reflection—beyond a few standout memories—for more than forty years. I had told those stories to myself and my family with the detachment, style, and well-rehearsed timing of a tour guide. It was emotionally safer that way, but I had not consciously and courageously analyzed my own liner notes about myself and all that Germany had taught me.

In the raw hours of menopausal insomnia . . . that is where the curtain came down for me, and my emotions poured forth. That's where I defused my previously buried metaphoric three thousand tons of live munitions. Those three years in Frankfurt had opened my eyes and my heart to art, to architecture, to music, to literature, to feminism, to social justice, and to people like no place ever had before.

I grew to know myself in my music, my room, and the byways of an ancient land. The menopausal insomnia, complete mental "boots down," often left me sobbing hour after hour while the rest of the house slept. Sometimes the tears were happy; sometimes they explored and purged the depths of long-stuffed sorrow.

I arrived in Germany in 1974 with a good heart and a mind just beginning to question things, and I left in 1977 with a heart that had been broken for the first time, with some answers, more questions, and with definitive likes, dislikes, and a raging desire to do something to establish my place in both my family and the world. But the culture shock of moving back to a location in the States where the mentality mimicked 1954 sent me reeling into survival mode. Not the stuff of internal growth.

My daughter's sudden debilitating onset of postural orthostatic tachycardia syndrome (POTS) during her junior year of high school in 2016 left me so raw and frightened that mentally returning to my Germany years provided the comfort I needed. I knew it on one level, but oh, the beauty of pain is that, if one lets it, it reveals a path to the discovery of self. My coming-of-age revelations finally became clear so many years later.

I was previously afraid to look back at myself and my choices. I really was. I was embarrassed at how boy crazy I had been, all the while railing against the limiting prescribed gender roles of the times. I burned to be a writer but kept my writing hidden or nonexistent for fear that I was B+ Ordinary and never as talented as April.

I wish I had come out from under April's shadow right when Alan had said those very words to me. I had not used the same compassionate understanding for my younger self that I had cultivated for my sister as we aged. Well, I have now. I love that younger me. I love her questions, her humor, her fear, her laughter, her heartbreak, her music, her clothes . . . She is truly adorable.

And since I have come to that deep belief, I am embracing the age I am now. I don't know what you call this age . . . I'm going to call it "wise, sprinkled with pixie dust."

I have let Dad, April, and Laura read my manuscript. But unfortunately, Mom is "not interested." It almost crushed me when she said that, but her memory issues have caused Mom to no longer be the person I grew up with. The only consolation is that she seems content. Her eyes look settled.

After reading this, Dad told me in an email, "I did not realize you were not a fan of me growing up. I'm glad we are both older and past all that. Good job," and then he noted where I needed to make corrections to information. I made the corrections. I also felt devastated that I had hurt his feelings. Honestly, I didn't know he had those feelings. It took me two days to work up the courage to call him to clarify and to apologize.

I was determined to do so without crying. I succeeded until I hung up the phone. Then I wept. I thought I had written a loving tribute to Germany and to my family. It's who we were. It was written as I saw it, felt it, heard it, tasted it, and processed it through the lens of ages thirteen to fifteen.

Laura quibbled a bit about "when" certain excursions took place. She also wondered why she "didn't feature more prominently in the manuscript." But I reminded her that she was in a different phase of her life from mine then. This did not seem to placate her, so I said, "So write your own damn memoir!"

April bravely read through and expressed deep remorse for her behavior toward me during those growing-up years. But the writing of those stories, for me, provided the compassionate understanding I needed. All the previous years, I had struggled mightily, thinking I needed to "forgive" her to find peace and my own personality, and I was unable to do so. As it turned out,

I just needed to tell our stories at this age where I understand myself and, therefore, her so well. We were just two teenagers.

There is a large part of me that wants to go back to Germany, to the street where I lived, but I know from Google Earth that the only buildings that remain are those Wismarer Strasse homes and the IG Farben Building. Everything else I knew is gone, replaced by buildings meeting the needs of the German people of today. I know that is how it should be, but if I returned in person, I'm afraid the visual reality might shatter me.

Fear, fear, fear . . . and yet I have this ever-hopeful heart that finds a streak of light, leading me forward with more questions, more understanding, more laughter, more tears, more staying, and more leaving. There is less of my life now than more. I cherish that young woman who navigated those Frankfurt years with such passion, such emotion, and such bravery to go on her quest of "self."

Here is what else I know:

I love and live in the veil of the bittersweet past, the present, and a hopeful future.

I am not here to fit in; I am here as a change maker.

I both love and hate my super ability to anticipate.

Give me a superb brunch menu at an outdoor café, and I am set.

I always need a cat by my side.

No one cares what my hair looks like, ever.

I will always advocate for the fair treatment of and justice for people, animals, and nature.

I do have the redeeming quality of humor.

I haven't become nasty, but I am so much more than sweet, quiet, and cute.

And when I lose my way, I go back . . .
across the ocean, in a time, in a country, in a family,
in a life that exists not in real time
but in truth and in memories that are forever a part of me.
No longer in up-close randomness
But in the perspective of stepping back
Walking in my clarity, in my light.

ACKNOWLEDGMENTS

NOTE: Both of my parents died in March 2024, twenty-five days apart from one another. Their loss in my life leaves me bereft and also hopeful that wherever they are, they are proud of this book.

To Mom, who made the world a better place for me and for all who have known you.

To Dad, who toughened me with the resolve that I can handle anything. Thank you.

To my sister Laura, who keeps me humble, keeps me on my toes, and was my first friend.

To my sister April, my dear, dear soul friend, and no more my adversary.

To Alan (RIP), whose kindness, books, and music forever opened my mind.

To the Motsko family: Nick (RIP), Greg, Mike, Colonel (RIP), and Mrs. Liz Motsko (RIP).

To Carl, Steve, and Ryan, who opened their home and hearts to me and to Sylvie.

To Bryan Henderson, for being my kind lab partner and being kind still.

To my coach, Susan Conley, for asking the questions that allowed me to banish the Censor.

To Brooke Warner and the talented staff at She Writes Press for believing in my story.

To my PR team at BookSparks for their tireless work in
    championing me and this book.

To Germany, for your kindness and culture, and for
    opening the world for this traveler.

To the friends and teachers who traveled beside me
    throughout those three years.

To the US Army for my well-traveled life.

And lastly, to my daughter Sylvie, who gave me the
    courage to show the gifts I always had inside.
    You *are* my *Wizard of Oz.*

To Grandma McKnight

We used to snuggle together and read Peanuts books
and share a laughter so sweet and innocent.
I told you, "Grandma, someday I'm going to write a book."
You answered, "I know you will."
I found a poem you had written when you were young,
tucked into a book of yours called *Heartthrobs.*
I know you wrote it, and I suspect you submitted it to
    them for publication
and were rejected.
Well, that ends today, because here it is. I love you.
You always, always believed in me, and I in you:

"I have to live with myself. And so
I want to be fit for myself to know:
I want to be able as days go by
Always to look myself in the eye.
I don't want to stand in the setting sun
And hate myself for the things I've done.
I want to go out with my head erect:
I want to deserve my own respect."

By Mary Klinger McKnight

SOUNDTRACK OF MY LIFE

"Wild World"—Cat Stevens
"I Got a Name"—Jim Croce
"Carefree Highway"—Gordon Lightfoot
"I Need You"—America
"Top of the World"—The Carpenters
"Rikki Don't Lose That Number"—Steely Dan
"Help Me"—Joni Mitchell
"The Joker"—Steve Miller Band
"Sundown"—Gordon Lightfoot
"Rock Your Baby"—George McCrae
"Rock the Boat"—The Hues Corporation
"Kung Fu Fighting"—Carl Douglas
"Mandy"—Barry Manilow
"Fire"—Ohio Players
"You're No Good"—Linda Ronstadt
"Pick Up the Pieces"—Average White Band
"Black Water"—The Doobie Brothers
"Lovin' You"—Minnie Riperton
"Midnight at the Oasis"—Maria Muldaur
"Shining Star"—Earth, Wind & Fire
"Sister Golden Hair"—America
"Jive Talkin'"—Bee Gees
"Get Down Tonight"—KC and the Sunshine Band
"Could It Be Magic"—Barry Manilow
"Car Wash"—Rose Royce

"Theme from *Mahogany* (Do You Know Where You're Going To)"—Diana Ross

"Love Rollercoaster"—Ohio Players

"Kiss and Say Goodbye"—The Manhattans

"Don't Go Breaking My Heart"—Elton John and Kiki Dee

"Play That Funky Music"—Wild Cherry

"If You Leave Me Now"—Chicago

"I Wish"—Stevie Wonder

"Don't Leave Me This Way"—Thelma Houston

"The Bitch Is Back"—Elton John

"Haven't Got Time for the Pain"—Carly Simon

"Angie"—The Rolling Stones

"Diamonds and Rust"—Joan Baez

"Tangled Up in Blue"—Bob Dylan

"Hurricane"—Bob Dylan

"If You See Her, Say Hello"—Bob Dylan

"Golden Lady"—Stevie Wonder

"Canon"—Johann Pachelbel

"The Stars and Stripes Forever"—John Philip Sousa

"Rockin' the Boogie"—Freddie Slack

"Old Man"—Neil Young

"Walk Don't Run"—The Ventures

"In My Life (The Beatles Cover)"—Madison Cunningham

"Black Dog"—Led Zeppelin

"Stairway to Heaven"—Led Zeppelin

"We May Never Pass This Way (Again)"—Seals and Crofts

"What Is Life"—George Harrison

"Band on the Run"—Paul McCartney and Wings

"Imagine"—John Lennon

"Sweet Home Alabama"—Lynyrd Skynyrd

"Spiders and Snakes"—Jim Stafford

"Some Kind of Wonderful"—Grand Funk Railroad

"Killing Me Softly"—Roberta Flack
"If"—Bread
"Growin' Up"—Bruce Springsteen
"Landslide"—Fleetwood Mac
"Waterloo"—ABBA
"Wish You Were Here"—Pink Floyd
"Barracuda"—Heart
"Abbey Road Medley"—The Beatles
"Free Man in Paris"—Joni Mitchell
"As"—Stevie Wonder
"At Seventeen"—Janis Ian
"I'll Be Good to You"—The Brothers Johnson
"South Side Soul"—The John Wright Trio
"Golden Years"—David Bowie
"The Moon Is a Harsh Mistress"—Judy Collins
"Magic Man"—Heart

ENDNOTES

Tor nach Europa (Gateway to Europe)

1. Nancy Shea, *The Army Wife* (New York: Harper, 1966).

Seltsam (Weird)

2. From the US Department of Transportation: Plans for the Autobahn date to the 1920s. Construction of the first segment (Cologne–Bonn) began in 1929 and was dedicated by Mayor Konrad Adenauer of Cologne on August 6, 1932. When Adolf Hitler assumed power as Chancellor of the Third Reich in 1933, he took over the program, claiming it for his own. "We are setting up a program," he said later that year, "the execution of which we do not want to leave to posterity."

   Hitler's Autobahn construction began in September 1933 under the direction of chief engineer Fritz Todt. The fourteen-mile expressway between Frankfurt and Darmstadt, which opened on May 19, 1935, was the first section completed under Hitler. By December 1941, when wartime needs brought construction to a halt, Germany had completed 2,400 miles (3,860 km), with another 1,550 miles (2,500 km) under construction. ("The Reichsautobahnen," US Department of Transportation, Federal Highway Administration, updated

June 30, 2023, https://www.fhwa.dot.gov/infrastructure/reichs.cfm)

3. This is a reference to Pat Conroy's *The Great Santini* (New York: Bantam, 1987).

Unsere Welterweitert Sich (Our World Expands)

4. For details of the occupation of Germany by the Allies post WWII–1962, see "Forging the Shield: The U.S. Army in Europe, 1951–1962," by Donald A. Carter, https://history.army.mil/html/books/045/45-3-1/cmhPub_45-3-1.pdf.

Der Trek (The Trek)

5. For more information about guest workers and their role in German society, see Deutsche Welle, "Turkish Guest Workers Transformed German Society," October 30, 2011, https://www.dw.com/en/turkish-guest-workers-transformed-german-society/a-15489210.

6. "German Word of the Week: Trinkhalle," *German Joys* (blog), January 26, 2014, https://andrewhammel.blog/2014/01/26/trinkhalle-the-neighborhood-nexus/.

7. To read about the interesting history of Eschenheimer Turm, see Kaushik Patowary, "Eschenheimer Turm: A Mediaeval Tower in the Middle of Frankfurt," *Amusing Planet*, July 9, 2015, https://www.amusingplanet.com/2015/07/eschenheimer-turm-mediaeval-tower-in.html.

Soundtrack Meines Lebens
(Soundtrack of My Life)

8. For more about the history of the American Forces Network, see "Democracy on a Dial: A Short History of AFN in Europe," The National WWII Museum, February 13, 2020, https://www.nationalww2museum.org/war/articles/democracy-dial-short-history-afn-europe.

Alles Dreht Sich um die Schuhe
(It's All about the Shoes)

9. To learn more about the evolution of the Adidas shoe company, beginning with its humble origins, see "Adidas: History," on the brand's website, https://www.adidas-group.com/en/about/history.

Innere Gedanken (Inner Thoughts)

10. For a more in-depth look at the book's predictions, see "*Future Shock* at 40: What the Tofflers Got Right (and Wrong)," Fast Company, October 15, 2010, https://www.fastcompany.com/1695307/future-shock-40-what-tofflers-got-right-and-wrong.

Tapfer Sein (Being Brave)

11. Henry David Thoreau, *Walden; or, Life in the Woods* (London: J.M. Dent, 1908).

Die Wand (The Wall)

12. To learn more about the significance of the Fulda Gap, see "Fulda Gap Is Key Point in NATO Defense Against Soviet Forces," *LA Times*, March 1, 1987, https://www.latimes.com/archives/la-xpm-1987-03-01-mn-6926-story.html.

Was Ist eine Nutte? (What's a Hooker?)

13. To read about the 1976 bombing by the Baader–Meinhof Gang, see "2 Bombs Injure 15 Americans and a German at U.S. Base," *New York Times*, June 2, 1976, https://www.nytimes.com/1976/06/02/archives/2-bombs-injure-15-americans-and-a-german-at-us-base.html.

Das Ist Also Freiheit (So This Is Freedom)

14. Albert Einstein, "Religion and Science," *New York Times Magazine*, November 9, 1930, https://static01.nyt.com/images/blogs/learning/pdf/2013/19301109Einstein.pdf.

15. Nebraska Curriculum for English: Grade Ten, Units 109–10, "Man, Society, Nature, and Moral Law," Nebraska Curriculum Development Center Staff (author), copyright 1965.

16. Simone Weil, *Waiting for God* (New York: Harper & Row, 1973), 165. First published 1951 by G. P. Putnam's Sons.

Ich Sehe Immer Noch Punkte (Still Seeing Dots)

17. Hugh Prather, *Notes to Myself: My Struggle to Become a Person* (New York: Bantam Books, 1976).

RESOURCES

Excellent site for the history of Frankfurt, Germany, past and present: https://www.frankfurthigh.com/history/subpages/Frankfurt_History.htm

Excellent wartime/'60s/modern photos of Frankfurt: http://www.columbia.edu/~fdc/family/frankfurt.html

Information about Eleanor Roosevelt's visit and speech at Zeilsheim (twelve miles from Frankfurt):
https://www.facinghistory.org/universal-declaration-human-rights/eleanor-visits-displaced-persons-camps

Hanau Displaced Persons Camp information (ten miles from Frankfurt):
https://www.germany-insider-facts.com/displaced-persons-camp-in-hanau-late-1940s.html

"Stumbling Stones" project honoring and marking where Jewish people were ripped from their lives and homes by the Nazi regime. (Note those from the West End . . . that's where I lived.):
https://www.stolpersteine-frankfurt.de/media/pages/dokumentation/4b862e67ad-1624115963/doku2019_web.pdf

THE FATE/HISTORY OF THE PEOPLE OF HANSA ALLEE

The people below, to whom I dedicated this book, all suffered unthinkable fates. The information below is courtesy of the "Stumbling Stones" project and the research I did through Yad Vashem. May their memory be a remembrance to us all, to never forget.

Information is courtesy of the Holocaust Survivors and Victims Database at ushmm.org.

HERMANN ALTSCHÜLER

Date of Birth:
26 Oct 1893

Previous Place:
Frankfurt, Germany

Place of Incarceration:
Litzmannstadt-Getto, Łódź, Poland
https://www.ushmm.org/collections/bibliography/od-ghetto

Occupation:
Bankbeamter

Source:
VI Transport A
https://www.ushmm.org/online/hsv/source_view.php?
SourceId=34933

Collection:
"The elders of the Jews in the Łódź ghetto"
https://www.ushmm.org/online/hsv/source_view.php?SourceId=
25274

ELISE HOFMANN

Sex:
Female

Maiden Name:
Elise Bloch

Date of Birth:
18 Jul 1872

Date of Transport:
19 Aug 1942

Date of Departure:
26 Sep 1942

Previous Place:
Frankfurt am Main

Destination:
Treblinka

Holocaust Fate:
Deceased

Transport Numbers:
- XII/1
- Br
- 868

Number of People in Transport:
315

RUTH COHNSTAEDT

Birth date:
17 Jun 1912

Birthplace:
Frankfurt a. Main, Hessen-Nassau, Germany

Source:
Das Bundesarchiv Memorial Book
https://www.ushmm.org/online/hsv/source_view.php?
SourceId=49492

FRIEDA ALTSCHÜLER

Birth date:
22 Apr 1894

Birth place:
Bonn, Rheinprovinz, Germany

Maiden name:
Frieda Apfel

Sources:
VI Transport A
https://www.ushmm.org/online/hsv/source_view.php?
SourceId=34933

Das Bundesarchiv Memorial Book
https://www.ushmm.org/online/hsv/source_view.php?
SourceId=49492

Collection:
"The elders of the Jews in the Łódź ghetto"
https://www.ushmm.org/online/hsv/source_view.php?
SourceId=25274

May your lives and your deaths be a reminder to us all to LIVE
and to treat others with mutual understanding, appreciation,
and respect.

ABOUT THE AUTHOR

Mary E. McKnight

Mary E. McKnight is an avid observer of people, a teacher of young children, a co-owner of an herb garden (Split Stone Farm LLC), a painter, and a lover of cats. She lives for kindness, creativity, and her amazing daughter. Her writing is the creative expression that feeds her soul, and she enjoys writing in a variety of genres. If she wasn't her, she would probably be the Lorax. She lives in Ellicott City, Maryland, with her partner and their tortie, Abbey Rhodes.

Looking for your next great read?

We can help!

Visit www.shewritespress.com/next-read
or scan the QR code below for a list
of our recommended titles.

She Writes Press is an award-winning
independent publishing company founded to
serve women writers everywhere.